Also by Katha Pollitt

Subject to Debate:
Sense and Dissents on Women, Politics, and Culture

Reasonable Creatures:
Essays on Women and Feminism

Antarctic Traveller
(POETRY)

Virginity or Death!

Random House Trade Paperbacks
New York

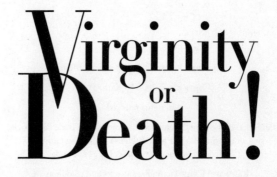

Virginity or Death!

And Other Social and Political
Issues of Our Time

Katha Pollitt

A Random House Trade Paperback Original

Copyright © 2006 by Katha Pollitt

All rights reserved.

Published in the United States by Random House Trade Paperbacks,
an imprint of The Random House Publishing Group,
a division of Random House, Inc., New York.

RANDOM HOUSE TRADE PAPERBACKS and colophon are
trademarks of Random House, Inc.

The essays that appear in this work were
originally published in *The Nation*.

LIBRARY OF CONGRESS CATALOGING-IN-PUBLICATION DATA

Pollitt, Katha.
Virginity or death!: and other social and political issues of our time/Katha Pollitt.
p. cm.
A collection of articles originally published in the author's column,
Subject to Debate, in *The Nation*.
ISBN 0-8129-7638-X
1. United States—Social conditions—1980–82. 2. United States—
Politics and government—2001–2003. 3. United States—
Politics and government—1993–2001. I. Title.
HN59.2.P653 2006   973.93—dc22   2006043886

Printed in the United States of America

www.atrandom.com

2 4 6 8 9 7 5 3 1

Book design by Mary A. Wirth

For Steven
and
for Sophie

Contents

Introduction

When I started writing my Subject to Debate column for *The Nation* in 1994, the magazine had around 80,000 subscribers, and even my friends didn't read me. Now it has 187,000 subscribers and a flourishing website where my column is always posted, so my friends have no excuse. As we like to say, George Bush has been a disaster for the nation, but he's been great for *The Nation*. Last year our Christmas party was even held in a restaurant! Perhaps the failure of the left end of the spectrum to lie down and die when requested is what drives right wingers so around the bend. Rush Limbaugh, Bill O'Reilly, Ann Coulter, Michael Savage, and similar—why are they so mad all the time? Nothing seems to satisfy them. Never mind that the Republican party controls the White House and both houses of Congress, and that seven out of nine Supreme Court justices are Republican nominees, to say nothing of a slew of judges on the federal bench and 28 out of 50 state governors. Forget their famous multimillion-member base in the Christian evangelical/fundamentalist churches, their huge money advantage over the Democrats, their think tanks churning out position papers that find their way into the mainstream media as if they were actual scholarly research, their heavy presence in every form of news and opinion media from bestseller to blog. Pass over the decline of unions, once a powerful political machine and counterweight to corporate power. Pay no attention to the haplessness and confusion of the Democrats. Despite the fact that conservatives control the discourse and run the country—and midcensus redistricting and other electoral power plays have made it likely that they'll keep doing so even if everyone decides to hate them tomorrow—conservatives are haunted by fear. Somewhere out in this big land of ours, an English professor has put an antiwar cartoon on his office door; a high school girl is wearing an anarchist T-shirt; a woman had an abortion and doesn't want to slit her wrists; Michael Moore—oh no!—is making another movie. Talk about sweating the small stuff. Lefties are always being accused of lacking joie de vivre, but it's obvious where the real anxieties are these days. Could it be that conservatives always sensed the party might not last so very long?

Politicians can win votes for a long time by wrapping themselves in God and Flag and Family Values, but eventually they have to deliver something to their constituents, even if it's just one of those bridges to nowhere in Alaska. Beyond protecting America from the twin plagues of gay marriage and embryonic stem cell research, it is hard to say what Republican hegemony has done for the ordinary people whose votes the party needs to stay in power. In foreign affairs, it has embroiled us in a disastrous war in Iraq, stained our reputation with indelible images of torture, and sends around the world a President so bumptious, so ignorant of history, he lectures Latin Americans on the importance of democratic elections—tell them about it! At home, we have more people in poverty, more people without health insurance, and a government that is stuffed with incompetent political appointees, of whom Michael "heckuva job" Brown of FEMA fame is only the most notorious, and which perverts science on practically a weekly basis to placate that section of the electorate that believes birth control is the root of all evil and the world is at most 10,000 years old.

The fecklessness of the current regime astonishes me, I admit. Hurricane Katrina displayed to the whole world the inability of the administration to do the bedrock job of government, which is to ensure public safety and protect people from catastrophe, while simultaneously revealing what should definitely not come as a surprise but somehow did to many: the deep poverty of the Gulf region and its racial nature. Surely— after botching the rescue in full view of the whole world, after Bush's unfortunate use of Trent Lott's beach house as the synecdoche for the towns and neighborhoods destroyed by storm and flood, and his mother's even more clueless remark that living in the Houston Astrodome was "working well" for the displaced, who were "underprivileged anyway"—surely, I thought, the Administration would pour on steam to show what a good job it could do to get the evacuees back on their feet. I forgot for a moment that this was the same administration that had shown nothing but contempt for professional expertise, whose answer to every question of public policy was tax cuts, and whose response to every crisis has been to leave people to their own devices, down to expecting soldiers on active duty in Iraq to supply their own body armor, like medieval knights.

Sometimes I wish I had spent more time ingratiating myself with powerful conservatives, like a real journalist, because I would truly like to know what the game plan is now. More torture? More Jesus? More shovelling tax cuts to the richest 1 percent? In an article in the *Weekly Standard,* "The Party of Sam's Club," Ross Douthat and Reihan Salam argue that Republicans must give up the idea of cutting government programs or lose the working class, especially the women. Working-class voters want government to help them; they didn't appreciate one bit, for example, President Bush's attempt to privatize Social Security, excellent idea though it was. Therefore, what the Republican Party should support now are family-friendly programs targeted at low-income people. For example, government could encourage larger families by offering significant cash payments and other benefits to parents who have three or more children. And why, you warily ask, should the government promote bigger families? Because, the authors reply, if people have lots of children, they won't need Social Security! Their kids will take care of them. Got it. As of this writing, that seems to be the plan: More babies now, less government later.

And speaking of babies, what about feminism? If you follow the media, the women's movement is well into the third decade of the longest funeral in history ("Is Women's Lib a Passing Fad?" *New York Times,* 1972). A torrent of books, articles, and popular entertainment tells women they don't really want equality, and if they get it they will only be miserable, because what makes women happy is nurturing men and children, or even, as a recent *New York Times* front-page story suggested, quitting their jobs—their empty, materialistic, meaningless jobs—to move back into their childhood bedrooms and tend their aging parents ("Forget the Career. My Parents Need Me at Home," November 24, 2005). When was the last time you saw a mass-market film with a "career woman" character who wasn't a bitch on wheels? In which the diamond-in-the-rough working-class beauty was a genius who needed a scholarship, not a stripper who needed a husband? As for sex, any number of writers, from right-wing Harvard political scientist Harvey Mansfield and novelist Tom Wolfe on down, are eager to warn young women of the horrors of the hookup. (Why young women should care what these septuagenarians think about their sex lives is a question not easily answered.)

If feminism—the idea that women are equal to men and that social arrangements should reflect that truth—was truly a doomed project, if it made women as lonely and twisted and frustrated as its opponents insist, if it violated fundamental laws of nature, as pop sociobiology insinuates, we would not even be talking about it today. Women themselves would have rejected it very quickly, and we would now be a nation of premarital virgins eager to fire up the crockpot the minute they found a fiancé manly enough to put "obey" back into the wedding vows. Despite the onslaught of negative media, and large audiences receptive to it, and despite the real-life opprobrium that can befall a woman perceived as uppity, promiscuous, or insufficiently shaven of leg, feminism persists because it fits the actual conditions in which women live. If women are educated, if they choose their own husbands (or choose to have none) and determine the size of their families, if they can support themselves or know that they could do so if they had to, then they are going to feel that they deserve the rights and privileges and respect society accords adult human beings. This is so, whether or not they call themselves feminists and even if they stay home taking care of children. Moreover, it's not only women who need feminism. America could not manage for a day if women reverted en masse to the norms of the 1950s, forgoing serious education or professional training, marrying by twenty-one, having many babies right away, working, if they worked at all, for low wages in a few low-skill and/or gender-segregated occupations. Who would support them and all those kids? Male wages have been stagnant or declining for thirty years, while the definition of the good life has been rising. And who would take the jobs women now have, jobs so necessary to the economy—and for those seventy-seven-cents-on-the-male-dollar salaries?

The trouble is, although the country can't afford to send women back half a century, it can't afford gender equality either, because that would mean providing socially all the services women now provide for free. Women are the great American free labor pool—even if they have full-time jobs. They raise the next generation, make possible the even more extensive working hours of their husbands, orchestrate the flow into their households of a vast array of commodities—new sofas! aromatherapy candles! fresh flowers!—put in millions of hours of volunteer work, care for the old and the sick. If women stopped performing those unpaid tasks, or even did only as much as men were willing to do, society could not function as we know it. We would have to have a giant social-welfare state. We would have to have an economy organized around some other principle than constant, daily mass consumerism on credit, all that shopping women do as entertainment and reward and theatre of the self. How often, after all, would men redo the kitchen, buy a baby outfit just because it was so adorable, or even so much as venture inside Bloomingdale's—or for that matter T. J. Maxx? Relations between men and women might be more pleasant, because the sexes would need each other less desperately, but for that very reason marriages would be even less permanent than they are now, which is saying a lot. And if men decided that rather than have society provide care collectively they would like to reorganize the work patterns of the business world so they could do more caregiving themselves, the economic and social disruption would arguably be even greater.

The solution is obvious. Women must live modern lives organized around principles of self-reliance and self-development, while at the same time they must feel endlessly guilty and uneasy about the ways in which doing so inconveniences those around them. They have to be independent, and they have to blame themselves if they enjoy it. That way, they can be moved around the chess board of the economy as business requires without ever being able to make the kinds of demands on society or family relationships that would make them truly equal either in the workplace or the home. The genius twist in the logic is to present social conditions as fixed, as offering an array of individual choices that it is up to the woman—and only the woman—to make. Job or baby? Promotion or mommy track? Middle-aged independence or moving in with your Alzheimered parents? It's up to you. What disappears from the media discussion of what women "choose" is the social matrix in which these decisions get made: inflexible hours, rigid career tracks, the lack of good, affordable, reliable child care, the unwillingness of many men to share domestic burdens equally, the perception that married women with employed husbands don't really need to work (but men, no matter how much money their wives make, really do), and of course, the constant cultural reinforcement of the belief that being a good mother—a *great* mother—means treating childrearing as something between curing cancer and a religious vocation. By today's standards, most stay-home 1950s mothers were neglectful slatterns. They didn't play Mozart to their fetuses; they didn't breast-feed; they let their kids play outside unsupervised; when a child complained of boredom they said, "Go clean your room."

It's not surprising that, caught between these crosscurrents, women are making slower progress along a more tortuous path than one might have predicted back in 1970 or even 1980. If you want, you can get rather depressed about it, like Maureen Dowd, who in her much discussed book *Are Men Necessary?* argues that young women are going retro in vast numbers and will live to rue the day. I'm not at all sure young women are going backward, even if they are more likely to take their husband's name than brides twenty years ago (the great majority of whom changed their names). I'm a total Lucy Stoner myself, but why should that one item be the benchmark of female progress? Isn't it a little more important in the grand scheme of things that 41 percent of young women are in college, that half of all medical students are female, that more and more girls are playing sports, that more women (and more men) are willing to vote for a woman, that a woman police officer or bus driver or unionized blue collar worker is no longer a rarity, that lesbians can come out of the closet, that a woman who is raped or abused is more likely to come forward and is more likely to get justice?

When women retreat on those fronts, it will be time to speak of the death of feminism. Meanwhile, I'd like to hear more about the *life* of feminism. It doesn't get nearly enough attention, but feminist activism continues to shape our political, social, and cultural landscape. A million-plus women, many of them young, gathered on the Washington Mall last spring in the pro-choice March for Women's Lives. This February, once again students on hundreds of campuses celebrated V-Day, performing their own versions of the Vagina Monologues as a fundraiser for groups that fight violence against women. Maybe, by the time you read this, emergency contraception—the morning-after pill—will be available over the counter, despite the heavy politicking against it by the Christian right, and it will actually be on sale at your local pharmacy. If that happens—*if*—it will be because of pressure from fed-up, outraged women—not just politicians, doctors, and other health workers, journalists, advocates, and pro-choice activists, but also the women we are always being told have no use for feminism, the "sex and the city" singles and soccer moms and waitress moms and other women who show up in the media mostly as demographic stereotypes in presidential campaign coverage. Who knows? Maybe even some of those future stay-home moms of the Ivy League the *New York Times* likes to write about.

It is hard to believe that modern American women are just going to let the Eagle Forum and the local anti-choice pharmacist decide whether they get pregnant when the condom slips. Just as it is hard to believe that women would rather their daughters get cervical cancer as adults than be immunized against the human papilloma virus at puberty, and supposedly, in some preacher's fantasy life, be thereby encouraged to have sex. Surely there is a limit to what women, and men, are willing to accept in the name of social purity, right order, family values, and "life," even in the fabled nutgroves of Kansas.

Women may not call themselves feminists when they fight for their rights, and their daughters' rights. But that is what they are. In the same way, conservatives may not call themselves liberals when they protest the Bush administration's invasions of our privacy in the name of fighting terrorism, and Christians may not think of themselves as secular humanists when they decide, as did the voters of Dover, Pennsylvania, that "intelligent design" should not be taught as science in the public schools. The requirements of real life count for something, no matter what ideology says. And yes, there are days when that is my most optimistic thought.

A FEW REMARKS about the book. The pieces collected here cover more than five years and a variety of different topics. I've avoided the temptation to fix and revise to make myself look prescient and wise, but in a few places I've made small alterations to incorporate into the text corrections that were noted in subsequent issues, to elucidate a topical reference, or to re-expand a too-tightly-edited sentence. (As always, I'm indebted to *The Nation*'s readers for pouncing on every sort of error, from grammatical to historical, as well as for the prayers some claim to be offering for my soul.) The dates follow *The Nation*'s strange system, by which each issue is given a date two and a half weeks later than its actual publication. That is why I seem to be complaining about media frivolity on September 17, 2001, and wrap up 2003 in mid-January of 2004. At the risk of reminding some of my friends why they were so mad at me, I've left in the most controversial column, "Put Out No Flags," which is constructed around a discussion with my daughter about why I didn't want to fly the flag from our window after 9/11. It got a lot of flak, and not just from the right-wing press, which mounted a not very successful campaign to send American flags to "young Miss Pollitt." (She only received one actual cloth flag, plus assorted flag-themed items: a paper cocktail decoration, a crayon drawing—and several letters congratulating her for having more sense than her mother. Still, the hate mail and hate messages left on my answering machine made her see what I meant about the connection between flag-waving, jingoism, and war.) The column even won me spot 74 in Bernard Goldberg's "100 People Who Are Screwing Up America." (Memo to self: must try harder.) Reading it over, I can see why the brisk, wry tone disturbed people, so soon after the tragedy. A better writer would have found words that spoke more clearly to the shock and sorrow of the moment. My basic point, though, was simply that nationalism fuels hatred and war and is too small a way to think about today's world. Considering how easily fear of terrorism, desire for vengeance, and calls for patriotic unity were soon to be manipulated to build support for the invasion of Iraq, I think I was on to something.

Virginity or Death!

Dear Larry, Thanks! John

Only yesterday pundits assured us that George W. Bush, who lost the popular election by half a million votes, would tread softly and govern meekly. "He has no mandate to do anything except Be Nice," Molly Ivins wrote in the December *Progressive*. But who needs a mandate, with the mainstream media resolutely ignoring the still-unfolding scandal of the Florida election? Bush is making hay while the sun shines—paying off his debt to business with the nominations of Elaine Chao, late of the Heritage Foundation, for Labor; Gale Norton, lead-paint champion, for Interior; and Christie Whitman, governor of the state with the second-worst air pollution in the country (Texas is first), for EPA. Over at HHS, anti-choicers get Tommy Thompson—whose devotion to welfare reform provides a note of continuity with the worst aspects of the outgoing Clinton administration. Most ominous, the Christian and loony right gets its reward for keeping quiet during the campaign: the nomination of John Ashcroft for Attorney General.

How far to the right is Ashcroft? As I write, the Democrats on the Judiciary Committee are doing their best to help him obscure his ghastly twenty-five-year record on abortion, guns, women's rights, gay rights, the separation of church and state. A rare exception was Ted Kennedy, who closely questioned the nominee on his crusade as Missouri's attorney general against voluntary school desegregation. But so far the only senator who has publicly said she will vote no is Barbara Boxer, never a *Nation* favorite, while "progressive" stalwarts like Paul Wellstone and Russell Feingold (who was particularly fawning and vacuous in his questioning), not to mention Tom Daschle and Joe Biden, have all said they were inclined to vote yes (Wellstone and Biden later backpedaled after an outcry). You'd think the Democrats had *lost* the popular election! Unless Ashcroft is discovered to be sleeping with Barney Frank, his confirmation looks assured. Who in the Senate can be expected to care that as governor of Missouri, Ashcroft twice vetoed bills that would have equalized voter-registration procedures in mostly black and mostly white counties, given that *not one* senator would sponsor the Congressional Black Caucus's January 6 protest of the Electoral College vote? The Republicans really are reactionaries, but the Democrats are only pretending to be liberals.

If Ashcroft is not too far out to be confirmed, who is? Accepting an honorary degree at Bob Jones University in 1999, Ashcroft proclaimed that in America "We have no king but Jesus." (Why aren't Jews up in arms about that?) This is a man who, on the eve of his swearing-in as a Missouri senator, anointed himself with Crisco, supposedly after the manner of the Hebrew kings. Can it be that Barbara Boxer is the only senator discomfited by the thought of an attorney general who thinks the Bible instructs him to put salad oil on his head?

John Ashcroft is not just a conservative: He stands at the place where Christian fanatics, anti-choicers, militiamen, gun nuts, and white supremacists come together. As Joe Conason reports, he has acknowledged meeting with the head of the St. Louis chapter of the racist Council of Conservative Citizens to discuss the case of a member jailed on federal charges of conspiring to murder an FBI agent. He defended the leaders of the Confederacy in *Southern Partisan,* the neo-Confederate magazine that has done a brisk business in T-shirts celebrating the assassination of Abraham Lincoln (Timothy McVeigh was wearing one when arrested). If *Southern Partisan* rings a bell, by the way, it's because when editor Richard Quinn was discovered to be managing John McCain's South Carolina campaign, a Bush spokesperson criticized McCain for associating with him.

Among Ashcroft's many connections on the far side is Larry Pratt, who, as head of Gunowners of America, functions as a kind of liaison between the militia movement and Capitol Hill. A handwritten note from Ashcroft is posted on Pratt's website (www.gunowners.org). According to the *Guardian,* "the two men know each other from a secretive but highly influential right-wing religious group called the Council for National Policy, of which Mr Pratt is a member and whose meetings Mr. Ashcroft has attended." Tom DeLay and Trent Lott also belong.

In a glowing profile in *CounterPunch* (July 1–15, 1999), Alexander Cockburn uncritically paraphrases the position for which Pratt is best known—that the surest proof against Columbine-type school shootings is to arm teachers to shoot students "just like they do in South Africa, where one instructor recently gunned down a bellicose student." South Africa is one of the world's most violent countries, with a long history of serious corporal punishment—with whips—in its dismal black schools, so it's not immediately obvious why the United States should follow its lead even if Pratt's tale is true. But the South African consul says there is no such policy and knows of no such incident having occurred, nor did a media search turn one up. Need one point out as well that millions of pistol-packing teachers present something of a danger to defenseless schoolchildren? On the other hand, since Pratt also believes in guns for kids (Ashcroft's note was to thank Pratt for enlightening him about the anti-gun provisions in the juvenile justice bill), the students could just shoot back.

Pratt's website is a grab bag of nuttiness ("What the Bible Says About Gun Control"; "Guns Save Health Care Costs"). But it would be wrong to see him as a marginal, if colorful, figure. *CounterPunch* doesn't mention it, but Pratt has been a leader of the hard-core Christian right for many years. He led the walkout of religious conservatives at the White House Conference on Families in 1980; he has fundraised for Operation Rescue. In 1996, he was cochairman of Pat Buchanan's presidential campaign until he was forced to resign when his links to Christian Identity and white-supremacist groups became public. Today Pratt pals around with Lott, DeLay, and Ashcroft—whom Bush Senior reportedly considered for the Attorney General post but rejected as too extreme to be confirmed.

That was then, this is now.

No Olive Branch

How many times did we hear during the endless campaign that Bush wouldn't go after abortion if elected? Republicans, Naderites, and countless know-it-alls and pundits in between agreed: Pro-choice voters were too powerful, the country was too divided, the Republicans weren't that stupid, and Bush didn't really care about abortion anyway. Plus, whoever won would have to (all together now) "govern from the center." Where are all those smarties now, I wonder? Bush didn't even wait for his swearing-in ceremony to start repaying the immense debt he owes to the Christian right, which gave him one in four of his votes, with the nominations of anti-choice diehards John Ashcroft for Attorney General and Tommy Thompson to head Health and Human Services.

On his first full day in office, Bush reinstated the "gag rule" preventing international family-planning clinics and NGOs from receiving U.S. funds if they so much as mention the word "abortion." (This action was widely misrepresented in the press as being a ban on funding for performing abortions; in fact, it bans clinics that get U.S. aid from performing abortions *with their own money* and prohibits speech— whether lobbying for legal changes in countries where abortion is a crime or informing women with life- or health-threatening pregnancies about their legal options.) A few days later, Thompson announced he would look into the safety of RU-486, approved by the FDA this past fall—a drug that has been used by half a million European women over twelve years and has been more closely studied here than almost any drug on the market. In the wake of Laura Bush's remark to NBC News and the *Today* show that she favored retention of *Roe v. Wade,* both the

President and the Vice President said the administration has not ruled out a legal challenge to it, placing them to the right of Ashcroft himself, who told the Judiciary Committee he regarded *Roe* as settled law (at least until the makeup of the Supreme Court changes, he did not add).

Don't count on the media to alert the public. The press is into champagne and confetti: Who would have thought Dick Cheney would be such an amiable talk show guest! Time to move on, compromise, get busy with that big tax cut. "Who in hell is this 'all' we keep hearing about?" a friend writes, "as in 'all agree' that the Bush transition has been a smashing success?" An acquaintance at the *Washington Post*, whose executive editor, Leonard Downie, Jr., claims to be so objective he doesn't even vote, says word has come down from "on high" that stories must bear "no trace of liberal bias"—interestingly, no comparable warnings were given against pro-Bush bias. So, on abortion, look for endless disquisitions on the grassiness of the anti-choice roots, the elitism of pro-choicers, and the general tedium of the abortion issue. Robin Toner could barely stifle a yawn as she took both sides to task in the *New York Times* ("The Abortion Debate, Stuck in Time," January 21): Why couldn't more anti-choicers see the worth of stem-cell research, like anti-choice senator Gordon Smith, who has several relatives afflicted with Parkinson's (but presumably no relatives unwillingly pregnant); and why can't more pro-choicers acknowledge that sonograms "complicate" the status of the fetus? In an article that interviewed not a single woman, only the fetus matters: not sexuality, public health, women's bodies, needs, or rights.

Now is the time to be passionate, clever, original, and urgent. I hate to say it, but pro-choicers really could learn some things from the antis, and I don't mean the arts of arson, murder, and lying to the Judiciary Committee. Lots of right-wing Christians tithe—how many pro-choicers write significant checks to pro-choice and feminist organizations? Why not sit down today and send President Bush a note saying that in honor of the women in his family you are making a donation to the National Network of Abortion Funds to pay for a poor woman's abortion (NNAF, Hampshire College, Amherst, MA 01002-5001)?

The antis look big and powerful because they have a built-in base in the Catholic and fundamentalist churches. But (aha!) pro-choicers have a built-in constituency too: the millions and millions of women who have had abortions. For all sorts of reasons (privacy concerns, overwork, the ideology of medicine) few clinics ask their patients to give back to the cause. Now some providers and activists are talking about changing that. "My fantasy," Susan Yanow of the Abortion Access Project wrote me, "is that *every* woman in this country gets a piece of paper after her procedure that says something like, 'We need your help. You just had a safe, legal abortion, something that the current Administration is actively trying to outlaw. Think of your sisters/mothers/daughters who might need this service one day. Please help yourself to postcards and tell your elected representatives you support legal abortion, join (local group name here), come back as a volunteer,' and so on." If every woman who had an abortion sent her clinic even just a dollar a year, it would mean millions of dollars for staff, security, and cut-rate or gratis procedures. Think how different the debate would be if all those women, and the partners, parents, relatives, and friends who helped them, spoke up boldly—especially the ones whose husbands are so vocally and famously and self-righteously anti-choice. If women did that, *we* would be the grassroots.

●◄ FEBRUARY 19, 2001 ►●

Vaginal Politics

Imagine Madison Square Garden brimming over with 18,000 laughing and ebullient women of every size, shape, age, and color, along with their male friends, ditto. Imagine that in that immense space, usually packed with hooting sports fans, these women are watching Oprah, Queen Latifah, Claire Danes, Swoosie Kurtz, Kathleen Chalfant, Julie Kavner (voice of Marge Simpson), Rosie Perez, Donna Hanover (soon-to-be-ex-wife of New York's semi-bigamous mayor), and sixty-odd other A-list divas put on a gala production of *The Vagina Monologues,* Eve Ensler's theater piece about women and their mimis, totos, split knishes, Gladys Siegelmans, pussycats, poonanis, and twats. Imagine that this extravaganza is part of a huge $2 million fundraising effort for V-Day, the antiviolence project that grew out of the show and that gives money to groups fighting violence against women around the world. That was what happened on February 10, with more donations and more performances to come as the play is produced by students at some 250 colleges around the country, from Adelphi on Long Island—where it was completely sold out, and where, sources assure me, the V-word retains every bit of its shock value—to Yale.

And they keep saying feminism is dead.

The Vagina Monologues, in fact, was singled out in *Time*'s 1998 cover story "Is Feminism Dead?" as proof that the movement had degenerated into self-indulgent sex chat. (This was a new departure for the press, which usually dismisses the movement as humorless, frumpish, and puritanical.) In her *Village Voice* report on the gala, Sharon Lerner, a terrific feminist journalist, is unhappy that the actresses featured at the Garden event prefer the V-word to the F-word. ("Violence against women is a feminist issue?" participant Isabella Rossellini asks her. "I don't think it is." This from the creator of a new perfume called "Manifesto"!) Women's rights aren't what one associates with postfeminist icons like Glenn Close, whose most indelible screen role was as the bunny-boiling man-stalker in *Fatal Attraction,* or Calista Flockhart, television's dithery microskirted lawyerette Ally McBeal. Still, aren't we glad that Jane Fonda, who performed the childbirth monologue, has given up exercise mania and husband-worship and is donating $1 million to V-Day? Better late than never, I say.

At the risk of sounding rather giddy myself—I'm writing this on Valentine's Day—I'd argue that the implied contradiction between serious business (daycare, abortion, equal pay) and sex is way overdrawn. Sexual self-expression—that's self-indulgent sex chat to all you old Bolsheviks out there—was a crucial theme of the modern women's movement from the start. Naturally so: How can you see yourself as an active subject, the heroine of your own life, if you think you're an inferior being housed in a shameful, smelly body that might give pleasure to others but not to you? The personal is political, remember that?

The Vagina Monologues may not be great literature—on the page it's a bit thin, and the different voices tend to run together into EveEnslerspeak about seashells and flowers and other lovely bits of nature. But as a performance piece it's fantastic: a cabaret floor show by turns hilarious, brassy, lyrical, poignant, charming, romantic, tragic, vulgar, sentimental, raunchy, and exhilarating. In "The Flood," an old woman says she thinks of her "down there" as a cellar full of dead animals, and tells of the story of her one passionate kiss and her dream of Burt Reynolds swimming in her embarrassing "flood" of sexual wetness. A prim, wryly clever woman in "The Vagina Workshop" learns how to give herself orgasms at one of Betty Dodson's famous masturbation classes. At the Garden, Ensler led the cast in a chorus of orgasmic moans, and Close got the braver members of the audience to chant "Cunt! Cunt! Cunt!" at the climax of a poetic monologue meant to redeem and reclaim the dirtiest of all dirty words.

How anyone could find *The Vagina Monologues* antimale or pornographic is beyond me—it's a veritable ode to warm, quirky, affectionate, friendly, passionate sex. The only enemies are misogyny, sexual shame, and sexual violence, and violence is construed fairly literally: A poor black child is raped by her father's drunken friend; a Bosnian girl is sexually tortured by Serbian paramilitaries. None of your ambiguous was-it-rape? scenarios here. Oprah performed a new monologue, "Under the *Burqa*," about the horrors of life for Afghan women under Taliban rule, followed by Zoya—a young representative of the Revolutionary Association of the Women of Afghanistan (RAWA)—who gave a heartbreaking, defiant speech. Three African women spoke against female genital mutilation and described ongoing efforts to replace cutting with new coming-of-age rituals, "circumcision by words."

I hadn't particularly wanted to see *The Vagina Monologues*. I assumed that it would be earnest and didactic—or maybe silly, or exploitative, or crude, a sort of *Oh! Calcutta!* for women. But I was elated by it. Besides being a wonderful night at the theater, it reminded me that after all the feminist debates (and splits), and all the books, and the Theory and the theories, in the real world there are still such people as women, who share a common biology and much else besides. And the power of feminism, whether or not it goes by that name, still resides in its capacity to transform women's consciousness at the deepest possible level: That's why Betty Friedan called her collection of letters from women not *It Got Me a Raise* (or a daycare center, or an abortion) but *It Changed My Life*. Sisterhood-is-powerful feminism may feel out of date to the professoriat, but there's a lot of new music still to be played on those old bones.

Besides, if feminists don't talk about sex in a fun, accessible, inspiring, nonpuritanical way, who will?

•◀ MARCH 5, 2001 ▶•

Anti-Catholic? Round Two

If a critic's clout can be measured by the ability to make an artist's name, the most important art critic in America today is clearly Rudolph Giuliani. Just over a year ago he excoriated the Brooklyn Museum of Art for including in its "Sensation" show Chris Ofili's *Holy Virgin Mary*—the elephant-dung-decorated painting of an African BVM, which the mayor found "anti-Catholic," blasphemous, and disgusting—and turned Ofili himself into a sensation overnight: One collector, I heard, complained that the media attention had driven Ofili's prices so high he couldn't afford him anymore. If I were Jake & Dinos Chapman, represented by a perverse sculpture of deformed and weirdly sexualized children, I would have been seriously peeved, and if I had been Richard Patterson, whose *Blue Minotaur,* a profound meditation on postmodernity and the heroic tradition, got no attention at all, I would have wept.

You'd think the mayor would have learned to stay his theocritical thunderbolts, but once again he has gone after the Brooklyn Museum for including an "anti-Catholic" work—Renee Cox's *Yo Mama's Last Supper*—in the new show of contemporary black photographers, "Committed to the Image." He's even suggested that what New York needs is a "decency commission," which got big laughs all around, since the mayor, a married man, is openly carrying on with his mistress, upon whom he has bestowed police protection worth some $200,000 annually at taxpayers' expense. As the whole world now knows, *Yo Mama* is a five-panel picture in which Cox appears naked, as Jesus, surrounded by male disciples—ten black, one white—at the Last Supper. As an artwork it's negligible, glossily produced but awkwardly composed and, to my eye, rather silly. Cox is thin and beautiful; the men, in robes and caftans, are handsome and buff—apparently the first Christians spent a lot of time in the gym and at the hair salon, getting elaborate dreadlocked coiffures. Unlike the figures in Leonardo's *Last Supper,* which are highly individualized and dramatically connected, the figures here are generic and stiff. My eye kept going to the limited food on offer: bowls of wax-looking fruit (did they have bananas in Old Jerusalem?), rolls, pita bread. Was the Last Supper a diet Seder?

If you want to see visually haunting work at "Committed to the Image," there's Gordon Parks, Albert Chong, Imari, Nathaniel Burkins, and many others. LeRoy W. Henderson's black ballet student, dressed in white and standing in front of a damaged classical frieze, interrogates the Western tradition much more deeply than *Yo Mama* does. Mfon's self-portraits of her mastectomized torso, meditations on beauty, heroism, and tragedy expressed through the female body, lay bare the high-fashion hokiness of Cox's costume drama. For fan and foe alike, the interest of *Yo Mama* appears to be political. Cox describes her art in ideological terms ("my images demand enlightenment through an equitable realignment of our race and gender politics"), and she has been quite pungent in defending it. As with *The Holy Virgin Mary,* the mayor hasn't actually seen it, nor had the numerous people who sent me frothing e-mails after I defended government support for the arts on *The O'Reilly Factor.*

Even the *New York Observer*'s famously conservative art critic, Hilton Kramer, who usually delights in withering descriptions of pictures he hates, apparently felt that depicting Christ as a naked black woman was so obviously, outrageously anti-Catholic he need say no more about the photo before embarking on his usual rampage. It would be interesting to know where the offense lies: Is it that Cox as Christ is naked, black, or female? All three? Two out of three? If one thinks of Catholics, the people, there's nothing bigoted about any of this. (Like Ofili, Cox is Catholic—as are most perpetrators of "anti-Catholic" works.) There is no ethnic stereotyping of the sort on view, for instance, on St. Patrick's Day, when the proverbial drunkenness of the Irish is the butt of endless rude humor, especially from the Irish themselves. While we're on the subject of ethnic stereotyping, it's worth noting that in a great deal of Christian art, Jesus and the disciples are portrayed as

Northern Europeans, while Judas is given the hooked nose and scraggly features of a cartoon Jew.

But if what is meant by anti-Catholic is anti-Catholic Church, why can't an artist protest its doctrines and policies? The Church is not a monastery in a wilderness, it's a powerful earthly institution that uses all the tools of modern politics to make social policy conform to its theology—and not just for Catholics, for everyone. It has to expect to take its knocks in the public arena. A church that has a 2,000-year tradition of disdain for women's bodies—documented most recently by Garry Wills (a Catholic) in his splendid polemic *Papal Sin*—and that still bars women from the priesthood because Jesus was a man, can't really be surprised if a twenty-first-century woman wonders what would be different if Jesus had been female, and flaunts that female body. And a church with a long history of racism—no worse than other mainstream American religions but certainly no better—can't expect the topic to be banned from discussion forever.

At the Brooklyn Museum, *Yo Mama's Last Supper* is in a separate room with its own security guard. On Sunday afternoon, it attracted blacks, whites, Asians, parents with small children, older women in groups, dating couples, students taking notes—*le tout* Brooklyn, which is turning out in large numbers for the show. I asked one black woman, who described herself as a Christian, what the picture meant to her. "It shows Life as a woman," she said. "It's beautiful." Her friend, who said he was a Muslim, liked the picture too.

If only I could get the mayor to review my book!

•◀ MARCH 19, 2001 ▶•

Letters to the Office of
Faith-Based Initiatives

HONORED INFIDEL,

In the near future we plan to expand our faith-based initiative, Holy Terror Sandblasting and Demolition Corp. New York City Mayor Rudolph Giuliani finds much merit in our proposal for a workfare program in which homeless people (men only, *naturellement!*) would be trained in medieval theology, art criticism, and the use of explosives. Please send dollars and the floor plan of the Brooklyn Museum. Or else.

> Thanks,
> *The Taliban*

DEAR PROFESSOR DiIULIO,

With medical costs going through the roof, you'd think there'd be a better way. And now, with the Lord's help, there is! Our idea is to buy up struggling inner-city hospitals and turn them into profit centers—no doctors, no nurses, no fancy-shmancy machines, and, best of all, no messy malpractice suits. Just the blessed healing power of prayer, provided 24 hours a day at bedside by recovering drug addicts as part of their therapy. It's total win-win—the government saves, the patient is saved—if not in this world, the next. And that's the world that counts, right?

> *Reverend Tommy Johnson*
> Pentecostal Holiness Church,
> Memphis, TN

DEAR DIRECTOR,

People say communism is just another religion, and they're right! We have everything the other faiths have—an all-encompassing worldview, sacred texts, meetings (and how!), schisms, excommunications, and declining numbers and influence. We'd like to reverse that last item with funding for our workfare proposal. First, we provide welfare mothers a crash course in job readiness, parenting skills, and the works of Karl Marx. Then, we get them jobs in daycare centers, where they pass their new "faith" on to the next generation, hopefully in time for the stock market crash. Don't count us out—a god that failed is still a god.

Call us,
The Communist Party, USA

DEAR BROTHER IN CHRIST,

Did you know the Chicago Archdiocese has an exorcist on staff? Our faith-based initiative, The Exercist™, would get this superbly trained but underutilized man out of the apse and into the community, where he'd help the so-called mentally ill get their sillies out with a carefully graduated low-impact aerobic workout that goes beyond head swiveling and projectile vomiting to get at the real nitty-gritty of diabolical possession. Then, everyone cools down with a sharing session, novena, and group hug: because admitting you're possessed by the Devil is half the cure!

Hope to hear from you soon,
Monsignor George O'Reilly
Roman Catholic Archdiocese of Chicago

DEAR PROF. DIIULIO,

For ten years we've been trying to get our own public school district so our kids wouldn't have to go to school with *goyim*. The courts keep turning us down. Then we wanted buses with only male drivers and sex-segregated seating, and the self-hating Jewish liberals said no to that too.

So we would like to become a Faith-Based Initiative with ourselves as clients. Our project is, we stay in our own town and only talk to each other. Because that's what G-d wants. Eventually we hope to get NEA funding as a conceptual art project ("The Choice: Chosen People Choose Themselves"), but a starter grant from your office would really put us on track.

> Let us know,
> *Rabbi Shlomo Greenblatt*
> Kiryas Joel, NY

DEAR MORTAL,

Ever wonder what's really behind that weird weather of recent years? Hint: It's a long time between burnt offerings. How about paying some deadbeat dads to slaughter a herd of oxen and throw those fabulous thighbones on the barbie? Everybody benefits: They learn the meat business, you get fruitful harvests, favorable winds, and calm, winedark seas, and we get a decent meal. Reply soonest—the wife is pushing me to zap you with a thunderbolt.

> *Zeus*

JACK,

Death Row Dad is a moving story of one father's embrace of capital punishment—*despite his own imminent execution*! While his ACLU lawyer tries frantically to turn up new evidence even as his own marriage unravels, and beautiful crusading nun Helen Prejean pleads with the governor for a stay, Leroy, who is in fact innocent, wants only that his son renounce his homosexual lifestyle and accept Christ as his personal savior. Soon the whole prison—even the crusty warden and a pair of racist guards—is praying for Leroy to get his wish. Jack, I promise you, when Leroy looks up from the gurney just before the lethal injection, sees his son standing there with his new girlfriend, and *rejects the last-minute stay of execution* ("I reckon the Lord is waitin' for my sorry self"), the audience won't know whether to cheer or go down on its knees. Morgan's people think yes for the lead, Julia's *very* interested in doing the nun. A major studio is ready to greenlight the minute your office comes through with co-financing.

Talk to you after the prayer meeting,

Howie

HEY,

How about a grant where I become a lay minister and practice laying on of hands? There's a whole heck of a lot of lonely women out there with big spiritual needs. I mean, really big.

Just kidding,
Bill Clinton

•◀ APRIL 2, 2001 ▶•

This Warning May Be
Hazardous to Your Health

A woman two months pregnant goes to see her ob-gyn for prenatal care. As required by law, her doctor informs her that her condition places her at greater risk for a wide range of medical problems: hypertension and diabetes if she is overweight; complications of surgery if, like one in four women, she has a cesarean section; permanent weight gain with its attendant problems, including heart disease; urinary tract infections and prolapsed uterus if she has had multiple pregnancies; postpartum depression or psychosis, leading in rare cases to suicide or infanticide; not to mention excruciating childbirth pain, stretch marks, and death. There are ominous social possibilities too, the doctor continues, reading from his state-supplied script: increased vulnerability to domestic violence; being or becoming a single mother, with all the struggles and poverty that entails; job and housing discrimination; the curtailment of education and professional training; and lowered income for life.

No state legislature would compel doctors to confront patients with the statistical risks of childbearing, serious though they are; a doctor who did so on his own would strike many as intrusive, offensive, and out of his mind. Should a woman seek abortion, however, anti-choicers are pushing state laws requiring that she be informed of a risk most experts do not believe exists: a link between abortion and breast cancer. Like the supposedly widespread psychological trauma of abortion, which even anti-choice surgeon general Dr. C. Everett Koop was unable to find evidence of, the abortion–breast cancer connection is being aggressively promoted by the anti-choice movement. (Even *Mother Jones* leapt on the bandwagon, with an April–May 1995 piece entitled "Abortion's Risk.")

"It's yet another example of efforts to encumber this legal choice and make it more difficult and painful for women," says Dr. Wendy Chavkin, professor of public health and clinical obstetrics and gynecology at New York's Columbia Presbyterian Hospital, and editor in chief of the *Journal of the American Medical Women's Association.* It's also an attempt by anti-choicers to reframe their opposition to abortion as concern for women's health, something not usually high on their list. These are, after all, the same people who fight health exceptions to "partial birth" abortion bans and who have successfully prevented poor women from receiving medically necessary abortions with Medicaid funds.

Nonetheless, such is the power of the anti-choice movement that laws have been passed in Montana and Mississippi, and bills are pending in fifteen other states, mandating a breast cancer warning (and in some cases, a waiting period for it to sink in). Along with laws come lawsuits: In Fargo, North Dakota, the Red River Women's Clinic is being sued for failing to give such a warning; a nineteen-year-old Pennsylvania woman is suing a New Jersey clinic for her abortion two years ago, which left her, she claims, with an overwhelming fear of contracting breast cancer. In ferociously anti-choice Louisiana, a new law permits women to sue for damages—including damages to the fetus!—up to ten years after their abortion. Given today's high rates of breast cancer, a deluge of litigation is in the making.

Does abortion cause breast cancer? Some studies have appeared to suggest a connection: Dr. Janet Daling, for example, an epidemiologist who says she is pro-choice, compared the abortion histories of 1,800 women with and without breast cancer and found that, among those who had been pregnant at least once, the risk of breast cancer was 50 percent higher for those who had abortions—but her cancer-free sample was obtained through telephone interviews with women chosen at random from the phone book. Not everyone has a phone, of course, which raises questions about the comparability of the samples; and besides, how many women would volunteer information about their abortion history to a voice on the phone? Like other studies showing a link, this one was marred by "recall bias": Cancer patients are more likely to volunteer negative information about themselves than healthy people. They are looking for an explanation for a disease—and one many feel must somehow be their fault. Demographic studies, which are free from recall bias, produce different results: Lindefors Harris, analyzing the national medical database of Swedish women in 1989, found that women did deny their abortions, that breast cancer patients were less likely to do so—and that women who had had abortions were *less* likely to get breast cancer. The largest study to date, of 1.5 million Danish women, found no correlation.

"The supposed link between breast cancer and abortion is motivated by politics, not medicine," says Dr. David Grimes, clinical professor of obstetrics and gynecology at the University of North Carolina. "The weight of the evidence at this time indicates no association. To force this on women is just cruel." Indeed, the National Cancer Institute, the American Cancer Society, and the World Health Organization, none of which have an ax to grind, reject the notion. The standard medical textbook, *Diseases of the Breast*, concurs. The main figure advocating the link is Dr. Joel Brind, professor of biology and endocrinology at Baruch College, who has done no original research on this issue but is a tireless anti-choice propagandist—plug "abortion breast cancer" into a search engine and the top half-dozen sites are his.

Abortion is just about the only medical procedure in which doctors and patients are hemmed about by lawmakers. No other operation has legally mandated waiting periods, although many are dangerous, life-altering, and irreversible. With no other operation are doctors legally required to give specific information—certainly not information that the vast preponderance of medical opinion believes to be false or at best unproven. Good medical practice calls for discussion of the pros and cons of particular courses of treatment, not burdening the patient's choice with unsubstantiated fears. Will we ever see a law requiring doctors to tell pregnant patients that abortion is statistically safer than carrying to term—which it is? Sure, the day state lawmakers put a waiting period on Viagra prescriptions, to let male patients really consider whether an erection is worth a heart attack.

●◄ APRIL 16, 2001 ►●

Analyze This

This is not going to be a column blaming Ralph Nader and the Greens for the daily disasters of the Bush administration, so don't stop reading—yet. That column has been written dozens of times, in every shade of emotion with which the words "I told you so" can be uttered, and I think it's been pretty well established that Tweedledum and Tweedledee are at best fraternal rather than identical twins. Or are there readers out there who think the Gore administration would be proposing a budget that would end contraceptive coverage for federal employees while angling for a huge tax cut for the richest 1 percent? If so, you won't have any problem washing your delicious school-lunch salmonellaburger down with a big glass of arsenic-laced water from one of our fine mining and timber states.

Nader's assistant called me recently to say that he had been misquoted last summer in *Outside,* which had him hoping for a Bush win. But those who thought the Democrats deserved to die seem to have gotten their wish. I mean, where *is* Al Gore? I've been an adjunct professor myself, and the duties are not all that taxing. He could be going on the Sunday-morning talk shows every week, rallying opposition to Bush's onslaught against the environment—the Kyoto treaty was supposedly his baby, after all. Maybe he read Alexander Cockburn's column in the testosterone-addled *New York Press* claiming the greenhouse effect is bunk and now thinks it's *good* that Bush slammed the door on the treaty. Clinton's off riding elephants in India, Hillary voted for the bankruptcy bill, nobody wants to pay to make sure votes get counted in poor neighborhoods (remember when voting-booth upgrades were definitely on the agenda, whoever won Florida?), and the McCain-Feingold cam-

paign finance reform bill, which was going to start the arduous process
of getting big money out of electoral politics, has morphed into a measure that doubles the Republican hard-money advantage while abolishing soft money, where the Democrats had edged ahead. Thanks a lot,
Senator Feingold! And you too, Senator Wellstone! Now advocacy organizations like the ACLU and NARAL will be barred from running issue
ads for sixty days before the election. Forget the First Amendment: Let
them buy their own radio and TV stations like the right-wingers do.

None of this cowardice, confusion, and collapse is the fault of
Ralph Nader or the Greens: Would the Republicans be quivering in fear
if they were the ones out of power? Still, the political landscape we confront today does call into question some of the arguments that were
made for the Nader candidacy. You will remember that I expressed a certain skepticism about these claims last spring and summer, for which I
was belabored with e-mails from *Nation* readers for months. Progressives don't like to analyze their past enthusiasms in the light of history,
preferring to move right along to the next glorious cause. So let's go to
the videotape and see what happened:

- I said the Greens would do poorly because that's the general fate of
  progressive third-party and symbolic presidential candidacies; for
  the decreasing number of Americans who actually vote, the two
  parties are not identical and each offers concrete rewards to its constituency. Perhaps nonvoters would bring a new set of concerns and
  demands to the electoral table—that was the thinking behind the
  motor voter bill—but to register nonvoters on a massive scale and
  get them to the polls was quite beyond the capacities (or radar
  screen) of the Greens. What happened: Nader polled 2.7 percent.

- I said that history suggested presidential candidacies did not build
  movements, as many supporters claimed Nader's run would do. I
  noted the rapid descent into nutty irrelevance of the most successful third-party candidate in modern history, Ross Perot, and his Reform Party. A party that cannot attract large sums of money and
  cannot deliver favors to its supporters is just not in the game. What
  happened: The Greens tool along at the same modest level as be-

fore, with eighty-one mostly low-level elected municipal officials thinly scattered around the country. Nader claims he is shut out by the media—surprise—but media never built a movement. Can you imagine Eugene Debs or Bob La Follette, to whom Nader is often compared, letting Rupert Murdoch or the *Washington Post* decide whether his message gets out or not?

- I pooh-poohed the Greens' somewhat contradictory prediction that Nader would attract new voters who would not have gone for Gore but would vote for "good Democrats" lower down on the ticket. Why would voters drawn to the polls by a candidate who spent months bashing the Democrats turn around and vote for them? What happened: Despite much spin on both sides, Nader votes were probably a wash for down-ticket Dems. There was no major influx of new voters lured by Nader. Youth voting went down.

- I took issue with the argument that the Nader candidacy would push the Democratic Party left. As the Greens themselves have observed in disclaiming responsibility for Bush's win, thirteen times as many registered Democrats (13 percent) voted for Bush in Florida as for Nader (1 percent). Nationally too, many more Democrats voted Republican than voted Green. So if you were thinking of running for President as a Democrat, where would you look for votes? Left to the Naderites, or right to the Dems and moderate Republicans who voted for Bush? Answer: Joe Lieberman's already exploring his options for 2004.

SPEAKING OF PAST ENTHUSIASMS, the Teamster-turtle alliance isn't looking too good: Teamsters president Jimmy Hoffa, Jr., supports Bush's proposal to drill for oil and gas in the Arctic National Wildlife Refuge. According to the *New York Times,* Hoffa said drilling would help stabilize the economy and create employment, including 25,000 Teamsters' jobs at a time when the nation appears near recession. Turtle soup, anyone?

●◀ APRIL 30, 2001 ▶●

Childcare Scare

Depending on who's counting, one in four, five, or six American children lives in poverty, the highest rate in the industrialized West. Nearly 11 million have no health insurance. Hundreds of thousands are in foster care. Five hundred thousand are homeless. The infant mortality rate in the inner cities of Washington, New Haven, East St. Louis, and Chicago rivals that of Malaysia. There is one thing America has, though, that you won't find in France or Denmark or Sweden or Italy, and that is the persistent conviction that children would be just fine if only their mothers would give up working and stay home.

Consider the media feeding frenzy around the latest research released by the National Institute for Child Health and Development. Just about every paper has given major play to its finding that 17 percent of children who regularly spend thirty hours or more a week in childcare between the ages of three months and four and a half years are aggressive, disobedient, and defiant in kindergarten, versus only 6 percent of children who have spent less than ten hours a week in childcare. (Childcare, by the way, is everybody but Mom, including nannies, Dad, and Grandma—so forget equal parenting, and forget, too, the nanas and bubbes and aunts and older sisters who have taken care of small children for centuries while mothers toiled in the fields or behind counters or over laundry vats long before "working mothers" existed.) Buried in the coverage is the study's other finding: that high-quality childcare is associated with better cognitive and linguistic skills. Unmentioned is the fact that only a few years ago welfare moms were lambasted as lazy and useless for staying home with their children by some of the same right-wing ideologues now crowing on TV about the NICHD study. The truth is, the daycare debate has always been about college-educated working moms—women with good jobs some think they shouldn't have, and children every quirk of whose development is of interest to the opinion classes.

As it happens, Jay Belsky, who has gotten the lion's share of the press attention and is often cited, incorrectly, as the study's lead or even sole author, has been warning against the dangers of early childcare since 1986, when he claimed it caused babies and toddlers to fail to bond with their mothers. That didn't pan out, but Belsky is all over the press now, boasting of his lack of political correctness in bringing people the unpleasant truth. "I won't lie down and play dead," he told the *New York Times*. Elsewhere, he has recommended not only parental leave but that mothers reconsider full-time work. Sarah Friedman, Kathleen McCartney, and other researchers on the study don't agree at all. "This study was conducted by a team of some thirty researchers," Friedman told me. "His view is not the majority view." And she adds, "the type of analysis does not allow us to infer causality." In other words, childcare may not cause aggression but may be associated with something else that does—family stress, exhausted parents. Says Deborah Vandrell of the University of Wisconsin, "Mothers should stay home? Childcare is bad for kids? The data don't support that." And indeed, the study isn't so dire: Most kids in childcare are fine; the problematic behavior falls within the normal range; moreover, kids kept out of childcare double their rate of aggression when they finally get to school, suggesting that Vandrell may be right when she theorizes that the results mostly reflect the opportunity for aggressive behavior, and that kids would benefit from better conflict-resolution skills. (In an all-caps e-mail to me, Belsky professed himself "appalled" that McCartney put this idea forward on *Face the Nation*—he claims the study refutes it—and accused his colleagues of focusing on childcare quality rather than quantity because they don't want to be "unpopular.")

It's easy to take potshots at social science, so I'll just note in passing that one of the criteria for "cooperation" is "keeps room neat and clean without being reminded." It does seem like yesterday, though, that Bruno Bettelheim was blaming the group care typical of an Israeli kibbutz for making kids *too sociable*, too compliant, not ruggedly individualist enough. I know, it sounds crazy now—have you ever met a laid-back Israeli? But then, as Caryl Rivers pointed out on *Women's E-News,* back in the 1950s stay-at-home moms were blamed for producing a generation of mollycoddled wimps unable to stand up to the communists. If middle-class working moms really did trade the briefcase for the stroller, not only would lots of them be poor and frustrated, but within five years we'd be reading about spoiled, feminized sons and angry, condescending daughters already plotting their escape to Lesbian Island.

My French friends find the American debate over childcare utterly mystifying—all French three-year-olds go to the *écoles maternelles,* and many are in crèches long before that. In European countries with long-established childcare systems, the American suspicion of daycare does not exist. (Vandrell noted that the European papers haven't even reported the NICHD study.) But then, why would it? European parents have government-paid parental leave and government-funded childcare systems staffed with well-trained and decently paid professionals. In this country, paid leave is a rarity, and daycare is like baby-sitting: Any warm body will do. Pay is abysmal, training rare, formal standards low. And, of course, the very conservatives who champion the NICHD study oppose every attempt to raise those standards, because that would cost money, encourage "bureaucracy," and go against the know-nothing faux libertarianism that is their political stock-in-trade.

There's another difference, though. Although everywhere childcare is connected to women's employment, in Europe childcare was developed as something that would be beneficial for children, like nursery school; in this country, it's seen as something for women—women, who if middle-class shouldn't have jobs and if low-income shouldn't have kids. Daycare in America is about feminism. That's why no matter how many studies appear touting the benefits of high-quality childcare, the ones that hit the headlines are always full of gloom.

•◀ MAY 14, 2001 ▶•

Happy Mother's Day

When we left that old journalistic evergreen, the evils of daycare, two weeks ago, the media hysteria over the NICHD study had just about peaked. The researchers had begun to turn on each other in public, never a good sign—Jay Belsky, a champion sound-biter who had seized the media initiative by strongly suggesting that the study showed that more than thirty hours a week with anyone but Mom would risk turning little Dick and Jane into obnoxious brats, was sharply challenged by numerous co-researchers, who claimed the study's results were tentative, ambiguous, and negligible, hardly results at all, really. After a few rounds of this, the media suddenly remembered that no one had actually seen the study, which won't be published for another year and which does seem on the face of it rather counterintuitive: Daddy care is bad? Granny care is bad? Quality of care makes *no* difference? What really did the trick, though, I suspect, was that every fed-up woman journalist in America sat down and bashed out a piece telling the doomsayers to lay off, already. With 13 million kids in daycare, and two-thirds of women with children under six in the workforce, working moms are a critical mass, and they are really, really tired of being made to feel guilty when they are, in fact, *still* the ones doing double duty at work and home.

Compare the kerfuffle over the quantity of hours spent in daycare with the ho-hum response to studies of its quality. On May 1, Worthy Wage Day for childcare workers, came a study from Berkeley and Washington, D.C., that looked at staffing in seventy-five better-than-average California daycare centers serving kids aged two and a half through five. According to *Then and Now: Changes in Child Care Staffing 1994–2000,* staffers and directors are leaving the field in droves. At the centers in the study, 75 percent of teachers and 40 percent of directors on the job in 1996 had quit four years later. Some centers had turnover rates of 100 percent or more (!) from one year to the next. Half the leavers abandoned the field entirely—raising their incomes by a whopping $8,000 a year compared with the other half, who remained in childcare. Nor were those who left easily replaced: Most of the centers that lost staffers could not fill all their job slots by the next year.

The demoralization and turmoil caused by constant turnover stresses both the workers who stay and the children. Making matters worse, the new workers are "significantly less well-educated" than those they replace—only a third have bachelor's degrees, as opposed to almost half of the leavers. Pay, say the researchers, is the main issue: Not only have salaries not risen with the rising tide supposedly lifting all boats; when adjusted for inflation, they have actually fallen. A daycare teacher works twelve months a year to earn $24,606—just over half the average salary of public-school teachers, who work for ten months (not that school-teachers are well paid, either). Center directors, at the top of the field, earn on average a mere $37,571; the recommended starting salary for elementary-school teachers in California is $38,000. (In France, which has a first-rate public daycare system, daycare teachers and elementary-school teachers are paid the same.) Daycare teachers love their work—two-thirds say they would recommend it as a career—but simply do not earn enough to make a life in the field.

It's a paradox: Even as more and more families, of every social class, rely on daycare, and even as we learn more and more about the importance of early childhood education for intellectual and social development, and even as we talk endlessly about the importance of "quality" and "stability" and "qualified" staff, the amount of money we are willing—or able—to pay the people we ask to do this demanding and important job goes down. Instead of addressing this reality, we endlessly distract ourselves with Mommy Wars. (You let your child have milk from the store? *My* child drinks nothing but organic goat milk from flocks tended by Apollo himself!) And because as Americans we don't really believe the rest of the world exists, when a study comes along suggesting that other-than-mother-care produces some nasty and difficult kids, we don't think to ask if this is a problem in Denmark or France, and if not, why not.

Two new books of great interest, Ann Crittenden's *The Price of Motherhood* and Nancy Folbre's *The Invisible Heart: Economics and Family Values,* point out that there is a crisis of care in America. Women are incredibly disadvantaged when they perform traditionally female work— childcare, housework, eldercare—unpaid within families. (According to Crittenden, motherhood is the single biggest cause of poverty for women.) The free market cannot replace this unpaid labor at decent rates, Folbre argues, because it would be too expensive: Even now, most families cannot afford tuition at a "quality" daycare center, any more than they can afford private school. And men are hardly falling over themselves to do their share—nobody's talking about the Daddy Track, you'll notice. Both writers call for recognizing the work of care as essential to the economy: Top-quality daycare should be funded by the government, like school, because it is a "public good."

Unfortunately, funding public goods is not exactly a high priority of government, which is busily cutting programs for children in favor of a huge tax cut for the rich. These days our main public goods seem to be prisons ($4.5 billion), the drug war ($19 billion, including $1 billion in military aid to Colombia), abstinence education ($250 million), and executing Timothy McVeigh ($50 million, not counting plane tix for celebrity death witness Gore Vidal). You can always find money for the things you really want.

•⊰ MAY 28, 2001 ⊱•

Cold Comfort

They were kidnapped on the street, or summoned to the village square, or lured from home with false promises of work, to be forced into the Japanese military's far-flung, highly organized system of sexual slavery throughout its occupied territories in the 1930s and forties. Of some 200,000 so-called comfort women only a quarter survived their ordeal; many of those died soon after of injuries, disease, madness, suicide. For years the ones who remained were silent, living marginal lives. But beginning in 1991, first one, then a trickle, then hundreds of middle-aged and elderly women from Korea, China, Taiwan, the Philippines, and other former Japanese possessions came forward, demanding that the Japanese government acknowledge its responsibility, apologize, and make reparations. Despite a vigorous campaign of international protest, with mass demonstrations in Korea and Taiwan, Japan has hung tough: In 1995, Prime Minister Tomiichi Murayama offered "profound"—but unofficial—apologies and set up a small fund to help the women, to be financed on a voluntary basis by business; this past March, the Hiroshima high court overturned a modest award to three Korean women. As if official foot-dragging weren't demeaning enough, a popular comic-book history of Japan alleges that the comfort women were volunteers, and ultra-right-wing nationalists have produced middle-school textbooks, approved for use in classrooms, that omit any mention of the government's role in the comfort-woman program.

Frustrated in Japan, the comfort women have now turned to the U.S. Court of Appeals for the Washington, D.C., Circuit. Under the 212-year-old Alien Tort Claims Act, foreigners may sue one another in U.S. courts for human-rights violations; the women are also relying on a law against sexual trafficking passed last year by Congress. In mid-May, however, the State Department asked the Justice Department to file a brief expressing its sympathies with the women's sufferings but urging that the case be dismissed as lacking jurisdiction: Japan has sovereign immunity, under which nations agree to overlook each other's wrongdoings, and, moreover, treaties between it and the United States put finis to claims arising from the war.

In other words, it's all right to seize girls and women and put them in rape camps—*aka* "comfort stations"—for the amusement of soldiers far from home, as long as it's part of official military policy. War is hell, as the trustees of the New School noted in their letter absolving their president, Bob Kerrey, of the killing of as many as twenty-one Vietnamese women and children. If it's okay to murder civilians, how wrong can it be to rape and enslave them?

"The Administration's position is particularly terrible and irresponsible when you consider the evolution of attitudes toward wartime rape over the last ten years," says Elizabeth Cronise, who with Michael Hausfeld is arguing the comfort women's case. Indeed, sexual violence in war has typically been regarded as the inevitable concomitant of battle, part of the spoils of war, maybe even, for the evolutionary-psychology minded, the point of it: Think of the rape of the Sabine women, or the plot of the *Iliad,* which is precipitated by a fight between Achilles and Agamemnon over possession of the captured Trojan girls Chryseis and Briseis, although my wonderful old Greek professor Howard Porter didn't quite put it like that. It was only this past February that an international tribunal brought charges solely for war crimes of sexual violence, when three Bosnian Serbs were convicted in The Hague of organizing and participating in the rape, torture, and sexual enslavement of Muslim women.

But even by these ghastly standards, the case of the comfort women stands out for the degree of planning and organization the Japanese military employed. Noting, for example, that subject populations tended to resent the rape of local women, authorities typically shipped the women far from home; although the women saw little or no money, "comfort stations" were set up as brothels with ethnically graduated fees, from Japanese women at the top to Chinese women at the bottom. The system was not, strictly speaking, a wartime phenomenon: It began in 1932, with the Japanese occupation of Manchuria, and continued after the war's end. In fact, according to Yoshimi Yoshiaki, whose *Comfort Women: Sexual Slavery in the Japanese Military During World War II* (Columbia University Press) is crucial reading, the Japanese military authorities set up comfort stations for the conquering American troops. As Cronise points out, even if the United States has closed the books on Japan's wartime atrocities, it could still side with the comfort women on the grounds that many of them were enslaved during peacetime.

"The government's position is technically defensible," says Widney Brown, advocacy director for women's rights at Human Rights Watch. "What's not defensible is the Department of Justice's giving as a reason that it doesn't want to jeopardize relations with Japan." Incredibly, the Justice Department is arguing just that, along with the further self-interested point that a ruling in favor of the comfort women would open the United States to human-rights lawsuits in other countries. (Remember that the United States has sabotaged the International Criminal Court.) Says Brown, "It shows a failure to understand the significance of the comfort women case as a major step in the development of human rights for women. After all, their case could have been brought up in the Far East tribunal right after World War II, but it wasn't. This is a major chance to move beyond that. You could even argue that the view of women as property—if not of one man, then another—was what prevented sexual slavery from being seen as a war crime until now."

The U.S. lawsuit may well be the comfort women's last chance. Now in their seventies and eighties, most will soon be dead, and since few married or had children, there won't be many descendants to continue the fight for reparations. By stonewalling, the Japanese government will have won. And the Bush administration will have helped it. All that's missing is the call for healing and mutual forgiveness.

•◀ JUNE 11, 2001 ▶•

Mad Bad Ads

Memo to editors of campus papers: When right-wing ideologues show up with an ad full of nonsense, just take the money and print it. That way, they will not be able to pose as the victim of "political correctness," they will not get millions of dollars' worth of free publicity, and their ideas will not acquire the glamour of the forbidden. By the same token, you will not look afraid of debate and controversy, nor will you have to explain why you rejected their ad while printing something equally false, offensive, or stupid on some previous occasion.

Never mind that the people accusing you of censorship practice it themselves. In an amusing riposte to David Horowitz's flamethrower ad opposing reparations for slavery, *Salon*'s David Mazel proved unable to place an enthusiastically pro-abortion ad in papers on conservative campuses; and as Fairness and Accuracy in Reporting points out, the *Boston Globe,* which editorialized against students who rejected the Horowitz ad, itself rejected an ad criticizing Staples, a major advertiser, for using old-growth forest pulp in its typing paper. So there, and so there! But you're in a better place to make such arguments stick if you can stand— however cynically and self-servingly—on the high ground of free speech yourself.

Just as Horowitz faded, having shot himself in the foot by refusing to pay the *Daily Princetonian* after it printed his ad but editorialized against it, up comes the *soi-disant* Independent Women's Forum—you know, that intrepid band of far-right free spirits funded by the ultraconservative Sarah Scaife Foundation—with an ad in the UCLA *Daily Bruin* and Yale *Daily News* urging students to "Take Back the Campus!" and "Combat the radical feminist assault on Truth." The IWF charges "campus feminism" with being "a kind of cult" in which "students are inculcated with bizarre conspiracy theories about the 'capitalist patriarchal hegemony,'" a fount of "Ms./Information," "male-bashing and victimology." Brainwashing isn't exactly what comes to mind when I think of the revolution in scholarship that has produced such celebrated historians as Linda Gordon, Ellen DuBois, Joan Scott, Rickie Solinger, Leslie Reagan, and Kathy Peiss. The sweeping, paranoiac language gives it away—this is IWF member Christina Hoff Sommers speaking from her perch at that noted institution of higher learning, the American Enterprise Institute.

The bulk of the ad consists of a list of "the ten most common feminist myths" and the "facts" that supposedly prove them false. Much of this is lifted from Sommers's *Who Stole Feminism?,* a book that attempted to deploy a few gotchas against hyperbolic statistics and questionable studies to deny the significance of violence, sexism, and discrimination in women's lives. I mean, how important is it that "rule of thumb" may not derive, as some feminist activists believe and some newspapers have printed, from an old legal rule permitting husbands to beat their wives with a stick no thicker than their thumb (Myth #4)? Feminists did not make this folk etymology up out of nothing—actually, according to Sharon Fenick of the University of Chicago, writing on the Urban Legends website, it probably goes back to the eighteenth century, when a respected English judge, Francis Buller, earned the nickname "Judge Thumb," for declaring such "correction" permissible. That it was legal for premodern English husbands to beat their wives within limits is not in dispute (in her book, Sommers obscures this fact by omitting the Latin phrases from a passage in Blackstone's *Commentaries*); nor is the fact that wife-beating, regardless of the law, was, and sometimes still is, treated lightly by the legal system under the rubric of marital privacy. Thus, in 1910 the Supreme Court, in *Thompson v. Thompson,* barred wives from suing husbands for "injuries to person or property as though they were strangers." (I learned this, and much else relating to the history of American marriage, from Yale feminist historian Nancy Cott's fascinating *Public Vows: A History of Marriage and the Nation.*)

And what about Myth #2, "Women earn 75 cents for every dollar a man earns." That doesn't come from some man-bashing fabulator squirreled away in a women's studies department. It comes from the U.S. government! The IWF argues that the disparity disappears when you take education, training, occupation, continuity of employment, motherhood, and other factors into account—but even if that were true, which it isn't, to overlook all those things is itself *advocacy,* a politicized way of defining sex discrimination in order to minimize it.

And then there's #1, the mother of all myths: "One in four women in college has been the victim of rape or attempted rape." The IWF debunks this number, which comes from the research of Mary Koss, by citing the low numbers of reported rapes on college campuses, but the one-in-four figure includes off-campus and pre-college rapes and rape attempts. Are Koss's numbers the last word? Of course not. In 1998 the Centers for Disease Control and Prevention found that among all women, one in five had experienced a rape or attempted rape at some point in her life. In January the Justice Department released a report claiming that 3 percent of college women experience rape or attempted rape per school year, which does add up over four years.

Does irresponsible, lax, or even slanted use of facts and figures exist in "campus feminism"? Sure—and out of it, too. (Try economics.) But what does that have to do with women's studies, a very large, very lively interdisciplinary field of intellectual inquiry, in which many of the supposed verities of contemporary feminism are hotly contested? The real debate isn't over the merits of this study or that, in social science, "results" are always provisional. Now that the IWF has thrown down the gauntlet, feminist scholars should call for that real debate. Resolved: Women's lives were more seriously studied and accurately understood when almost no tenured professors were female. Or, Resolved: Violence against women is not a major social problem. Or, Resolved: If women aren't equal, it's their own darn fault.

●◀ JUNE 25, 2001 ▶●

It's a Bird, It's a Plane,
It's . . . Superclone?

Is human cloning a feminist issue? Two cloning bans are currently winding their way through Congress: In the Senate, the Human Cloning Prohibition Act seeks to ban all cloning of human cells, while a House version leaves a window open for cloning stem cells but bans attempts to create a cloned human being. Since both bills are the brainchildren of anti-choice Republican yahoos, who have done nothing for women's health or rights in their entire lives, I was surprised to get an e-mail inviting me to sign a petition supporting the total ban, organized by feminist heroine Judy Norsigian of the Boston Women's Health Book Collective (the producers of *Our Bodies, Ourselves*) and signed by Ruth Hubbard, Barbara Seaman, Naomi Klein, and many others. Are feminists so worried about "creating a duplicate human" that they would ban potentially useful medical research? Isn't that the mirror image of anti-choice attempts to block research using stem cells from embryos created during in vitro fertilization?

My antennae go up when people start talking about threats to "human individuality and dignity"—that's a harrumph, not an argument. The petition raises one real ethical issue, however, that hasn't gotten much attention but by itself justifies a ban on trying to clone a person: The necessary experimentation—implanting clonal embryos in surrogate mothers until one survives till birth—would involve serious medical risks for the women and lots of severely defective babies. Dolly, the cloned Scottish sheep, was the outcome of a process that included hundreds of monstrous discards, and Dolly herself has encountered developmental problems. That's good reason to go slow on human research—especially when you consider that the people pushing it most aggressively are the Raelians, the UFO-worshiping cult of technogeeks who have enlisted the services of Panayiotis Zavos, a self-described "cowboy" of assisted reproduction who has been fired from two academic jobs for financial and other shenanigans.

Experimental ethics aside, though, I have a hard time taking cloning seriously as a threat to women or anyone else—the scenarios are so nutty. Jean Bethke Elshtain, who took a break from bashing gay marriage to testify last month before Congress against cloning, wrote a piece in *The New Republic* in 1997 in which she seemed to think cloning an adult cell would produce another adult—a carbon of yourself that could be kept for spare parts, or maybe a small army of Mozart Xeroxes, all wearing knee breeches and playing *The Marriage of Figaro*. Actually, Mozart's clone would be less like him than identical twins are like each other: He would have different mitochondrial DNA and a different prenatal environment, not to mention a childhood in twenty-first-century America with the Smith family rather than in eighteenth-century Austria under the thumb of the redoubtable Leopold Mozart. The clone might be musical, or he might be a billiard-playing lounge lizard, but he couldn't compose *Figaro*. Someone already did that.

People thinking about cloning tend to imagine *Brave New World* dystopias in which genetic engineering reinforces inequality. But why, for example, would a corporation go to the trouble of cloning cheap labor? We have Mexico and Central America right next door! As for cloning geniuses to create superbabies, good luck. The last thing most Americans want are kids smarter than they are, rolling their eyeballs every time Dad starts in on the gays and slouching off to their rooms to I-M other genius kids in Sanskrit. Over nine years, only 229 babies were born to women using the sperm bank stocked with Nobel Prize winners' semen—a tiny fraction, I'll bet, of those conceived in motel rooms with reproductive assistance from Dr. Jack Daniel.

Similarly, cloning raises fears of do-it-yourself eugenics—designer babies "enhanced" through gene manipulation. It's hard to see that catching on, either. Half of all pregnancies are unintended in this country. People could be planning for "perfect" babies today—preparing for conception by giving up cigarettes and alcohol and unhealthy foods, reading Stendhal to their fetuses in French. Only a handful of yuppie control freaks actually do this, the same ones who obsess about getting their child into a nursery school that leads straight to Harvard. Those people are already the "genetic elite"—white, with lots of family money. What do they need genetic enhancement for? They think they're perfect now.

Advocates of genetic tinkering make a lot of assumptions that opponents tacitly accept: for instance, that intelligence, talent, and other qualities are genetic, and in a simple way. Gays, for example, worry that discovery of a "gay gene" will permit selective abortion of homosexual fetuses, but it's obvious that same-sex desire is more complicated than a single gene. Think of ancient Greece, or Smith College. Even if genetic enhancement isn't the pipe dream I suspect it is, feminists should be the first to understand how socially mediated supposedly inborn qualities are—after all, women are always being told anatomy is their destiny.

There's a strain of feminism that comes out of the women's health movement of the seventies that is deeply suspicious of reproductive technology. In this view, prenatal testing, in vitro fertilization, and other innovations commodify women's bodies, are subtly coercive, and increase women's anxieties, while moving us steadily away from experiencing pregnancy and childbirth as normal, natural processes. There's some truth to that, but what about the side of feminism that wants to open up new possibilities for women? Reproductive technology lets women have children, and healthy children, later; have kids with lesbian partners; have kids despite disabilities and illness. Cloning sounds a little weird, but so did in vitro in 1978, when Louise Brown became the first "test tube baby." True, these technologies have evolved in the context of for-profit medicine; true, they represent skewed priorities, given that 43 million Americans lack health insurance and millions worldwide die of curable diseases like malaria. Who could argue that the money and brain power devoted to cloning stem cells could not be better used on something else? But the same can be said of many aspects of American life. The enemy isn't the research, it's capitalism.

•◄ JULY 23, 2001 ►•

Baby, It's Cold Inside!

The President now says he will make the decision on federal funding of embryonic stem cell research before Labor Day—in time to catch the wave of his just-announced refocusing of his administration on "values." (Apparently tax cuts for the rich and drilling in the Arctic aren't catnip to women voters. Who knew? Bring on that all-abstinence-all-the-time cable station America's soccer moms are clamoring for!) Perhaps revealing more than he intended about customary decision-making procedures at the White House, Bush has said that his administration is being "unusually deliberative" about stem cells. Most people, not to mention the powerful biotech industry, say they want the research to go forward, even though it involves the destruction of four- to six-day-old blastocysts left over from fertility treatments. However, Bush not only promised during the campaign that he would eliminate the funding, he went to the Vatican in July for direction, as any good Methodist would do, where the pope declared that "a tragic coarsening of consciences accompanies the assault on innocent human life in the womb," and out of it, too. If only Bush had gone to a rabbi—modern medicine practically *is* the Jewish religion.

In a rational world, the President would decide on funding by thinking about whether this was the best use of the country's money and brainpower—but then, in a rational world, the President would not be making this decision at all, as if he were a medieval king dispensing largesse and boons. In this world, the stem-cell debate is not about health policy, it's about abortion: Is a 150-cell blastocyst—the equivalent of a fertilized egg not yet implanted in the womb—a person or not?

Many people usually lined up on the anti-choice side have a hard time visualizing a frozen speck as a baby, especially since, as my friend Dr. Michele Barry pointed out, that frozen speck could be helping to cure diseases Republican men get, like Alzheimer's and Parkinson's. (Would we be having this debate if the research showed promise to cure Chagas disease and sleeping sickness?)

According to Orrin Hatch, it's okay to destroy a frozen embryo because the embryo is only a person if it's in a woman. This location theory of personhood is obviously unsatisfactory. You put the cells in the woman, it's a person; you take them out, it's not a person; you put them back in, *voilà!*—it's a person again. You might as well say Orrin Hatch is a person in his office but not in his car. If, as anti-choicers like to claim, what makes personhood is a full set of chromosomes—rather than, say, possession of a gender, a body, a head, a brain—then a clump of cells in an ice-cube tray is at least as much a person as Trent Lott. Maybe more.

I think I see a way to help the president out of his difficulties. The White House should ask opponents of embryonic stem-cell research to sign a legally binding pledge forgoing any treatment or procedures derived from it, both for themselves and their minor offspring. If they really believe that frozen embryos are children, they should have no problem with this. An impressive list of right-wing pundits have laid out the argument in characteristically colorful fashion: Andrew Sullivan, for instance, insisted in *The New Republic* that the blastocyst is "the purest form of human being" and to kill it is to "extinguish us." (Someone should tell him that nearly half of all fertilized eggs fail to implant and are washed out with menstruation—maybe there should be funerals for tampons, just to be on the safe side.) In the *Washington Times,* Michael Fumento writes that stem-cell research "rightly or wrongly" summons up visions of Dr. Mengele's Auschwitz experiments. Who, after all, would be willing to treat their illness with a potion of boiled five-year-olds? Well, maybe some very bad five-year-olds, already set on the path to crime and low SAT scores by single mothers, but you see my point. As Eric Cohen put it in *The Weekly Standard,* "to ask the sick and dying to love the mystery of life more than their own lives" is a bit like asking comfortable Americans to sacrifice themselves in wars against tyranny around the globe: "Both require a courageous commitment to something larger than self-interest." The mystery of life versus, well, life. Let's put people on record.

If frozen embryos really are children, though, is it enough not to kill them? Don't we need to rescue them from the icy wasteland to which they have been consigned? Their selfish yuppie biological parents may have abandoned them, but the Family Research Council says that every frozen embryo should have "an opportunity to be born" and I am surprised that the anti-choicers haven't yet rallied to the cause. True, a few women unable to conceive naturally have been implanted with the leftover embryos of others, but there are some 100,000 frozen embryos in need of homes—it's like a whole other foster-care system.

Anti-choice women are the only hope to get those embryos out of Frigidaire limbo. As they like to say, an extra pregnancy is just an inconvenience, its health dangers much exaggerated by pro-choice babykillers and its opportunities for moral growth scorned by our culture of death. So, Concerned Women for America, give a frozen embryo the gift of gestation! Mona Charen, Ann Coulter, it isn't enough to write columns comparing stem-cell research to tearing transplantable organs out of freshly killed prisoners—you could be leading the way! Think of the talk-show opportunities. ("Chris, some people think we right-wing women are a pack of peroxided harpies, but when I thought of those adorable cells just *trapped* in there with the yogurt, I knew I had to help!") They can always put the baby up for adoption so it will be raised by normal people, as they think pregnant singles ought to do. Frozen embryo rescue would be an interesting project for the Sisters of Life, the anti-choice order of nuns founded by the late John Cardinal O'Connor. Sort of a virgin birth kind of thing.

In a pinch, the President can always call on welfare moms laid off from their jobs at Wendy's in the looming recession. It would be a natural extension of his plan to offer healthcare directly to poor fetuses, a sort of housing program for blastocysts. Compassionate conservatism at its best!

●◄ AUGUST 20, 2001 ►●

Summer Follies

The best thing about my summer in the country was that I didn't have a TV and usually got to the market after the tiny clutch of papers had already been snatched up by the local information junkies. So I missed a lot of Really Important News. Gary Condit, who? Most of my friends believe he had "something to do" with Chandra Levy's disappearance, despite the lack of any evidence or motive or even credible scenario for same. This shows how desperately we long for life to be more interesting than it really is, but will somebody please tell me why the people at Buzzflash.com and other hardcore Democratic propagandists want progressives, liberals, Dems—whatever *Nation* readers are calling themselves these days—to rally to the defense of this slimeball? He doesn't even have a good voting record! (During the Contract with America years he voted with Newt Gingrich 77 percent of the time, and he has often been pressed to switch parties.) Count me out—I used up all my humor and worldliness on Bill and Monica, not to mention their numerous real-life equivalents. My position on sexually predatory politicians and their interns (and aides and flight attendants) is the same as for the ever-popular aging male professor/bushy-tailed young grad student combo: These people, both the men and the women, are *on their own.* If half of Congress had to go home in disgrace to Modesto, and half the intern pool learned the hard way that there's more to getting ahead than giving head, why would that be bad?

In sports news, we had the story of Danny Almonte, the fourteen-year-old twelve-year-old who pitched a perfect game for his Bronx Little League team, leading them to a third-place finish in the international championship. Bring on President Bush and Mayor Giuliani, the television cameras and the ticker-tape parade! The unearthing of Danny's true birth certificate, showing he was born in 1987, not 1989, was spun out in the press for days on end, with vast quantities of shocked, fake-solicitous moralizing ladled on by every sports commentator in America and then some. Said sports agent Drew Rosenhaus on CNN's *TalkBack Live,* "If you start cheating and start making excuses for that, you're destroying the American dream here." In quest of baseball glory, Danny's parents lied and exploited him, messed with his head, and, it was believed at one point, hadn't even enrolled him in school—all very bad. But what do you expect in our sports-and-entertainment-addled country? As Joyce Purnick pointed out in an acid column in the *New York Times,* no one makes a fuss over New York City public school kids who, against great odds, win writing competitions or debating championships or excel academically (not even the Board of Education, which had trouble coming up with a list of relevant names)—and then we wonder why so many inner-city kids blow off their education in favor of a "dream" about being a rapper, a movie star, a model, a sports hero. The Bronx is full of teenage Dominican immigrants like Danny who've dropped out of their awful schools, where they learned nothing, to face bleak futures in the subproletariat, without even a chance at getting their pictures in the paper unless they happen to be run over by a drunken policeman. Where's the outrage about that?

Perhaps it's being expended on superpublicist-to-the-stars Lizzie Grubman's automotive rampage in the parking lot of the Hamptons' Conscience Point Inn. Or perhaps it's been kidnapped by the Reverend Al Sharpton, who's taking a break from black-Hispanic bridge-building over target practice on Vieques to feud with right-wing *New York Post* columnist Rod Dreher, who questioned the good taste of twenty-two-year-old singer Aaliyah's funeral procession down Fifth Avenue: "A traffic-snarling, horse-drawn cortege in honor of a pop singer most people have never heard of? Give us a break!" Dreher went on to cruelly contrast Aaliyah's song lyrics with the poetry of Byron, deserving recipient of lavish obsequies from a grateful nation. In response Sharpton called for a boycott of the *Post* and its advertisers: "It was ugly and divisive. She was degraded," he said. "What would make her not worthy of this type of funeral?"

Too right. I can't think of a more important issue than celebrity funerals for a self-described national black leader to be addressing right now! Unless, of course, it is the absence of black faces on television, the pet cause of Kweisi Mfume, president of the NAACP. Syndicated columnist Cynthia Tucker and others have charged that Mfume was pushing this issue in order to promote himself as a talk-show host, although media imagery and representation is a standard issue for identity-based organizations from NOW to the Anti-Defamation League. In any case, Mfume, a national figure and former congressman who appeared on cable for years, would make at least as worthy a regular commentator as, oh I don't know, the racially humorous Don Imus, or Rush Limbaugh, or Chris Matthews. I'd watch.

The real issue, though, is that television is the least of black America's problems. Sure, it's absurd that all the young nudniks on *Friends, Will & Grace, Dawson's Creek,* and other top-ranked shows my daughter loves are white, but life is short and time's a-wasting. How much energy does the nation's largest black organization want to spend shoehorning an African-American best friend into *Dharma & Greg* or getting Clarence Page more face time on CNN? It was left to one Emory Curtis, whose essay "Blacks on TV or Educate Our Kids?" was posted on the Black Radical Congress e-mail list in August, to make the obvious point. For three years the NAACP has been making a major issue out of the prime-time lineup. Where is its crusade against the terrible state of education for black children? Curtis notes that black kids trail by almost every measure. On last year's National Assessment of Educational Progress, one in three white fourth-graders performed at grade level, which is itself pretty shocking—but only one in twenty black fourth-graders did. In California, three out of four black fourth- and eighth-graders were at the lowest level, "below basic"—about the same as eight years ago.

Well, summer's over. Time to turn off the set?

•◄ SEPTEMBER 17, 2001 ►•

Put Out No Flags

My daughter, who goes to Stuyvesant High School, only blocks from the World Trade Center, thinks we should fly an American flag out our window. Definitely not, I say: The flag stands for jingoism and vengeance and war. She tells me I'm wrong—the flag means standing together and honoring the dead and saying no to terrorism. In a way we're both right: The Stars and Stripes is the only available symbol right now. In New York City, it decorates taxicabs driven by Indians and Pakistanis, the impromptu memorials of candles and flowers that have sprung up in front of every firehouse, the chi-chi art galleries and boutiques of SoHo. It has to bear a wide range of meanings, from simple, dignified sorrow to the violent anti-Arab and anti-Muslim bigotry that has already resulted in murder, vandalism, and arson around the country and harassment on New York City streets and campuses. It seems impossible to explain to a thirteen-year-old, for whom the war in Vietnam might as well be the War of Jenkins' Ear, the connection between waving the flag and bombing ordinary people half a world away back to the proverbial stone age. I tell her she can buy a flag with her own money and fly it out her bedroom window, because that's hers, but the living room is off-limits.

There are no symbolic representations right now for the things the world really needs—equality and justice and humanity and solidarity and intelligence. The red flag is too bloodied by history; the peace sign is a retro fashion accessory. In much of the world, including parts of this country, the cross and crescent and Star of David are logos for nationalistic and sectarian hatred. Ann Coulter, fulminating in her syndicated column, called for carpet-bombing any country where people "smiled" at news of the disaster: "We should invade their countries, kill their leaders, and convert them to Christianity." What is this, the Crusades? The Reverend Jerry Falwell issued a belated mealy-mouthed apology for his astonishing remarks immediately after the attacks, but does anyone doubt that he meant them? The disaster was God's judgment on secular America, he observed, as famously secular New Yorkers were rushing to volunteer to dig out survivors, to give blood, food, money, anything—it was all the fault of "the pagans, and the abortionists, and the feminists, and the gays and the lesbians . . . the ACLU, People for the American Way." That's what the Taliban think too.

As I write, the war talk revolves around Afghanistan, home of the vicious Taliban and hideaway of Osama bin Laden. I've never been one to blame the United States for every bad thing that happens in the Third World, but it is a fact that our government supported militant Islamic fundamentalism in Afghanistan after the Soviet invasion in 1979. The mujahedeen were freedom fighters against communism, backed by more than $3 billion in U.S. aid—more money and expertise than for any other cause in CIA history—and hailed as heroes by tag-along journalists from Dan Rather to William T. Vollmann, who saw these lawless fanatics as manly primitives untainted by the West. (There's a story in here about the attraction Afghan hypermasculinity holds for desk-bound modern men. How lovely not to pay lip service to women's equality! It's cowboys and Indians, with harems thrown in.) And if, with the Soviets gone, the vying warlords turned against one another, raped and pillaged and murdered the civilian population, and destroyed what still remained of normal Afghan life, who could have predicted that? These people! The Taliban, who rose out of this period of devastation, were boys, many of them orphans, from the wretched refugee camps of Pakistan, raised in the unnatural womanless hothouses of fundamentalist boarding schools. Even leaving aside their ignorance and provincialism and lack of modern skills, they could no more be expected to lead Afghanistan back to normalcy than an army made up of kids raised from birth in Romanian orphanages.

Feminists and human-rights groups have been sounding the alarm about the Taliban since they took over Afghanistan in 1996. That's why interested Americans know that Afghan women are forced to wear the total shroud of the burqa and are banned from work and from leaving their homes unless accompanied by a male relative; that girls are barred from school; and that the Taliban—far from being their nation's saviors, enforcing civic peace with their terrible swift Kalashnikovs—are just the latest oppressors of the miserable population. What has been the response of the West to this news? Unless you count the absurd infatuation of European intellectuals with the anti-Taliban Northern Alliance of fundamentalist warlords (here we go again!), not much.

What would happen if the West took seriously the forces in the Muslim world who call for education, social justice, women's rights, democracy, civil liberties, and secularism? Why does our foreign policy underwrite the clerical fascist government of Saudi Arabia—and a host of nondemocratic regimes besides? What is the point of the continuing sanctions on Iraq, which have brought untold misery to ordinary people and awakened the most backward tendencies of Iraqi society while doing nothing to undermine Saddam Hussein? And why on earth are fundamentalist Jews from Brooklyn and Philadelphia allowed to turn Palestinians out of their homes on the West Bank? Because God gave them the land? Does any sane person really believe that?

Bombing Afghanistan to "fight terrorism" is to punish not the Taliban but the victims of the Taliban, the people we should be supporting. At the same time, war would reinforce the worst elements in our own society—the flag-wavers and bigots and militarists. It's heartening that there have been peace vigils and rallies in many cities, and antiwar actions are planned in Washington, D.C., for September 29–30, but look what even the threat of war has already done to Congress, where only a single representative, Barbara Lee, Democrat from California, voted against giving the President virtual carte blanche.

A friend has taken to wearing her rusty old Women's Pentagon Action buttons—at least they have a picture of the globe on them. The globe, not the flag, is the symbol that's wanted now.

•◄ OCTOBER 8, 2001 ►•

Where Are the Women?

A re there any people on earth more wretched than the women of Afghanistan? As if poverty, hunger, disease, drought, ruined cities, and a huge refugee crisis weren't bad enough, under Taliban rule they can't work, they can't go to school, they have virtually no health-care, they can't leave their houses without a male escort, they are beaten in the streets if they lift the mandatory burqa even to relieve a coughing fit. The Taliban's crazier requirements have some of the obsessive par-ticularity of the Nazis' statutes against the Jews: no high heels (that lust-inducing *click-click!*), no white socks (white is the color of the flag), windows must be painted over so that no male passerby can see the dread female form lurking in the house. (This particular stricture, com-bined with the burqa, has led to an outbreak of osteomalacia, a bone dis-ease caused by malnutrition and lack of sunlight.)

Until September 11, this situation received only modest attention in the West—much less than the destruction of the giant Buddha stat-ues of Bamiyan. The "left" is often accused of "moral relativism" and a "postmodern" unwillingness to judge, but the notion that the plight of Afghan women is a matter of culture and tradition, and not for West-erners to judge, was widespread across the political spectrum.

Now, finally, the world is paying attention to the Taliban, whose days may indeed be numbered now that their foreign supporters—Saudi Arabia, the United Arab Emirates, Pakistan—are backing off. The connections between religious fanaticism and the suppression of women are plain to see (and not just applicable to Islam—show me a major re-ligion in which the inferiority of women, and God's wish to place them and their dangerous, polluting sexuality under male control, is not a central original theme). So is the connection of both with terrorism, war, and atrocity. It's no accident that so many of the young men who are foot soldiers of Islamic fundamentalism are reared in womanless religious schools, or that Osama bin Laden's recruiting video features bikinied Western women as symbols of the enemy.

But if fundamentalism requires the suppression of women, offering desperate, futureless men the psychological and practical satisfaction of instant superiority to half the human race, the emancipation of women could be the key to overcoming it. Where women have education, healthcare, and personal rights, where they have social and political and economic power—where they can choose what to wear, whom to marry, how to live—there's a powerful constituency for secularism, democracy, and human rights. What educated mother engaged in public life would want her daughter to be an illiterate baby machine confined to the four walls of her husband's house with no one to talk to but his other wives?

Women's rights are crucial for everything the West supposedly cares about: infant mortality (one in four Afghan children dies before age five), political democracy, personal freedom, equality under the law—not to mention its own security. But where are the women in the discussion of Afghanistan, the Middle East, the rest of the Muslim world? We don't hear much about how policy decisions will affect women, or about what women want. Men have the guns and the governments. Who asks the women of Saudi Arabia, our ally, how they feel about the Taliban-like restrictions on *their* freedom? In the case of Afghanistan, the Northern Alliance presents itself now to the West as women's friend. A story in the *New York Times* marveled at the very limited permission given to women in NA-held territory to study and work and wear a less restrictive covering than the burqa. Brushed aside was the fact that many warlords of the Northern Alliance are themselves religious fighters who not only restricted women considerably when they held power from 1992 to '96 but plunged the country into civil war, compiling a record of ethnically motivated mass murder, rape, and other atrocities and leaving the population so exhausted that the Taliban's promise of law and order came as a relief. It's all documented on the Human Rights Watch website (www.hrw.org).

Now more than ever, the Revolutionary Association of the Women of Afghanistan (RAWA), which opposes both the Taliban and the Northern Alliance as violent, lawless, misogynistic, and antidemocratic, deserves attention and support. "What Afghanistan needs is not more war," Tahmeena Faryel, a RAWA representative currently visiting the United States, told me, but massive amounts of humanitarian aid and the disarming of both the Taliban and the Northern Alliance, followed by democratic elections. "We don't need another religious government," she said. "We've had that!" The women of RAWA are a different model of heroism than a warlord with a Kalashnikov: In Afghanistan, they risk their lives by running secret schools for girls, delivering medical aid, documenting and filming Taliban atrocities. In Pakistan, they demonstrate against fundamentalism in the "Talibanized" cities of Peshawar and Quetta. Much as the victims of the World Trade Center attack need our support, so too do Afghans who are trying to bring reason and peace to their miserable country.

I GOT MORE negative comment on my last column, in which I described a discussion with my daughter about whether to fly an American flag in the wake of the WTC attack, than on anything I've ever written. Many people pitied my commonsensical, public-spirited child for being raised by an antisocial naysayer like me. And if *The Weekly Standard* has its way—it's urging readers to send "young Miss Pollitt" flags c/o *The Nation*—she will soon have enough flags to redecorate her entire bedroom in red, white, and blue, without having to forgo a single Green Day CD to buy one for herself.

•⊣ OCTOBER 22, 2001 ⊢•

War and Peace

How depressing was the October 13 peace rally in Washington Square? Well, the Bread and Puppet Theater performed—that should give you an idea. "It's the sixties all over again," murmured the portly graybeard standing next to me as the funereal drum thudded and the players, holding their papier-mâché body masks, paraded glumly through the crowd of perhaps five hundred people—most, by the look of them, veterans of either the peace-and-justice or sectarian left. Look on the bright side, I thought: At least we don't have to sing "Down by the Riverside," as happened at the peace rally in Union Square on October 7, a few hours after bombs started falling on Afghanistan.

I don't like to criticize the activists who put together what little resistance to the bombing there is. But the 2000s aren't the 1960s, and whatever else Afghanistan is, it isn't Vietnam, any more than international terrorism or Islamic extremism is the new communism. Essential to the movement against the war in Vietnam was the pointlessness of our involvement: What had Ho Chi Minh ever done to us? The Vietcong never blew up American office buildings and murdered thousands of ordinary American working people. You didn't have to be a pacifist or an opponent of all intervention everywhere to favor getting out of Vietnam—there were dozens of reasons, principled, pragmatic, humanitarian, self-serving, to be against the war. This time, our own country has been attacked, and the enemies are deranged fanatics. No amount of military force short of nuclear weapons would have defeated the North Vietnamese and Vietcong, who really did swim like fish in the sea of the people and had plenty of help from the Soviet Union besides. The Taliban, by contrast, are widely, although not universally, hated in Afghanistan, and Osama bin Laden's men, known as the Arab-Afghans, are viewed there by many as a hostile foreign presence.

Faced with a popular air war conducted, at least on paper, in such a way as to minimize civilian casualties, the peace movement falls back on boilerplate: All war everywhere is wrong, no matter what evils pertain; any use of force merely perpetuates the "cycle of violence"; the war is "racist," whatever that means; it's a corporate plot. The most rousing and focused speech at Washington Square was physicist Michio Kaku's denunciation of Star Wars—but no one I heard (I missed the noted foreign-policy experts Al Sharpton and Patti Smith) grappled with the central question: If not war, what? Realistically, some of the alternatives that have been proposed would also involve military action. Osama bin Laden is not likely to mail himself to the International Criminal Court to be tried for crimes against humanity; the disarming of both the Taliban and the Northern Alliance by United Nations peacekeepers, followed by free and democratic elections—the course favored by the Revolutionary Association of the Women of Afghanistan—is not likely to happen peacefully either.

The attack on the World Trade Center, an unspeakable and unjustifiable crime, created a sense of urgency and feelings of fear and anger that do not easily accord with calls for a deeper understanding of America's role in the Muslim world. It's hard to care that the U.S. government armed and bankrolled the fundamentalist mujahedeen in Afghanistan to fight the Soviets, or that it supports clerical-fascist Islamic governments like the one in Saudi Arabia, when you're afraid to fly in an airplane or open your mail. Say for the sake of argument that the "chickens" of American foreign policy "are coming home to roost": You can see why many would answer, Well, so what? Why not just kill the chickens and be done with it? That may prove much more difficult than today's prowar pundits acknowledge—what if one only hatches more chickens?—but it's not totally off the wall, like Alice Walker's embarrassing and oft-cited proposal that bin Laden be showered with love and "reminded of all the good, nonviolent things he has done."

Right now, the argument that the war will have unforeseen and disastrous consequences may sound like handwringing, but it is doubtless true. Given the millions who are starving in Afghanistan, the 37,500 mini-meals that have fallen from the sky are a cruel joke. And even if the Al Qaeda network is destroyed and the Taliban overthrown, the circumstances that created them will remain. This is the case whether one sees the attack on the WTC as inspired by religiously motivated hatred of modernity and Enlightenment values, like Christopher Hitchens, or as a response to particular American policies in Israel, Iraq, and Saudi Arabia, as Noam Chomsky argues. Experts can debate the precise amount of motivation this or that factor contributes to terrorism—but unless the Muslim world is transformed on many levels, it is hard to see how the bombing of Afghanistan will keep Americans safe or prevent new Al Qaedas and Talibans from forming. For that we would have to be able to look down the road ten years and see a peaceful, well-governed, rebuilt Afghanistan; a Pakistan in which the best chance for a poor boy or girl is public school, not a *madrassah* for him and nothing for her; a Saudi Arabia with a democratic, secular government; an Egypt without millions living in abject poverty and a hugely frustrated middle class. This is all the more true if militant Islam is relatively independent of concrete grievances like Israel and Iraq.

Unfortunately, anyone who tries to talk about the WTC attack in this way—as Susan Sontag did in her entirely reasonable but now infamous *New Yorker* piece—is likely to find themselves labeled a traitor, a coward, anti-American, or worse. (I found this out myself when I made the mistake of going on the radio with mad Andrew Sullivan, who has said the "decadent left . . . may well mount a fifth column" and who accused me of objectively supporting the Taliban and likened me to someone who refuses to help a rape victim and blames her for wearing a short skirt.) But a war can be "just" in the sense that it is a response to aggression—as Vietnam was not—and also be the wrong way to solve a problem.

•◀ NOVEMBER 5, 2001 ▶•

After the Taliban

W hat if Hillary Clinton, not Laura Bush, had taken to the airwaves during her husband's first year in office and become the first First Lady to deliver the entire weekly presidential radio address—about women's rights, no less? Dragon lady! Castrating feminist manhating bitch! All together now: Who Elected *Her*? The Republicans would have started impeachment proceedings that very day. In fact, the down-to-earth and nonthreatening Laura Bush spoke so eloquently in support of Afghan women's rights I actually found myself not wanting to believe the Democratic Party accusation that this was a cynical attempt to appeal to women and narrow the eleven-point gender gap that bedeviled Bush in the 2000 election—not that a shortage of votes turned out to matter, but that's another story. Perhaps Mrs. Bush—like Cherie Blair, who gave a similar speech on November 19—was sending a message to the sorry collection of warlords and criminals, powergrabbers and back-stabbers vying for power in the new Afghanistan: This time around, women must have a seat at the table. As I write, Afghan women are swinging into action, with a major conference planned for early December in Brussels to insist on equality and political power in their post-Taliban nation.

Wouldn't it be wonderful if the defeat of the Taliban also marked the end of the cultural-relativist pooh-poohing of women's rights? Only a few weeks ago, a Bush administration spokesperson was refusing to promise that women would play a role in a new Afghan government: "We have to be careful not to look like we are imposing our values on them." A week before it began, no women had been mentioned as participants in the UN-sponsored Bonn conference to plan for a postwar

Afghanistan. As it turned out, there are three among the twenty-eight delegates: two in the delegation of the former king and one in that of the Northern Alliance, plus at least two more attending as advisers. Whether it means anything, who knows—of the four factions gathered in Bonn, only the Northern Alliance controls any actual territory, and its record with regard to women's rights and dignity is nothing to cheer about. While some Alliance leaders speak encouragingly of girls' education and women's right to work, early signs are mixed: In Kabul, women can once more freely walk the streets, but the newly reopened movie theater is off-limits and a women's rights march was halted by authorities; in late November, according to the *Los Angeles Times,* women were banned from voting for mayor in Herat, whose de facto ruler, Ismail Khan, has presented himself as sympathetic to women's rights.

Still, whatever government takes shape in Afghanistan will probably be better for women than the Taliban—how could it be worse?—as long as the country does not degenerate into civil war, as happened the last time the Northern Alliance was in power. But let's not kid ourselves: This war is not about freeing women from government-mandated burqas, or teaching girls to read, or improving Afghan women's ghastly maternal mortality rate of 17 in 1,000 births—the second highest in the world. Those things may happen as a by-product of realpolitik, or they may not. But if women's rights and well-being were aims of U.S.–Afghan policy, the Carter, Reagan, and Bush administrations would never have financed the mujahedeen, whose neanderthal treatment of women, including throwing acid at unveiled women, was well documented from the start; the Clinton administration would not have initially accepted the Taliban even after they closed the girls' schools in Herat; and the current Bush administration would have inundated the millions of Afghan women and girls in Pakistan's refugee camps with teachers, nurses, doctors, and food.

As other commentators have pointed out, if Laura Bush wants to make women's rights a U.S. foreign-policy goal, she's got her work cut out for her. Saudi Arabia, our best friend, is positively Talibanesque: Women are rigidly segregated by law, cannot drive, cannot travel without written permission from a male relative; top-to-toe veiling is mandated by law and enforced by a brutal religious police force. In a particularly insulting twist, U.S. women soldiers stationed there are compelled to wear the veil and refrain from driving when off base; so far, the Bush administration has refused to act on soldiers' objections to these conditions.

One can go on and on about the situation of women in Muslim countries—unable to vote in Kuwait; genitally mutilated in Egypt and Sudan; flogged, jailed, murdered with impunity, and even stoned to death for sexual infractions in a number of countries—and Muslim women everywhere are fighting back. (For a serious, nonsensationalist approach, check out the website of Women Living Under Muslim Laws, www.wluml.org.) But the Islamic world is hardly the only place where women are denied their human rights. How would you like to have to get a divorce in an Israeli rabbinical court or need an abortion in Chile, where it's illegal even to save your life? The United States makes no bones about using its economic and political might against illegal drugs—in fact, the administration rewarded the Taliban for banning opium production by making a $43 million donation to the World Food Program and humanitarian NGOs (not, as is usually reported, to the Taliban proper). If it cared to do so, the United States could back the global women's movement with the same zeal.

Instead, it does the opposite. In order to curry favor with conservative Catholics at home, Laura Bush's husband has shown callous disregard for women's rights and health abroad. He reinstated the Mexico City policy, which bars family-planning groups receiving U.S. funds from discussing abortion; he sent anti-choice delegations to wreck the consensus at international conferences on children's rights and public health; he tried to nominate John Klink, former adviser to the Holy See, to head the State Department's Bureau of Population, Refugees, and Migration, which would have thrown the United States behind the pope's call to deny emergency contraception to raped women in refugee camps.

That the Taliban are gone is cause for joy. A world that cared about women's rights would never have let them come to power in the first place.

•◄ DECEMBER 17, 2001 ►•

$hotgun Weddings

What would the government have to do to convince you to get married when you otherwise wouldn't? More than pay you $80 a month, I'll bet, the amount Wisconsin's much-ballyhooed "Bridefare" pilot program offered unwed teen welfare mothers beginning in the early nineties, which is perhaps why then-governor Tommy Thompson, now Health and Human Services Secretary, was uninterested in having it properly evaluated and why you don't hear much about Bridefare today. Okay, how about $100 a month? That's what West Virginia is currently offering to add to a couple's welfare benefits if they wed. But even though the state has simultaneously cut by 25 percent the checks of recipients living with adults to whom they are not married (including, in some cases, their own grown children, if you can believe that!), results have been modest: Only around 1,600 couples have applied for the bonus, and presumably some of these would have married anyway. With the state's welfare budget expected to show a $90 million shortfall by 2003, the marriage bonus is likely to be quietly abolished.

Although welfare reform was sold to the public as promoting work, the Personal Responsibility and Work Opportunity Reconciliation Act of 1996 actually opens with the declaration that "marriage is the foundation of a successful society." According to Charles Murray, Robert Rector, and other right-wing ideologues, welfare enabled poor women to rely on the state instead of husbands; forcing them off the dole and into the rigors of low-wage employment would push them into marriage, restore "the family," and lift children out of poverty. That was always a silly idea. For one thing, as any single woman could have told them, it wrongly assumed that whether a woman married was only up to her; for another, it has been well documented that the men available to poor women are also poor and often (like the women) have other problems as well: In one study, 30 percent of poor single fathers were unemployed in the week before the survey and almost 40 percent had been incarcerated; drugs, drink, violence, poor health, and bad attitudes were not uncommon. Would Murray want *his* daughter to marry a guy with even one of those strikes against him? Not surprisingly, there has been no upsurge of marriage among former welfare recipients since 1996. Of all births, the proportion that are to unwed mothers has stayed roughly where it was, at 33 percent.

Since the stick of work and the carrot of cash have both proved ineffective in herding women to the altar, family-values conservatives are calling for more lectures. Marriage promotion will be a hot item when welfare reform comes up for reauthorization later this year. At the federal level, conservatives are calling for 10 percent of all Temporary Assistance for Needy Families (TANF) money to be set aside for promoting marriage; Utah, Arizona, and Oklahoma have already raided TANF to fund such ventures as a "healthy marriage" handbook for couples seeking a marriage license. And it's not just Republicans: Senator Joe Lieberman and Representative Ben Cardin, the ranking Democrat on the House Ways and Means Committee, are also interested in funding "family formation." In place of cash bonuses to individuals, which at least put money in the pockets of poor people, look for massive funding of faith-based marriage-preparation courses (and never you mind that pesky separation of church and state), for fatherhood-intervention programs, classes to instruct poor single moms in the benefits of marriage (as if they didn't know!), for self-help groups like Marriage Savers, abstinence education for kids and grown-ups alike, and, of course, ingenious pilot projects by the dozen. There's even been a proposal to endow pro-marriage professorships at state universities—and don't forget millions of dollars for evaluation, follow-up, filing, and forgetting.

There's nothing wrong with programs that aim to raise people's marital IQ—I love that journalistic evergreen about the engaged couple who take a quiz in order to qualify for a church wedding and call it off when they discover he wants seven kids and she wants to live in a tree. But remember when it was conservatives who argued against social en-

gineering and micromanaging people's private lives and "throwing
money at the problem"?

Domestic violence experts have warned that poor women may find
themselves pushed into marrying their abusers and staying with them—
in a disturbing bit of Senate testimony, Mike McManus of Marriage
Savers said domestic violence could usually be overcome with faith-
based help. Is that the message women in danger should be getting? But
there are even larger issues: Marriage is a deeply personal, intimate matter, involving our most private, barely articulated selves. Why should the
government try to maneuver reluctant women into dubious choices just
because they are poor? Even as a meal ticket wedlock is no panacea—
that marriage is a cure for poverty is only true if you marry someone
who isn't poor, who will share his income with you and your children,
and who won't divorce you later and leave you worse off than ever. The
relation between poverty and marriage is virtually the opposite of what
pro-marriage ideologues claim: It isn't that getting married gives feckless
poor people middle-class values and stability, it's that stable middle-class
people are the ones who can "afford" to be married. However marriage
functioned a half-century ago, today it is a class marker. Instead of marketing marriage as a poverty program, how much better to invest in
poor women—and poor men—as human beings in their own right:
with education, training for high-paying jobs, housing, mental-health
services, really good childcare for their kids. Every TANF dollar spent
on marital propaganda means a dollar less for programs that really help
people.

The very fact that welfare reformers are reduced to bribing, cajol-
ing, and guilt-tripping people into marriage should tell us something.
Or have they just not hit on the right incentive? As a divorced single
mother, I've given some thought to what it would take for me to marry
against my own inclination in order to make America great again. Here's
my offer: If the government brings Otis Redding back to life and books
him to sing at my wedding, I will marry the Devil himself. And if the
Devil is unavailable, my ex-husband says he's ready.

Pierre Bourdieu, 1930–2002

●

The death on January 23 of the French philosopher and sociologist Pierre Bourdieu came as the American chattering classes were busy checking the math in Richard Posner's *Public Intellectuals: A Study of Decline*—an unintentional parody of sociology in which Posner presents a top-100 list ranking writers and professors according to the number of times they turned up on television or in Internet searches. Bourdieu, whose heaviest passages crackled with sardonic wit, would have had a wonderful time exploring this farcical project, which takes for granted that Henry Kissinger (no. 1), Sidney Blumenthal (no. 7), and Ann Coulter (no. 74) are in the Rolodex because they are leading the life of the mind—why not include Dr. Ruth or, as one wag suggested, Osama bin Laden? In tacitly conceding the fungibility of celebrity even while decrying it, Posner confirms Bourdieu's gloomy predictions about the direction modernity is swiftly taking us: away from scholarship and high culture as sources of social prestige, and toward journalism and entertainment.

Bourdieu himself argued that scholars and writers could and should bring their specialized knowledge to bear responsibly and seriously on social and political issues, something he suspected couldn't be done on a talk show. His involvement during the 1990s in campaigns for railway workers, undocumented immigrants, and the unemployed, and most recently against neoliberalism and globalization, was the natural outgrowth of a lifetime of research into economic, social, and cultural class domination among peoples as disparate as Algerian peasants and French professors, and as expressed in everything from amateur photography to posture. It's hard to think of a comparable figure on the American left.

Noam Chomsky's academic work has no connection with his political activities, and it's been decades since his byline appeared in the *New York Review of Books* or the *New York Times*. One friend found himself reaching all the way back to C. Wright Mills.

Bourdieu, who loved intellectual combat, called himself "to the left of the left"—that is, to the left of the ossified French left-wing parties and also to the left of the academic postmodernists *aka* antifoundationalists, about whose indifference to empirical work he was scathing. Reading him could be a disturbing experience, because the explanatory sweep of his key concept of "habitus"—the formation and expression of self around an internalized and usually accurate sense of social destiny— tends to make ameliorative projects seem rather silly. Sociology, he wrote, "discovers necessity, social constraints, where we would like to see choice and free will. The habitus is that unchosen principle of so many choices that drives our humanists to such despair." Take, for example, his attack on the notion that making high culture readily available—in free museums and local performances—is all that is necessary to bring it to the masses. (In today's America, this fond hope marks you as a raving Bolshevik, but in France it was the pet conviction of de Gaulle's minister of culture, André Malraux.) In fact, as Bourdieu painstakingly demonstrated in *Distinction,* his monumental study of the way class shapes cultural preferences, or "taste," there is nothing automatic or natural about the ability to "appreciate"—curious word—a Rothko or even a Van Gogh: You have to know a lot about painting, you have to feel comfortable in museums, and you have to have what Bourdieu saw as the educated bourgeois orientation, which rests on leisure, money, and unselfconscious social privilege and expresses itself as the enjoyment of the speculative, the distanced, the nonuseful. Typically, though, Bourdieu used this discouraging insight to call for more, not less, effort to make culture genuinely accessible to all: Schools could help give working-class kids the cultural capital—another key Bourdieusian concept—that middle-class kids get from their families. One could extend that insight to the American context and argue that depriving working-class kids of the "frills"—art, music, trips—in the name of "the basics" is not just stingy or philistine, it's a way of maintaining class privilege.

Although Bourdieu has been criticized as too deterministic—a few years ago *The New Yorker* characterized his views, absurdly, as leading "inexorably to Leninism"—he retained, in the face of a great deal of contrary evidence, including much gathered by himself, a faith in people's capacities for transformation. He spent much of his life studying the part played by the French education system in reifying class and gender divisions and in selecting and shaping the academic, technocratic, and political elite—the "state nobility"—that runs France, but he believed in education; he railed against the popularization and vulgarization of difficult ideas, but he believed in popular movements and took part in several. In one of his last books, *Masculine Domination,* he comes close to arguing that male chauvinism is a cultural universal that structures all society and all thought; he is that rare man who chastises feminists for not going far enough—but the book closes with a paean to love.

Bourdieu's twenty-five books and countless articles represent probably the most brilliant and fruitful renovation and application of Marxian concepts in our era. Nonetheless, he is less influential on the American academic left than the (to my mind, not to mention his!) obscurantist and, at bottom, conservative French deconstructionists and antifoundationalists. Perhaps it is not irrelevant that Bourdieu made academia and intellectuals a major subject of withering critique: You can't read him and believe, for example, that professors (or "public intellectuals," or writers, or artists) stand outside the class system in some sort of unmediated relation to society and truth. The ground most difficult to see is always the patch one is standing on, and the position of the intellectuals, the class that thinks it is free-floating, is the most mystified of all. It was not the least of Bourdieu's achievements that he offered his colleagues the means of self-awareness, and it's not surprising either that many decline the offer. His odd and original metaphor of the task of sociology holds both a message and a warning: "Enlightenment is on the side of those who turn their spotlight on our blinkers."

Egg on the Brain

It may look as if domestic politics no longer exists in the new America—the one in which there is no money for anything besides guns and prisons but we don't care because we are all bowling together against the Axis of Evil. But that's not true. As long as there is a fertilized egg somewhere in this great land of ours, there will be domestic politics. George Bush may not be able to bring about the Kingdom of Heaven on Earth for the religious right, who gave him one in four of his votes. He may even realize that a serious victory for religious conservatives—significantly restricting the legality of abortion, say—would hurt the Republican Party, because California has more people than Utah. But he is doing what he can to keep the fundamentalists happy.

It must be frustrating for him—just when we're all supposed to pretend to love our differently faithed neighbor even if we know he's bound for hell, Christians keep saying weird things. First there was Jerry Falwell's remark that God let terrorists blow up the World Trade Center because he was fed up with "the pagans, and the abortionists, and the feminists, and the gays and the lesbians . . . [and] the ACLU"; Falwell apologized, only to express the same thought a bit more obliquely on November 11 at a Florida church: "If the church had been awake and performing that duty"—proselytizing the ungodly—"I can tell you that we wouldn't be in the mess we're in today." God, says Falwell, "even loves the Taliban"—it's just liberals he can't stand.

And then there's Attorney General John Ashcroft, who burqaed the semi-nude statue of the Spirit of Justice because he felt upstaged by her perky breast at press conferences, and who thinks calico cats are emissaries of the devil, when everyone knows it's black cats. Ashcroft is in trouble with Arab-Americans for offering this proof of the superiority of Christianity to Islam, as quoted by conservative columnist Cal Thomas on his radio show on November 9 (and belatedly denied by a Justice Department spokeswoman): "Islam is a religion in which God requires you to send your son to die for him. Christianity is a faith in which God sends his son to die for you." Not to get too wound up in theology here, but if the Christian God sent his own son to die, doesn't that make him, according to Ashcroft's definition, a Muslim?

Fortunately, the fertilized egg can be rolled onstage to distract us from such knotty questions. In keeping with the strategy of rebranding anti-choice as pro-child, the Bush administration plans to use the Children's Health Insurance Program for poor children to provide healthcare "from conception to age nineteen," a neat way of defining zygotes as kids. The women in whom these fine young people are temporarily ensconced will remain uninsured—perhaps they can apply for federal funds by redefining themselves as ambulances or seeing-eye dogs. After all, somebody has to get those fetuses to the doctor's office.

But wait, there's more. In a highly unusual move, the Justice Department has weighed in on the side of Ohio's "partial-birth abortion" ban, which has been on ice thanks to a federal court ruling that found it did not make enough allowance for a woman's health, as required by the 2000 Supreme Court decision in *Stenberg v. Carhart.* The Ohio law would permit the operation only to save her life or avoid "serious risk of the substantial and irreversible impairment of a major bodily function." Gee, what about considerable risk of moderate and long-term impairment of a bodily function of only middling importance? Should the Ohio state legislature (seventy-five men, twenty-four women) decide how much damage a woman should suffer on behalf of a fetus? Shouldn't she have something to say about it?

To please fanatical anti-choicer Representative Chris Smith of New Jersey, Bush is holding back $34 million from UN family planning programs. To return the favor, congressional Republicans have revived the Child Custody Protection Act, which would bar anyone but a parent from taking a minor across state lines for an abortion. The parental-notification-and-consent laws of a pregnant teen's home state would follow her wherever she goes, like killer bees, or the Furies—and unlike any other law.

Bush is also stacking with social conservatives commissions that have nothing to do with abortion per se but raise issues of sex, gender, and reproduction. The cloning commission, called the Council on Bioethics (fourteen men, four women), is headed by bioethicist Leon Kass, a former opponent of in vitro fertilization who's associated with the American Enterprise Institute. There's room around the table for anti-choice columnist Charles Krauthammer; anti-choice law professor Mary Ann Glendon, the Vatican's representative at the UN conference on women in Beijing; and social theorist Francis Fukuyama, who wrote in a *New York Times* op-ed that the thirty-years-overdue introduction of the pill in Japan in 1999 spelled the downfall of the Japanese family, because now women will just run wild. But there are only four research scientists, and no advocates for patients with diseases that the cloning of stem cells might someday help cure. Similarly, the newly reconfigured AIDS commission is said to be stacked with religious conservatives and will be headed by former representative Tom Coburn, whose claim to fame is his rejection of condoms, which sometimes fail, in favor of "monogamy," which never does.

Finally, there's the nomination of Charles Pickering for the Court of Appeals for the Fifth Circuit. Rated unqualified by the Magnolia Bar Association of Mississippi, Pickering, an ardent segregationist when it counted, opposed the ERA, has been a lifelong opponent of legal abortion, and won't discuss his anti-choice record in Senate hearings. The Fifth Circuit includes Texas, Louisiana, and Mississippi, states where the right to abortion is already compromised by conservative legislatures; in 1999 Texas tied with Michigan for the most new anti-choice laws enacted (seven). Traditionally the federal courts offer hope of redress for victims of state laws—in this case, some of the poorest women in the country. What are the chances that Pickering will champion their rights and their health?

My money's on the fertilized egg.

●◄ MARCH 4, 2002 ►●

Justice, Not So Swift

On October 31 Governor Jane Swift of Massachusetts pardoned five women who had been convicted and executed in the Salem witch trials in 1692. Well, better late than never—what's a few centuries one way or another? Once you're dead you have all the time in the world. It's the living for whom justice delayed is justice denied, and on that score Governor Swift is not doing so well. On February 20 she rejected the recommendation of the state parole board, known for its sternness and strictness, and refused to commute the thirty-to-forty-year sentence of Gerald Amirault, who was convicted in the 1986 Fells Acre Day School child sex abuse case and who has already served sixteen years in prison. Violet Amirault and Cheryl Amirault LeFave, his mother and sister, who were convicted with him, served eight years before being released.

Since the 1980s, when a wave of now notorious prosecutions of alleged ritual child sex abuse swept the country, many of the techniques used to elicit children's stories of abuse have been discredited: leading and coercive questions, multiple reinterviews, promises of rewards, suggestive use of anatomical dolls. It's no longer iron-clad doctrine that certain behaviors, like bed-wetting, masturbation, and sexualized play, reliably indicate sex abuse. The slogan of the prosecution and the media was "believe the children"—but what that really meant was *don't* believe the children if they insist that nothing happened, if they like going to daycare and readily hug their alleged abusers; only believe the children when, after relentless questioning by interviewers, therapists, and parents, they agree that something terrible happened and eventually come to believe it, as the Fells Acre children, now young adults, still do. As

Dan Finneran, the Amiraults' lawyer until 2000, puts it, the case represents "a closed system of thought: denials, recantations and failure to remember are categorized as manifestations of repression and fear and thus stand as confirmations of actual abuse." If no means yes, and yes means yes, how do you say no?

All these issues featured in the Amirault case. The result was that a respected working-class family who had run a popular daycare center in Malden for twenty years—a place that parents were constantly popping in and out of—was convicted of a total of twenty-six counts of child abuse involving nine children in trials that included accusations of extravagant and flamboyant sadistic behavior: children being anally raped with butcher knives (which left no wounds), tied to trees on the front lawn while other teachers watched, forced to drink urine, thrown about by robots, tortured in a magic room by an evil clown. One child claimed sixteen children had been killed at the center. Obvious questions went unasked: How come no kids who went to Fells Acre in previous years had these alarming experiences? Why was an expert witness permitted to testify about a child-pornography ring when no pornographic photos of the Fells Acre kids were ever found?

Governor Swift made a big show of looking seriously and long at Gerald Amirault's case, but she failed to consider the central question, that of whether he was guilty of any crime. Indeed, Swift made Gerald's refusal to admit guilt and get treatment as a dangerous sexual predator a centerpiece of her decision—but why should an innocent man have to say he's guilty to get out of jail? Gerald has been a model prisoner: He's taken college courses, he has worked, he has a flawless record. He has the total support of his wife and children and a job lined up in anticipation of his release.

Swift claims that her main consideration was whether Amirault's sentence was in line with those of others convicted of similar crimes. She cited the case of Christopher Reardon, a lay Catholic church worker who last summer pled guilty to seventy-five criminal counts of abusing twenty-nine boys and received a forty-to-fifty-year sentence. But the case against Reardon was open and shut; he took photos and videos, and even kept spreadsheets detailing his crimes. The real cases to compare with Amirault's are those of his mother and sister, who were convicted of the same crimes, although slightly fewer of them. Cheryl Amirault LeFave and Violet Amirault received sentences half as long and were released after serving half as many years as Gerald. Does Gerald's being a man have something to do with these disparate outcomes? Absolutely. The women benefited from the leniency still—if fitfully—bestowed by the justice system on women. Moreover, as the case against the Amiraults came to look more and more troubling with hindsight, the original scenario, in which the three were equally involved in molesting children, was replaced by a theory, never put forward during the trials, that Gerald was the ringleader and the women his dupes. How could this be? The evidence against the three was the same.

At her press conference, Governor Swift refused to discuss the case against Gerald and three times declined to respond when asked how he had failed to demonstrate good behavior in prison. The clear implication is that her motives were political: With Massachusetts in an uproar over the ongoing scandal of pedophile priests, to commute Gerald Amirault's sentence would have made her vulnerable in November, when, as a not very popular or experienced Republican appointee, she faces an uphill struggle for election. What an irony—the Catholic Church protects genuine child molesters for decades and thereby creates a political situation in which an innocent man is trapped in jail. But Swift's calculation is backfiring. The *Boston Globe,* the *Boston Herald,* the Boston-based *Christian Science Monitor,* and the *Berkshire Eagle* in Swift's home county have all editorialized against her decision; polls show wide support for Amirault's release.

Massachusetts—liberal, modern, technocratic Massachusetts—is the only state in which people convicted in the 1980s' wave of ritual child abuse cases are still in prison. Bernard Baran, whose case shares many features with that of the Amiraults, with the added strike against him of being homosexual, has been incarcerated for almost half his life. Meanwhile, Scott Harshbarger, the DA who originally prosecuted the Amirault case, is now head of Common Cause. Will it take another 300 years for the state to acknowledge that Salem was not its last miscarriage of justice?

•◄ MARCH 18, 2002 ►•

God Changes Everything

Let's say there was a school system or a chain of clinics on whose professional staff were a certain number of men who molested the children in their care and who, whenever this behavior came to the attention of their superiors, were shifted to another school or clinic, with parents and colleagues, not to mention the justice system, kept in the dark whenever possible. Imagine that this practice continued for thirty years through a combination of out-of-court settlements, sympathetic judges and politicians, stonewalling lawyers, suppression of information, fulminations against the media. Don't you think that when the story finally broke, the men who had made and implemented the policy would be held legally responsible—for *something*? Certainly they would lose their jobs.

Bring God into the picture, though, and everything changes. The bishops who presided over the priestly pedophilia in the Catholic Church's ever-expanding scandal are not likely to follow Boston's Father Geoghan, convicted and sentenced to nine to ten years and facing more charges, into the dock, much less the cellblock. After all, they are men of God. Thanks to God, the Catholic Church can run a healthcare system—10 percent of private hospitals in the United States—that refuses to practice modern medicine where women are concerned: not just no abortion, but also no birth control, no emergency contraception for rape victims, no sterilization, no in vitro fertilization. The Church can agitate against the use of condoms to prevent the spread of AIDS, even in desperate Africa, a position as insane as South African president Thabo Mbeki's stance against antiretroviral AIDS drugs, but that generates a lot less outrage in the West. It can lobby in Ireland against allowing suicidal women to have abortions and intimidate a fourteen-year-old rape victim in Mexico into carrying to term. It can practice total sex discrimination, barring women from the priesthood and therefore from sharing in the political life of the Church, and still demand to be taken seriously when it speaks of human rights or ethics—rather like the Philadelphia parochial school recently reported as giving academic extra credit to students who march in anti-abortion-rights demonstrations even as the Church goes after public funding through vouchers. No secular institution could get away with any of this, any more than a secular psychotherapist or family counselor could get away with telling poor mad Andrea Yates what the Protestant evangelist Michael Peter Woroniecki did: that Eve was a witch whose sin required atonement in the form of perfect motherhood and that working mothers are "wicked."

Another example: Let's say a group of Americans decide that they would like to live where they believe their ancestors lived 2,000 years ago, even though other people have been living there for centuries and don't like the idea one bit. If these people were Cajuns who wanted to park themselves in the Bois de Boulogne, everyone would think they were out of their minds. If they were American blacks taking over swatches of Ghana, people—including many black people—would laugh at their historical pretensions and militaristic grandiosity. It would certainly be a relevant point that these settlers are not displaced persons or refugees—they have perfectly good homes already. But once again, God changes everything. The former Brooklynites, Philadelphians, and Baltimoreans now camping out in "Judea" and "Samaria" (the West Bank, to you) wave the Bible and the Israeli government lavishes on them all sorts of privileges—cheaper mortgages, income tax breaks, business development and housing grants—with results that are disastrous for Israel and Palestinians alike and that now threaten the peace of the entire world. In a recent front-page story, the *New York Times* treated the longing of Palestinians in the West Bank and Gaza to return to their homes in Israel proper as a psychological obstacle to their forging any kind of rational future, individual or collective, and maybe it is—maybe it would be better for them to forget the old homestead and demand reparations. But at least the old woman mourning a sewing machine left behind when she fled Beersheba fifty years ago really, personally owned that sewing machine; the family picnicking year after year in the ruins of its former property has living memories of farming that plot of land. It is not a notional "ancestral" possession supposedly guaranteed in perpetuity by God. In this case, the religious fanaticism is not coming from the Muslims.

Elsewhere, of course, it is. God has been particularly busy in the Islamic world, building *madrassah*s, issuing *fatwa*s, bringing in Sharia with its bloody stumps and beheadings and floggings and stonings—seventeen people have been stoned to death so far under the "progressive" Khatami regime in Iran—and underwriting a wide variety of dictators and monarchs and warlords. When gods start multiplying, matters don't improve: Polytheistic Hindu zealots have slaughtered 700 people, including many children, in revenge for the torching by Muslims of a train carrying Hindus from the site of the Ayodhya mosque, destroyed by a Hindu mob in 1992 because it supposedly occupied the site where the god-king Rama was supposedly born. As I write, Hindu fanatics are threatening to fight Muslims for a strand of beard hair preserved in a Muslim shrine in Srinagar, which they claim belongs not to Mohammed but to Hindu religious leader Nimnath Baba. How many children will be burned to death over the proper attribution of that holy facial hair?

Think of all the ongoing conflicts involving religion: India versus Pakistan, Russia versus Chechnya, Protestants versus Catholics in Northern Ireland, Muslim guerrillas in the Philippines, bloody clashes between Christians and Muslims in Indonesia and Nigeria, civil war in Sudan and Uganda and Sri Lanka, where Buddhist Sinhalese show a capacity for inflicting harm on the admittedly ferocious Hindu Tamils who might surprise Western admirers of that ancient Eastern creed. It's enough to make one nostalgic for the cold war—as if the thin film of twentieth-century political ideology has been stripped away like the ozone layer to reveal a world reverting to seventeenth-century-style religious warfare, fought with twenty-first-century weapons. God changes everything.

Backlash Babies

A long time ago I dated a twenty-eight-year-old man who told me the first time we went out that he wanted to have seven children. Subsequently, I was involved for many years with an already middle-aged man who also claimed to be eager for fatherhood. How many children have these now-gray gentlemen produced in a lifetime of strenuous heterosexuality? None. But because they are men, nobody's writing books about how they blew their lives, missed the brass ring, find life a downward spiral of serial girlfriends and work that's lost its savor. We understand, when we think about men, that people often say they want one thing while making choices that over time show they care more about something else, that circumstances get in the way of many of our wishes and that for many "have kids" occupies a place on the to-do list between "learn Italian" and "exercise."

Change the sexes, though, and the same story gets a different slant. According to Sylvia Ann Hewlett, today's fifty-something women professionals are in deep mourning because, as the old cartoon had it, they forgot to have children—until it was too late, and too late was a whole lot earlier than they thought. In her new book, *Creating a Life: Professional Women and the Quest for Children,* Hewlett claims she set out to record the triumphant, fulfilled lives of women in mid-career only to find that success had come at the cost of family: Of "ultra-achieving" women (defined as earning $100,000-plus a year), only 57 percent were married, versus 83 percent of comparable men, and only 51 percent had kids at forty, versus 81 percent among the men. Among "high-achieving" women (at least $65,000 or $55,000 a year, depending on age), 33 percent are childless at forty versus 25 percent of men.

Why don't more professional women have kids? Hewlett's book nods to the "brutal demands of ambitious careers," which are still structured according to the life patterns of men with stay-at-home wives, and to the distaste of many men for equal relationships with women their own age. I doubt there's a woman over thirty-five who'd quarrel with that. But what's gotten Hewlett a cover story in *Time* ("Babies vs. Careers: Which Should Come First for Women Who Want Both?") and instant celebrity is not her modest laundry list of family-friendly proposals—paid leave, reduced hours, career breaks. It's her advice to young women: Be "intentional" about children—spend your twenties snagging a husband, put career on the back burner, and have a baby ASAP. Otherwise you could end up like world-famous playwright and much-beloved woman-about-town Wendy Wasserstein, who we are told spent some $130,000 to bear a child as a single forty-eight-year-old. (You could also end up like, oh I don't know, me, who married and had a baby nature's way at thirty-seven, or like my many successful-working-women friends who adopted as single, married, or lesbian mothers and who are doing just fine, thank you very much.)

Danielle Crittenden, move over! Hewlett calls herself a feminist, but *Creating a Life* belongs on the backlash bookshelf with *What Our Mothers Didn't Tell Us, The Rules, The Surrendered Wife, The Surrendered Single* (!), and all those books warning women that feminism—too much confidence, too much optimism, too many choices, too much "pickiness" about men—leads to lonely nights and empty bassinets. But are working women's chances of domestic bliss really so bleak? If 49 percent of ultra-achieving women don't have kids, 51 percent do—what about them? Hewlett seems determined to put the worst possible construction on working women's lives, even citing the long-discredited 1986 Harvard-Yale study that warned that women's chances of marrying after forty were less than that of being killed by a terrorist. As a mother of four who went through high-tech hell to produce last-minute baby Emma at age fifty-one, she sees women's lives through the distorting lens of her own obsessive maternalism, in which nothing, but nothing, can equal looking at the ducks with a toddler, and if you have one child, you'll be crying at the gym because you don't have two. For Hewlett, childlessness is always a tragic blunder, even when her interviewees give more equivocal responses. Thus she quotes academic Judith Friedlander calling childlessness a "creeping non-choice," without hearing the ambivalence expressed in that careful phrasing. Not choosing—procrastinating, not insisting, not focusing—is often a way of choosing, isn't it? There's no room in Hewlett's view for modest regret, moving on, or simple acceptance of childlessness, much less indifference, relief, or looking on the bright side—the feelings she advises women to cultivate with regard to their downsized hopes for careers or equal marriages. But Hewlett's evidence that today's childless "high achievers" neglected their true desire is based on a single statistic, that only 14 percent say they knew in college that they didn't want kids—as if people don't change their minds after twenty.

This is not to deny that many women are caught in a time trap. They spend their twenties and thirties establishing themselves professionally, often without the spousal support their male counterparts enjoy, perhaps instead being supportive themselves, like the surgeon Hewlett cites approvingly who graces her fiancé's business dinners after thirty-six-hour hospital shifts. By the time they can afford to think of kids, they may indeed have trouble conceiving. But are these problems that "intentionality" can solve? Sure, a woman can spend her twenties looking for love—and show me one who doesn't! But will having a baby compensate her for blinkered ambitions and a marriage made with one eye on the clock? Isn't that what the mothers of today's fifty-somethings did, going to college to get their Mrs. degree and taking poorly paid jobs below their capacities because they "combined" well with wifely duties? What makes Hewlett think that disastrous recipe will work out better this time around?

More equality and support, not lowered expectations, is what women need, at work and at home. It's going to be a long struggle. If women allow motherhood to relegate them to secondary status in both places, as Hewlett advises, we'll never get there. Meanwhile, a world with fewer female surgeons, playwrights, and professors strikes me as an infinitely inferior place to live.

Regressive Progressive?

As chairman of the fifty-nine-member Congressional Progressive Caucus and potential candidate for the Democratic presidential nomination, Ohio congressman Dennis Kucinich has been quite visible lately. At a time when few Democrats are daring to question the war aims of the Bush administration—or even to ask what they are—Kucinich has spoken eloquently against the Patriot Act, the ongoing military buildup, and the vague and apparently horizonless "war on terrorism." From tax cuts for the rich and the death penalty (against) to national health insurance and the environment (for), Kucinich has the right liberal positions. Michael Moore, who likes to rib progressives for favoring white wine and brie over hot dogs and beer, would surely approve of Kucinich's man-of-the-people persona—he's actually a New Age–ish vegan, but his website has a page devoted to "Polka, Bowling and Kielbasa."

One thing you won't find on Kucinich's website, though, is any mention of his opposition to abortion rights. In his two terms in Congress, he has quietly amassed an anti-choice voting record of Henry Hyde–like proportions. He supported Bush's reinstatement of the gag rule for recipients of U.S. family planning funds abroad. He supported the Child Custody Protection Act, which prohibits anyone but a parent from taking a teenage girl across state lines for an abortion. He voted for the Unborn Victims of Violence Act, which makes it a crime, distinct from assault on a pregnant woman, to cause the injury or death of a fetus. He voted against funding research on RU-486. He voted for a ban on dilation-and-extraction (so-called partial-birth) abortions without a maternal health exception. He even voted against contraception coverage in health insurance plans for federal workers—a huge workforce of some 2.6 million people (and yes, for many of them, Viagra *is* covered). Where reasonable constitutional objections could be raised—the lack of a health exception in partial-birth bans clearly violates *Roe v. Wade,* as the Supreme Court ruled in *Stenberg v. Carhart*—Kucinich did not raise them; where competing principles could be invoked—freedom of speech for foreign health organizations—he did not bring them up. He was a cosponsor of the House bill outlawing all forms of human cloning, even for research purposes, and he opposes embryonic stem-cell research. His anti-choice dedication has earned him a 95 percent position rating from the National Right to Life Committee, versus 10 percent from Planned Parenthood and 0 percent from NARAL.

When I spoke with Kucinich by phone, he seemed to be looking for a way to put some space between himself and his record. "I believe life begins at conception"—Kucinich was raised as a Catholic—"and that it doesn't end at birth." He said he favored neither a Human Life Amendment that would constitutionally protect "life" from the moment of conception, nor the overturning of *Roe v. Wade* (when asked by Planned Parenthood in 1996 whether he supported the substance of *Roe,* however, he told them he did not). He spoke of his wish to see abortion made rare by providing women with more social supports and better healthcare, by requiring more responsibility from men, and so on. He presented his votes as votes not against abortion per se but against federal funding of the procedure. Unfortunately, his record does not easily lend itself to this reading: He voted specifically against allowing Washington, D.C., to fund abortions for poor women with *nonfederal* dollars and against permitting female soldiers and military dependents to have an abortion in overseas military facilities even if they paid for it themselves. Similarly, although Kucinich told me he was not in favor of "criminalizing" abortion, he voted for a partial-birth-abortion ban that included fines and up to two years in jail for doctors who performed them, except to save the woman's life. What's that, if not criminalization?

"I haven't been a leader on this," Kucinich said. "These are issues I would not have chosen to bring up." But if he plans to run for president, Kucinich will have to change his stance, and prove it, or kiss the votes of pro-choice women and men goodbye. It won't be enough to present himself as low profile or, worse, focused elsewhere (he voted to take away abortion rights inadvertently? in a fog? thinking about something more "important" than whether women should be forced to give birth against their will?). "I can't tell you I don't have anything to learn," Kucinich told me. Okay, but shouldn't he have started his education *before* he cast a vote barring funds for abortions for women in prison? (When I told him the inhumanity of this particular vote made me feel like throwing up—you're not only in jail, you have to have a baby too?—he interjected, "But there's a rape exception!") Kucinich says he wants to "create a dialogue" and "build bridges" between pro-choicers and anti-choicers, but how can he "heal divisions" when he's so far on one side? The funding issue must also be squarely faced: As a progressive, Kucinich has to understand that denying abortion funding to poor women is as much a class issue as denying them any other kind of healthcare.

That a solidly anti-choice politician could become a standard-bearer for progressivism, the subject of hagiographic profiles in *The Nation* and elsewhere, speaks volumes about the low priority of women's rights to the self-described economic left, forever chasing the white male working-class vote. Supporting an anti-choice congressman may have seemed pragmatic; trying to make him president would be political suicide. Pregnant prisoners may not vote, but millions of pro-choice women do.

•◄ MAY 27, 2002 ►•

Special Rights for the Godly?

Let's say I'm a Jehovah's Witness, and I get a job in an understaffed emergency room where, following the dictates of my conscience, I refuse to assist with blood transfusions and try my best to persuade my fellow workers to do the same. How long do you think I'd last on the job? And after my inevitable firing, how seriously do you think a jury would take my claim that my rights had been violated? Five minutes and not very, right? A similar fate would surely await the surgeon who converts to Christian Science and decides to pray over his patients instead of operating on them, the Muslim loan officer who refuses to charge interest, the Southern Baptist psychotherapist who tells his Jewish patients they're bound for hell. The law rightly requires employers to respect employees' sincerely held religious beliefs, but not if those beliefs really do prevent an employee from performing the job for which she's been hired.

Change the subject to reproductive rights, though, and the picture gets decidedly strange. In 1999 Michelle Diaz, a born-again Christian nurse who had recently been hired by the Riverside Neighborhood Health Center, a public clinic in Southern California, decided that emergency contraception (EC), the so-called morning-after pill that acts to prevent pregnancy if taken within seventy-two hours of unprotected intercourse, was actually a method of abortion. She refused to dispense it or give referrals to other providers. The clinic offered her a position that did not involve reproductive healthcare, but when she told temporary nurses at the clinic that they too would be performing abortions by dispensing EC, Diaz, who was still on probation as a new hire, lost her job. She sued with the help of the American Center for Law and Justice

(ACLJ), the religious-right law firm headed by Jay Sekulow. At the end of May a jury agreed that her rights had been violated and awarded her $47,000.

Excuse me? A nurse at a public health clinic has the right to refuse to provide patients with legally mandated services, give out misleading health information in order to proselytize her coworkers to refuse as well, and keep her job? The low-income women who come to Riverside desperately in need of EC and abortion referrals are flat out of luck if they happen to turn up when the anti-choicers are on shift? Riverside is the largest public health clinic in the county, serving 150–200 patients a day, but it operates with a staff of four nurses—should those four people decide what services the clinic can offer? What about the patient's right to receive standard medical care? Or the clinic's responsibility to deliver the services for which they receive government funds?

Some states, California among them, have "conscience laws," permitting anti-choice healthworkers to refuse to be involved in abortions. EC, however, is just a high dose of regular birth-control pills that prevents ovulation and implantation.* It is not abortion, because until a fertilized egg implants in the womb, the woman is not pregnant. A long list of medical authorities—the American Medical Association, the American Medical Women's Association, the American College of Obstetricians and Gynecologists, and Harvard Medical School—agree that EC is not an abortifacient, and a 1989 California court decision itself distinguishes abortion from EC. There are lots of mysteries about the Diaz case, ranging from why Diaz took a job she knew involved practices she found immoral in the first place, to how the jury could possibly have come up with a decision so contrary to law and public policy. Did Diaz take the job with the express intention of disrupting services? Was the jury anti-choice? Interestingly, the jury pool was partly drawn from San Bernardino County, which last year unsuccessfully tried to bar its public health clinics from dispensing EC.

Whatever the jury's thinking, the Diaz case represents the latest of numerous attempts by the anti-choice movement to equate EC with

---

*In May 2005, the Population Council reported that studies show that EC does not affect implantation, but works entirely by inhibiting ovulation.

abortion and move it out of normal medical practice. Pharmacists for Life International, a worldwide organization that claims to have some 1,500 members, calls it "chemical abortion" and urges pharmacists to refuse to dispense it. The ACLJ is currently litigating on behalf of one who did. Wal-Mart refuses to stock it at all. Anti-choicers in Britain made an unsuccessful attempt to prevent EC from being dispensed over the counter by placing it under an archaic law that prohibits "procuring a miscarriage." Some anti-choicers have long argued that not just EC but conventional birth-control methods—the pill, Norplant, Depo-Provera, and the IUD—are "abortifacients": In northern Kentucky, anti-choice extremists are campaigning to force one local health board to reject Title X family-planning funds. According to the Lexington *Herald-Leader*, the board's vote, scheduled for June 19, is too close to call.

Although secular employers are expected to make reasonable accommodations to religious employees—or even, if the Diaz verdict is upheld, unreasonable ones—religious employers are not required to return the favor. On the contrary, the Supreme Court, in *The Church of Jesus Christ of Latter Day Saints v. Amos,* permits them to use religious tests to hire and fire personnel as far from the sacred mission as janitorial workers; if a Methodist church wants to refuse to hire a Muslim security guard, it has the blessing of the Constitution to do so. As often noted in this column, religious organizations can and do fire employees who violate religious precepts on and even off the job. A pro-choice nurse could not get a job at a Catholic hospital and declare that her conscience required her to go against policy and hand out EC to rape victims, or even tell them where to obtain it—even though medical ethics oblige those who refuse to provide standard services for moral reasons to give referrals, and even though Catholic hospitals typically get about half of their revenue from the government.

According to the ACLJ, however, secular institutions should be sitting ducks for any fanatic who can get hired, even provisionally. The Riverside clinic has asked the judge to set aside the Diaz verdict. If that bid is unsuccessful, it will appeal. I'll let you know what happens.

Ashcroft ♥ Iran

W hat would the world look like if women had full human rights? If girls went to school and young women went to college in places where now they are used as household drudges and married off at eleven or twelve? If women could go out for the whole range of jobs, could own the land they work, inherit property on equal terms with men? If they could control their own sexuality and fertility and give birth safely? If they had recourse against traffickers, honor killers, wife beaters? If they had as much say and as much power as men at every level of decision-making, from the household to the legislature? If John Ashcroft has his way, we may never find out. After twenty years of stalling by Jesse Helms, the Senate Foreign Relations Committee in early June held hearings on the Convention for the Elimination of All Forms of Discrimination Against Women (CEDAW), an international treaty ratified by 169 nations. (President Carter signed CEDAW in 1980, but the Senate blocked it.) George W. Bush originally indicated that he would sign it—that was when he was sending Laura onto the air-waves to blast the Taliban—but under the influence of Ashcroft, he's since been hedging. Naturally, the religious right has been working the phones: According to one e-mail that came across my screen, the opera-tor who answers the White House comment line assumed the writer was calling to oppose CEDAW, so heavily were the calls running against it. The reasons? CEDAW would license abortion, promote homosexuality and teen sex, and destroy The Family. In 2000, Helms called it "a terrible treaty negotiated by radical feminists with the intent of enshrin-ing their anti-family agenda into international law."

How radical can CEDAW be, you may ask, given that it's been ratified by Pakistan, Jordan, and Myanmar? Genderquake is hardly around
the corner. Still, across the globe women have been able to use it to improve their access to education and healthcare as well as to raise their legal
status. In Japan, on the basis of a CEDAW violation, women sued their
employers for wage discrimination and failure to promote; the Tanzan-
ian High Court cited CEDAW in a decision to overturn a ban on clan
land inheritance for women. Given the dire situation of women worldwide, it is outrageous to see U.S. policy in the grip of Falwell, James
Dobson, and Ralph Nader's good friend Phyllis Schlafly. Like the Vatican, which uses its UN observer status to make common cause with Islamic fundamentalist governments on behalf of fetus and family, on
CEDAW the Bush administration risks allying itself with Somalia,
Qatar, and Syria to promote the religious-right agenda on issues of sexuality. In the same way, at the recent UN General Assembly Special Session on the Child—where the United States opposed providing girls
with sex education beyond "just say no," even though in much of the
Third World the typical "girl" is likely to be married with children—the
Bush administration allied itself with Libya, Sudan, and evil axis member Iran. Some clash of civilizations.

Given this season's spate of popular books about mean girls and in-
humane women, it might seem starry-eyed to suppose that more equality for women would have a positive general social effect. Where women
are healthy and well educated and self-determined, you can bet that
men are too, but the situation of women is not only a barometer of a society's general level of equality and decency—improving women's status
is key to solving many of the world's most serious problems. Consider
the AIDS epidemic now ravaging much of the Third World: Where
women cannot negotiate safe sex, or protect themselves from rape, or
expect fidelity from their male partners, where young girls are sought
out by older, HIV-positive men looking for tractable sex partners, where
prostitution flourishes under the most degraded conditions, and where
women are beaten or even murdered when their HIV-positive status becomes known, what hope is there of containing the virus? Under these
circumstances, "just say no" is worse than useless: In Thailand, being

married is the single biggest predictor of a woman's testing positive. As long as women are illiterate, poor, and powerless, AIDS will continue to ravage men, women, and children.

Or consider hunger. Worldwide, women do most of the farming but own only 2 percent of the land. In many areas where tribal rules govern inheritance, they cannot own or inherit land and are thrown off it should their husband die. Yet a study by the Food and Agriculture Organization shows that women spend more time on productive activities than men do, and according to the International Center for Research on Women, spend more of their earnings on their children. Recognizing and maximizing women's key economic role would have a host of benefits—it would lessen hunger, improve women's and children's well-being, improve women's status in the family, lower the birth rate, and promote development.

And then there's war and peace. I don't think it's an accident that Islamic fundamentalism flourishes in the parts of the world where women are most oppressed—indeed, maintaining and deepening women's subjugation, the violent rejection of everything female, is one of its major themes. (Remember Mohammed Atta's weird funeral instructions?) At the same time, the denial of education, employment, and rights to women fuels the social conditions of backwardness, provincialism, and poverty that sustain religious fanaticism.

If women's rights were acknowledged as the key to human progress that they are, we would look at all these large issues of global politics and economics very differently. Would the U.S. government have been able to spend a billion dollars backing the fundamentalist warlords who raped and abducted women and threw acid at their unveiled faces while "fighting communism" and destroying Afghanistan? At the recently concluded *loya jirga,* which featured numerous current and former warlords as delegates, a woman delegate stood up and denounced former president Burhanuddin Rabbani as a violent marauder. For a moment, you could see that, as the saying goes, another world is possible.

•◄ JULY 8, 2002 ►•

School's Out

When the New York City Board of Education called on public schools to bring back the Pledge of Allegiance in the wake of 9/11, my daughter, a freshman at Stuyvesant High, thought her big chance to protest had finally come. Have you thought about what you'll say if you have to justify not reciting it? I asked. "Sure," she replied. "I'll say, there's such a thing as the First Amendment, you know—separation of church and state? I mean, *under God*? Duh!" Judge Alfred Goodwin of the Court of Appeals for the Ninth Circuit, meet my Sophie, future president of the ACLU if the punk-rock-guitarist plan doesn't work out.

Virtually every politician in the country has issued a press release deploring Judge Goodwin's ruling that the words "under God" constituted a coercive endorsement of religion. "Ridiculous!" said the President. Tom Daschle led the Senate in a stampede to condemn the ruling 99 to 0, after they recited the pledge together. The *Times* editorial expressed the standard liberal line, mingling world-weariness and fear: "under God" is a trivial matter, so why arouse the wrath of the mad Christians? You can turn that argument around, though—if it's so trivial, why not do the right, constitutional thing? Let the nonbelieving babies have their First Amendment bottle! The very fact that the vast majority of Americans believe in God counts against inserting expressions of religious faith into civic exercises for kids—civil liberties are all about protecting unpopular minorities from being steamrollered by the majority. The history of "under God" is not very edifying or even very long: It was added to the original pledge—written in 1892 by Francis Bellamy, a socialist—by Congress in 1954 as a means "to deny the atheistic and materialistic concept of communism." If that was the purpose, it worked. The new Evil Ones, however, have no quarrel with being "under God"; it's the "liberty and justice for all" they disapprove of. If we really want to drive them nuts, we should change "under God" to "with equality between men and women." Or better yet, retire the pledge as an exercise in groupthink unbefitting a free people.

Something tells me we haven't seen the last classroom invocation of the divine umbrella—Judge Goodwin has already stayed his own ruling—but even if the decision is upheld, it's unfortunately the least significant in a number of recent rulings about education. The Supreme Court decision upholding the Cleveland school voucher program is a real, nonsymbolic triumph for organized religion, which stands to reap millions of dollars in public funds, taken directly from the budgets of the weakest school systems. Theoretically, your tax dollars can now support the indoctrination of every crackpot religious idea from creationism to stoning, with extra credit for attending rallies against legal abortion and for the retention of "Judea" and "Samaria" as God's gift to the Jewish people. What happened to *"e pluribus unum"*? (Interestingly, as David Greenberg notes in *Slate*, *"e pluribus unum"* was replaced as the national motto in 1956 by . . . "In God We Trust"!) And what about that pesky First Amendment? Writing for the 5–4 majority, Chief Justice Rehnquist argues that separation of church and state is preserved because it is the parent, not the state, who actually turns the voucher over to the religious school. By the same logic, why not a health system in which patients get vouchers good either for surgery or a ticket to Lourdes?

The same day brought the court's decision upholding random drug testing of students who want to take part in after-school activities. Now there's a great idea—take the kids who could really use something productive to do with their afternoons, kids who, whatever mischief they're up to, actually want to run track or sing in the chorus or work on the yearbook, and don't let them do it! God forbid some sixteen-year-old pothead should get a part in the drama club production of *Arsenic and Old Lace*. The harm of the ruling isn't just that kids who do drugs will now have yet more time on their hands and yet more reason to bond with their fellow slackers, it's that everyone gets a lesson in collective humiliation and authoritarianism—stoned or straight, the principal can make you pee in a cup. Consider too that one-third of schools now offer abstinence-only sex education, in which kids are told that contraception doesn't work and having sex before marriage is likely to be fatal—if the kids don't go to parochial school, apparently, parochial school comes to them.

The prize for the worst school-related decision, though, has to go to the panel of New York State appeals court judges that reversed Justice Leland DeGrasse's brave and noble ruling invalidating the state's school funding formula, which gives less money per child to New York City schools despite the fact that city schools have disproportionate numbers of poor and non-English-speaking children. According to Justice Alfred Lerner, author of the court's majority opinion, the state is required to provide its young only the equivalent of a middle-school education— enough for them to sit on a jury, vote, and hold down a menial job. Anything more is optional and can be distributed at will. (Why not let kids drop out after eighth grade, you may ask? Well, then they'd miss abstinence classes and drug tests and reciting the Pledge of Allegiance!) The world needs workers at the lowest levels, the judge observes, so let the black and Hispanic kids of New York City be the hewers of wood and drawers of water and flippers of burgers. Somebody's got to do it— and it's a safe bet it won't be the judge's children.

Maybe the critical legal theorists are right and the law is merely a form of words into which can be poured whatever meaning the ruling class wants it to have. It's hard to understand in any other way the court's willful misunderstandings of the actual conditions of city public schools, so that the judge could respond to plaintiffs' evidence of schools with decades-old outmoded science textbooks by harrumphing that there's nothing wrong with libraries full of "classics."

●◀ JULY 22, 2002 ▶●

Beyond Good and Evil

So now it's official. If a foreign government does not offer its people "the rewards and challenges of political and economic liberty," an eternal value that all people everywhere espouse, we can "take action." If we deem a nation a threat to our safety, we can even "take action" "preemptively," on the basis of a possibility that it may harm us in the future. We do this to preserve "a balance of power that favors human freedom"—although "our forces will be strong enough to dissuade potential adversaries from pursuing a military buildup in hopes of surpassing, or equaling, the power of the United States"—strong enough, in other words, to preserve an *im*balance of power. This is the Bush doctrine, as revealed in *National Security Strategy of the United States* (NSSUS), a thirty-three-page administration document submitted to Congress and released on September 20. It's a sort of long-winded version of Ann Coulter's famous suggestion about the 9/11 terrorists, that we "invade their countries, kill their leaders, and convert them to Christianity."

Have it your way, Francis Fukuyama. Let's say that there is only one happy way to organize society, that, as the NSSUS claims, "People everywhere want to say what they think; choose who will govern them; worship as they please; educate their children—male and female; own property; and enjoy the benefits of their labor." Let's even say that "the duty of protecting these values against their enemies is the common calling of freedom-loving people across the globe and across the ages." Are we going to invade Saudi Arabia, where speech is anything but free, voting unheard of, Christianity illegal, and converting a Muslim a crime? Or northern Nigeria, where militant Muslims have installed Sharia law and propose to stone women who have sex outside marriage? And what about China—who elected Jiang Zemin? And do the slaves of Sudan and Mauretania, the indentured and child laborers of India, Pakistan, and Bangladesh—millions of people—enjoy "the benefits of their labor"?

These are not rhetorical or frivolous questions. If the U.S. government wants to promote humane and democratic values, there's no lack of peaceful ways to do so—we could start by pouring on the billions needed to make Afghanistan a livable country again. But what the Bush doctrine is really about is whipping up moral fervor for war against Iraq and who knows where else. Defense Secretary Donald Rumsfeld's desk bears a plaque imprinted with a quotation from Theodore Roosevelt: "Aggressive fighting for the right is the noblest sport the world affords." Never mind that the war party in the administration consists almost entirely of men who avoided military service—Bush took a sheltered position with the Texas National Guard; Cheney didn't enlist, citing "other priorities"; Paul Wolfowitz and Richard Perle were both at the University of Chicago. It's interesting too that it's the military men—Colin Powell, Anthony Zinni, Wesley Clark, Norman Schwarzkopf—the ones who've played that particular sport before, who have wanted to go slow and think about consequences. What wusses!

Saddam Hussein is a murderous, seemingly insane dictator who tortures and kills, perhaps even children in front of their parents, as Paul Wolfowitz claims, perhaps even for fun, as a woman who says she was his mistress told ABC News. But there are others—the government of Myanmar for example—who are as bad. Saddam gassed "his own people," actually Kurds, who would prefer not to be his people, and who can blame them? But Hafez Assad of Syria killed as many as 20,000 people when he shelled Hama, and Sudan's Omar el-Bashir has killed, displaced, and enslaved tens of thousands in the south. Iraq may be developing weapons of mass destruction, perhaps even a nuclear bomb—but Pakistan and India already have nuclear weapons aimed at each other, and nobody's talking about overthrowing their governments. As for Al Qaeda and terrorism and the world that will never be the same, Osama bin Laden seems to have functioned a bit like the flashy item in a bait-and-switch scheme that gets you into the grocery store, only to find yourself manipulated into buying something else. Saddam Hussein, so far as we know, had nothing to do with 9/11, barring one possible meeting between Mohammed Atta and Ahmed Al-Ani, an Iraqi agent, in Prague. There were no Iraqis among the 9/11 attackers: All but one hailed from our delightful allies Saudi Arabia and Egypt. Nor is Iraq, one of the more secular states in the Muslim world, a promoter of the Wahhabi strain of Islamic fundamentalism; it's Saudi Arabia that exports that particular brand of "worship" around the globe. Indeed, Osama bin Laden regards Saddam Hussein as an infidel.

None of this is to excuse or wave away or minimize or justify the wrongdoings and the dangers of Saddam Hussein, although I'm sure Andrew Sullivan will read it that way. But that Saddam is evil does not mean invading Iraq is good. Nor does it explain why the Bush administration is in such a huge, unilateral hurry. What's the rush? One of the functions of the Bush doctrine's language of moral absolutism is to discredit other moral concerns. Multilateralism can be dismissed as multiculturalism: Why should we care what the French and Germans think in their soft, snooty welfare states? To query the premises—do we know that Saddam wants to attack the United States? or does he want to defend himself from us?—can be tarred as pussyfooting. To raise commonsense concerns—do we want to occupy Iraq for years? what if Iraq attacks Israel and Israel retaliates? will we produce more terrorism by enraging the Muslim world?—can be portrayed as cowardly, feminine, "sissified," as right-wing columnist Walter Williams put it on townhall.com.

You can't have a debate in a black-and-white world—maybe that's the real aim of the Bush doctrine.

I AM VERY SAD to learn that Christopher Hitchens has given up his column, which for so many years has been one of the defining features of the magazine. He is a brilliant writer, and I will miss him.

•◄ OCTOBER 14, 2002 ►•

Letter to an Ex-Contrarian

DEAR CHRISTOPHER,

I was very sad when you left the magazine, but I was puzzled too. What kind of contrarian leaves a column—called "Minority Report," no less—because too many of the readers disagree with him? Quite apart from the fact that some readers share your views on Iraq, the precipitating subject, aren't contrarians supposed to relish the combat? To enjoy stomping about the lonely platform and hectoring the resistant multitudes? Let's say you wanted to persuade those opposed to invading Iraq that the cause of Iraqi democracy and Kurdish self-determination require it. What better pulpit than here?

But of course there was more to it than that. On the radio, on *Hardball*, in a long interview in *Salon*, in a *Washington Post* essay redolently titled "So Long, Fellow Travelers," you've offered a view of those who oppose Bush's military plans that is seriously at odds with reality: The antiwar movement equals the left and the left equals the followers of Ramsey Clark, defender of Slobodan Milosevic and assorted Hutu *genocidaires* and other thugs, who is the founder of the International Action Center, which is closely linked to ANSWER, a front for the Workers World Party. Your picture of the big antiwar demo in October could have come straight out of David Horowitz's column: "100,000 Communists March on Washington to Give Aid and Comfort to Saddam Hussein."

Now, it is a fact that ANSWER called the big demonstration in Washington, it arranged for the permits, organized many buses, and brought on all those speakers no one listens to. That's not the same as controlling the movement—99 percent of the people who go to those demonstrations don't even know ANSWER exists—but of course it's galling that this tiny group of sectarian throwbacks play any kind of leadership role. That's why numerous lefties you know well—David Corn, Marc Cooper, Todd Gitlin—have written polemics calling for their ouster, and various efforts are afoot to out-organize them. I think those writers exaggerate ANSWER's influence—I can't tell you how many people I've spoken with who do not recognize in Corn's *LA Weekly* description the D.C. event they attended. But the important point is, those writers and those organizers oppose ANSWER because they know it doesn't represent either the left or the antiwar movement. You seem to think it does.

What I don't understand is how you can believe that. You've spent decades on the left you now despise. You know that Edward Said, Ann Snitow, Doug Henwood, Laura Flanders, and Adolph Reed care as much about human rights as you do; don't regard Saddam Hussein as a people's hero; don't secretly gloat over 9/11 (you, weirdly, told *Salon* that the event filled you with "exhilaration"—the battle between fundamentalism and secularism had been joined). Why do you write as if these antiwar voices—or Vietnam Veterans Against the War, or the National Organization for Women, or your presidential candidate of choice, Ralph Nader—did not exist? You are doing to the American left exactly what Martin Amis did to you when he laid the crimes of Stalin at your Trotskyist feet. Sure, there are plenty of people (not all of whom are leftists) who oppose this war because they oppose all U.S. military intervention on principle, and maybe there is even some graduate student out there, mind addled by an all-Ramen diet, who believes that Osama bin Laden is merely a "misguided anti-imperialist." But surely you know that lots of people oppose invading Iraq who supported the war in Afghanistan and intervention in Kosovo—why aren't Mark Danner, Aryeh Neier, and Ronald Dworkin on your radar screen? Who died and made Ramsey Clark commissar?

As the polls, which show declining support for war, should suggest, many people oppose military action in Iraq who are not leftists. They are the troops at those big demonstrations—ordinary people from unions and high schools and churches, piling into buses with their handmade signs. Why? They're afraid of big casualties, American and Iraqi; they fear it will turn the whole region into a bloodbath; they fear Saddam Hussein will attack Israel, and Israel will strike back; they believe it will mean long-term occupation of Iraq, with terrible consequences for our own society; they fear it will backfire, increasing terrorism against the United States and fueling Islamic fundamentalism. They think it's a substitute for, and diversion from, the more difficult task of going after Al Qaeda. They oppose the whole concept of preemptive war, and see it as a violation of international law that will license other countries to do the same. They don't like the bellicose tone of the Bush administration, distrust its constantly shifting rationales and apparent willingness to go it alone. They do not believe, as you apparently do, that the administration cares about Iraqi democracy or the Kurds—who, by the way, are hardly united in welcoming the prospect of war.

These people are mostly not pacifists, whom this year you say you respect but last year jeered at in the *Guardian* (in a piece titled "Ha Ha Ha to the Pacifists"). But they see a world that bristles with arms and is run by men of limited vision on behalf of narrow economic and ideological interests—probably not many would agree with your statement in the London *Observer* last January that, Ashcroft excepted, Bush's early appointments were "statesmanlike." They see a world in which invading other countries often doesn't work out too well and has unintended consequences. You ought to understand all that—after all, you opposed the Gulf War, which had much more justification than the current proposal.

Well, I'm sorry you're not here to discuss all this further—although your current style of debate relies perhaps too heavily on words like "idiot" and "moron" to shed much light. Next time you put on your Orwell costume for the TV cameras, I hope you'll put on his fairness and modesty too. You may have spent years as a man of the left in America, but I don't think you really knew the American left.

Your ex-colleague,
Katha

•◁ NOVEMBER 25, 2002 ▷•

Raise a Glass to the
Stay-at-Home Voter?

How dismal was election night 2002? At the party I attended, the mood was so glum that one young man stood up in the TV room and announced that he had just the thing to cheer us up: a five-minute compilation of commercials from Paul Wellstone's first campaign. He popped it into the VCR, and we all stared at the screen as the dead candidate ran for the Senate in 1990.

I know what I'm supposed to say about the Democratic losses: The Dems stood for nothing/were indistinguishable from Republicans, so why not vote for the real thing? The last part of that argument has never made much sense to me—why would you vote for the more intense version of something you supposedly don't like in the first place? True, overall the Dems fumbled just about every issue in hot pursuit of the ever-rightward-moving center. But may I play devil's advocate for a moment? As *Nation* readers were endlessly informed, there were a number of contests in which the differences between candidates were quite marked. In the Florida gubernatorial contest, could you really mistake labor-backed Bill McBride for Jeb Bush, the dark prince of election 2000? Walter Mondale may not have had Paul Wellstone's populist fire, but he was hardly a carbon copy of Norm Coleman. Rhode Island's liberal Myrth York blasted her conservative, business-backed opponent in the gubernatorial race for his retrograde positions on abortion and gun control. Chellie Pingree, the Democrat who challenged moderate GOP incumbent Susan Collins for the Senate in Maine, was a classic progressive with strong positions on corporate reform, education, the environment, and healthcare, an attractive personality, and had a record of public service as a state legislator. Like other progressive-endorsed Democrats—

Iowa's John Norris, Oregon's Bill Bradbury, South Dakota's Stephanie Herseth, Arizona's George Cordova, and Illinois's Hank Perritt—they all went down to defeat.

And what about the referendums and ballot initiatives? Ohio voters could have said a modest, humane no to the insane drug war by requiring treatment for nonviolent drug offenders instead of jail; they voted to keep locking 'em up. (Voters in the District of Columbia went the other way.) In Oregon, voters had a chance to seize the holy grail of progressive politics, government-funded universal healthcare, something Americans famously tell pollsters they want. Seventy-nine percent of the voters said no thanks. A ban on gay marriage passed in Nevada; a living-wage proposal lost in Santa Monica; Massachusetts voted to abolish bilingual education; instant runoff voting was defeated in Alaska; and Colorado voters rejected same-day voter registration.

Of course, each of these contests had its own dynamic. In Oregon, the insurance industry spent a fortune on Harry and Louise–style ads; Mondale ran up against the mighty Republican spin machine's ridiculous attack on Paul Wellstone's memorial service (Omigod! They talked politics!); a Maine friend claims voters in her state just like to keep their incumbents unless they've totally screwed up. But isn't that the same as saying that the majority of Maine voters are satisfied with a moderate Republican? If Minnesotans were so turned off by the Wellstone memorial that they voted for Coleman or stayed home, their commitment to Wellstone's successor could not have been deep to begin with. And if universal healthcare loses its appeal the minute opponents say it will raise taxes, hurt business, and drive doctors out of state, it will never win.

True, the Republicans had more money, not to mention Rush and his ilk, Fox, and much of the mainstream media, plus a popular President who campaigned tirelessly round the country, plus the discombobulation of 9/11 and the prospect of invading Iraq. But it's hard to look at the election results and see much confirmation for the view that voters are panting to surge left but the Democratic Party won't let them. It would be nice to report that centrist Georgia senator Max Cleland lost because he supported the Bush tax cut. Unfortunately, this disabled Vietnam vet lost to a hawkish gun nut and religious zealot, Saxby Chambliss, who charged him with lack of patriotism for voting against the creation of a Department of Homeland Security that would bar union protection for workers. Georgia governor Roy Barnes, another centrist Dem, lost to Sonny Perdue after proposing a state-flag redesign that would have minimized its Confederate elements. I don't believe for a minute that most voters are raving reactionaries yearning to give humongous tax cuts to the richest Americans, criminalize abortion, bust labor, fill the garage with submachine guns and the judiciary with Scalias-in-waiting. But passion counts: Where is the evidence that the majority of voters who oppose these things care as much as the minority who favor them?

Maybe we need new voters, better voters. American turnout is famously low and getting lower—this year it was around 40 percent of the voting-age population. In *The Vanishing Voter,* a fascinating and multi-layered examination of the causes of declining turnout, Thomas Patterson argues that nonvoters—disproportionately poor, working-class, minority—are much more likely to support Democratic politics; if everyone voted, Democrats, not Republicans, would control the White House, Senate, and Congress today. I heard a lot of stories about people who say they didn't vote because of one inconvenience or another—not Florida-style shenanigans but everyday problems with schedules and transportation—to which my friend Josh Freeman acerbically replied: In East Timor, people walked barefoot for miles and stood in line for hours to vote. If people thought it mattered, they'd figure out a way to get to the polls, the way they figure out how to get to the post office.

So which is it: People don't vote because there's no one to vote for (except when there is)? People don't vote because it's too much trouble (except when it isn't)? Let's find out. Let's move Martin Luther King Day to the first Tuesday in November, so that Election Day is a paid national holiday and King's memory is honored with something more real than uplifting bromides. Or maybe, it will turn out, not more real.

•◀ DECEMBER 9, 2002 ▶•

As Miss World Turns

The war between religious fanaticism and secular modernity is fought over women's bodies. Feminists have been saying this for years, not that anyone important was listening, but the Miss World riots in Kaduna, Nigeria, should make it obvious even to the dead white males at the *Washington Post*. Muslims, already on edge due to the presence in their country of so many lovelies on display, were apparently driven out of their minds by journalist Isioma Daniel's suggestion in the Lagos-based newspaper *ThisDay* that Mohammed "would probably have chosen a wife among them." By the time the smoke cleared and the bloody knives were put away, the local offices of the paper had been destroyed; more than 200 people, mostly Christian, had been murdered; hundreds more had been injured; and at least 4,500 were left homeless. Nothing for the contestants to worry about, though: According to President Olusegun Obasanjo, "It could happen any time irresponsible journalism is committed against Islam." When in doubt, blame free speech. Nonetheless, the pageant relocated to London, while the governor of Zamfara State issued a *fatwa* (later rescinded) against Ms. Daniel, urging Muslims to kill her—"Just like the blasphemous Indian writer Salman Rushdie, the blood of Isioma Daniel can be shed." She fled the country.

Not a good week for cultural relativism, on the whole.

Militant Islam may be the beginning of the end for multicultural-ism, the live-and-let-live philosophy that asks, Why can't we all enjoy our differences? Ethnic food and world music are all very well, but *fat-wa*s and amputations and suicide bombings just don't put a smile on the day. In twelve Nigerian states, Sharia is now the law of the land, and in the background of the Miss World fiasco lies the case of Amina Lawal, condemned to death by stoning by a Sharia court for the crime of having a baby out of wedlock. Because of the shocking brutality of the verdict and its blatant misogyny—needless to say, the man who impregnated her was not charged—some feminists had unsuccessfully urged the Miss World Pageant to boycott Nigeria, and a number of contestants—Misses Denmark, Panama, Costa Rica, Switzerland, and South Africa—refused to take part. They are the true heroines of this discouraging episode.

Say what you will about beauty pageants, if it's bikinis versus burkas, you've got to be for bathing suits. British feminists who condemned the pageant as a sexist cattle call seemed to be missing the point, somehow. Yes, it's a sexist cattle call. And yes, the Miss World Pageant, seen each year by more than 2 billion viewers around the globe, helps disseminate white Western ideals of female beauty—and the concomitant body-image problems—to yet more distant lands (last year's winner, Miss Nigeria, the first black African winner, is, unlike most Nigerian women, *Vogue*-model slim). But that is not the big story right now. The big story is the growing power of fundamentalist maniacs.

Speaking of whom, no one is getting more mileage out of Islamic fundamentalism than Christian fundamentalists. Many divines have been quick to portray Christianity as the religion of peace and love as opposed to the murderous, false teachings of Islam. Franklin Graham, Billy's son, who spoke at Bush's inauguration, said Islam is "a very evil and wicked religion." Jerry Falwell has called Mohammed a "terrorist"—a "pedophile," too, chimed in the Reverend Jerry Vine. While President Bush keeps gamely asserting that Islam is a religion of peace, the foreign-policy hard right rolls its eyes. The Koran inherently leads to terrorism, Norman Podhoretz argues, because it commands Muslims "to wage holy war, or jihad, against the 'infidels.'" Does that make the Gospels responsible for anti-Semitism? Not as long as right-wing Christians are Israel's best friends.

And what do Muslim feminists, caught in the middle, make of all this? Given the bad image of Western feminism in the Muslim world, it's not surprising that they make their way carefully. On a recent segment of *Democracy Now!* Fawzia Afzal-Khan and Azizah al-Hibri insisted passionately that the conviction of Amina Lawal was against Islamic law—where were the four male witnesses to the act of penetration? Why wasn't the man charged too? What about the doctrine of the sleeping fetus (don't ask)? The problem wasn't the Koran but its corruption, both agreed, going on to energetically bash Western feminists for obsessing about the veil instead of poverty and the United States for promoting Islamic extremists from General Zia ul-Haq of Pakistan to bin Laden himself. "Islam," said al-Hibri, "gives women all the rights we are calling for." And yet, by the end of the program, Afzal-Khan was speaking sympathetically of separating mosque and state.

I'm no expert—to me the Koran, like the Old and New Testaments, seems both implicitly and explicitly sexist, and retrograde in other ways as well. Still, the human mind is a wonderful thing and modernity is a powerful force. We don't kill witches anymore, although Exodus explicitly bids us to, or cite the Bible to justify slavery, indentured servitude, polygyny, forcibly marrying widows to their brothers-in-law, or impregnating the maid if the wife is infertile, after the example of Abraham. Even the humiliating Jewish menstrual laws have been reinterpreted under the pressure of feminism and the sexual revolution: Suddenly, after thousands of years, they're not about pollution and uncleanness, they're about giving women more power in the bedroom and having a more meaningful marriage. Moreover, they are retroactively understood to have always contained this meaning. Christian feminists have no trouble contextualizing out of existence even the most plainly worded of Saint Paul's numerous male-supremacist commands: Women, obey your husbands, keep silent in church, cover your heads, and all the rest. Religious texts mean what people want them to mean, and always have. If the whole elaborate institution of the papacy can be balanced on a single remark of Jesus to Peter (a remark that to Protestants, of course, means something quite different), Islamic feminists can surely find in the Koran proof of Allah's commitment to women's rights. It won't be a perfect fit, any more than modern feminist readings of the Bible are a perfect fit, but it will do for the time being.

•◄ DECEMBER 23, 2002 ►•

They Know When
You Are Sleeping

One of my cherished childhood memories is of my petite, polite mother closing the front door firmly on two hulking FBI agents who wanted to come in and ask her questions. "I don't have to talk to you," she informed them in a steely voice, and she didn't. Wow, Mom! I can't swear to all the details—were the agents really so big, or was I just little? and did they really wear hats and trench coats, or have I dressed them to fit the 1950s stereotype?—but I do have a distinct memory of them casually lifting the lids from our streetside garbage cans as they left and peering inside, like cooks checking the stockpot. I doubt they really expected to find secret papers tossed in with the banana peels and steak bones; they were simply making a point. After my mother died, I sent away for her FBI file, which revealed, among other more serious invasions of privacy, that every year the FBI would phone our house on a pretext to make sure we still lived there. Honestly, hadn't they noticed that the phone book has addresses too? Your government dollars at work.

But why wallow in ancient history? In the wake of September 11, spying on citizens is back in all its careless glory. Indeed, it appears it never really went away. For example, my old friend Barbara Levy Cohen and her husband, Mark Cohen, are among the many represented by an ACLU lawsuit against the Denver Police Department. The Colorado branch of the ACLU announced last March that it had learned that the DPD had conducted surveillance and maintained "criminal intelligence files" since the 1950s (!) on people engaged in constitutionally protected political activities. Soon after, Mayor Wellington Webb admitted that "the issues that have been raised by the ACLU as well as others are legitimate" and that files existed on 3,200 individuals and 208 organizations, from the Million Mom March to the "criminal extremist" American Friends Service Committee, the Rocky Mountain Peace and Justice Center and NARAL.

As always seems to be the case with police files, the Denver dossiers are full of egregious misinformation and dark comedy. Barbara, a serious, mild-mannered secretary who, when not organizing around Native American and fair-trade issues, likes to read and go to the movies, is identified as having a "direct relationship" with an "outlaw biker" gang involved with "narcotics, weapons." (Not true, Barbara says, for the record.) Mark's file contains a group photograph with an arrow pointing to him—only it's not him. Margaret Taniwaki, a Japanese-American woman who spent time as a child in a World War II internment camp in California, is identified as "Caucasian" (maybe they meant to write "Asian"?); her ex-husband of twenty years has a file because she drove a car registered in his name. Sister Antonia Anthony, a seventy-four-year-old nun who belonged to a pro-Zapatista organization called the Chiapas Coalition, was cited as supporting the overthrow of the Mexican government—which would make her more of a firebrand than the Zapatistas themselves.

But there are more serious items too. Glenn Morris, chair of the political science department at the University of Colorado, Denver, and member of the leadership council of the Colorado American Indian Movement (AIM), had a death threat listed in his files: The police knew about it but never passed it on. While Cassandra Medrano and Pavlos Stavropoulos were in Greece, another couple used their car to drive to an antiglobalization demonstration; that couple's nine-year-old child—listed as a "reliable" source in the files—gave a police officer information about her parents that the DPD misassigned to Medrano and Stavropoulos; using this "information," the DPD started a file on Medrano and added to its file on Stavropoulos. Do we want to live in a society where fourth-graders are considered reliable sources, and in which cops probe children for information about their parents on the basis of political beliefs and activities that are legal?

What causes do "criminal extremists" favor in Denver? Besides reproductive rights, good works, and pacifism, apparently they are keen on Native American rights. "Of the files I've seen," Barbara tells me, "three-quarters mention AIM and protests against Columbus Day, which is a big issue here in Denver." The Direct Action Network, an antiglobalization/fair trade group, also caught the inquisitorial eye: So much so that at one point the DPD, aware that its usual infiltrators had become familiar faces, asked a detective from the vice and drugs control bureau to attend a DAN meeting undercover. Given such practices, it's not surprising that another popular cause is protesting abuses of the citizenry by the Denver Police Department. Barbara's and Mark's files note that in 1991 they cosigned a letter published in the *Colorado Statesman,* a local weekly, criticizing the police for racism. Why does this classic exercise of the First Amendment belong in secret dossiers?

Not that spying on the nonviolent would ever be right, but it's worth noting that the Denver debacle was facilitated by the police's lack of training in the use of the Orion Scientific Systems software program. Crucial decisions about how to categorize and input information (what constituted "criminal extremism," for example) were made in an unprofessional, whimsical way. Other cities in which secret police files have been uncovered tell a similar story of inept paranoia. Until the mid-1980s, four years after passage of a state law barring police spying on nonviolent political activities, Portland police kept tabs on a wide variety of groups, including the Northwest Oregon Voter Registration Project, a food co-op, a bicycle-repair collective, a group setting up a rape hotline, and a battered women's shelter.

These days, local authorities are eager to jettison longstanding restraints imposed after abuses in the 1970s and go back to their old-fashioned ways. The New York City Police Department, for example, announced that it wants to be able to spy on citizens without having to persuade an official three-member panel that it has just cause—even though it cited no examples of this process hindering an investigation. In a fine twist, the NYPD plans to use an updated version of the Orion software employed to such notable effect by the Denver PD.

Just remember: You don't have to talk to them.

•◄ JANUARY 27, 2003 ►•

War. What Is It Good For?

By the time you read this, the invasion of Iraq may have begun—or it may be over. The Iraqi military may have put daisies in their gun barrels—a London-based Kurdish journalist I know has received dozens of reports of soldiers in northern Iraq deserting or trying to surrender—or Republican Guard troops loyal to Saddam Hussein may be putting up ferocious street-by-street resistance in Baghdad. Thousands of civilians may be dead, and since U.S. plans for bombing entail leveling one in ten buildings in Iraq, it's hard to imagine less carnage. But perhaps the number of casualties will be surprisingly low.

Saddam Hussein may torch oilfields or use biological or chemical weapons against U.S. troops—or the United States may deploy sinister new weapons of its own, like the 21,000-pound MOAB bomb the *New York Times* says sends "a devastating wave of fire and blast," an electromagnetic pulse bomb that crashes entire computer networks, even a nuclear "bunker buster." Or both. Or neither. People like to predict, whether to strengthen their convictions or to prepare themselves psychologically, but war is inherently unpredictable. The Afghans were supposed to be formidable mountain fighters who would rally round the Taliban and hold out fiercely against the hated foreigner, and World War I was supposed to last six weeks.

Unless the worst predictions prove true, the antiwar movement—not to mention the United Nations—is sure to be scorned as crying wolf when it warned of hundreds of thousands of dead Iraqi children and thousands of U.S. body bags. I sometimes thought that too much stress was laid, at antiwar protests and candlelight vigils, on the simple fact that people—yes, even children—are killed in war. After all, people—

including children—are killed by tyrannical regimes too. Had the Taliban remained in power, torturing, massacring, executing, they might have killed outright as many people by now, or even more, as were killed by American bombs, while continuing to poison Afghan society with illiteracy, ignorance, ill health, brutality, fanaticism, and the most extreme misogyny the world has seen. Saddam Hussein has been a disaster for Iraq, and no doubt would continue to be so if left in power. Whether the Iraqis greet U.S. troops with cheers and confetti or with sullen, resentful glares, you can be sure that they won't be singing "Last Night I Had the Strangest Dream" or "Where Have All the Flowers Gone?"

According to polls, most Americans now believe that Saddam Hussein was behind the September 11 attacks and support the war—however anxiously and unhappily—in the mistaken belief that it is necessary for self-defense. The 9/11 connection is ceaselessly, demagogically promoted by the administration. In his speech warning of imminent invasion if Saddam failed to leave Iraq in forty-eight hours, George W. Bush alluded to this discredited canard seven times.

Liberal prowar intellectuals, though, don't talk so much anymore about self-defense as a motive for war—avoiding any embarrassment about the nuclear weapons Saddam turns out not to have, for example, or his decrepit military that is supposed to threaten world security even as it is on the brink of collapse. They know that Iraq has far less to do with terrorism than, say, Pakistan or Saudi Arabia, and that there are plenty of other sources for weapons of mass destruction. Their chief cause—I'm thinking here of Michael Ignatieff, for example, the most eloquent exponent of humanitarian imperialism—is "regime change." They argue the moral rightness of overthrowing Saddam by force and setting Iraq on the path to democracy and normality.

This is a seductive vision indeed—who wouldn't like to see Saddam in the dock at The Hague? I'd be surprised if the Iraqis got real democracy out of U.S. invasion and occupation, but maybe the next strongman or puppet or junta will be an improvement, the way Karzai is an improvement on the Taliban. It could be that, as Samantha Power (author of *"A Problem from Hell": America and the Age of Genocide*) told the *New York Times* in early February, "a unilateral attack would make Iraq a more humane place, but the world a more dangerous place."

Humane? Maybe. More dangerous, for sure. Whatever the immediate results—this many dead children versus that much freedom from repression—the fundamental issue has to be the perils of "preemptive war" in volatile times. However it works out for the Iraqis, invading their country will be bad for the rest of the world. It will aid terrorist recruitment, it will license other countries—India and Pakistan, for example—to wage preemptive wars of their own, it may even consolidate Islamic fundamentalism as the only alternative to American power in the Middle East. Those are the fears not just of the American antiwar movement but of the majority of people around the world, even in the nations whose leaders have joined with ours.

But who cares about the majority of the world's people? We'll go to war unilaterally, with our pathetic collection of allies (Britain, okay; but Spain? Italy? Latvia?), while the rest of the world stands by appalled. We'll boycott the Dixie Chicks, eat our freedom fries, and even, as documented in the *New York Times,* pour Dom Perignon by the gallon down the toilet ("I'll bet it was just water," said the manager of my local liquor store. "Nobody would waste great champagne like that!"). People will be called traitors if they wear peace T-shirts, fail to salute the flag, or dare to suggest that anyone in the administration has lower motives than the selfless salvation of humanity. Journalists "embedded," as the odd phrase goes, in military units will send back an endless stream of heartwarmers that will reinforce the confusion of "support the troops" with "support the war." If, in the end, the Iraqis turn out to hate and resent the nation that bombed them into freedom, we'll shake our heads in angry bewilderment: After all we did for you, this is the thanks we get!

The issue raised by the invasion of Iraq is American imperialism. That won't go away, no matter how this particular adventure turns out. See you at the demonstration.

•⊰ APRIL 7, 2003 ⊱•

Pride and Prejudice

How do we know the economy is in bad shape? Unemployed white male hotshots are back in the news. "This man used to make $300,000 a year," reads the *New York Times Magazine*'s cover. "Now he's selling khakis." The grim black-and-white cover photo shows a resentful-looking bald man with a clipboard and Gap tag, sporting a Silicon Alley hipster's five-day-old beard. He's "interactive industry pioneer" Jeff Einstein, one of three men profiled in "Commute to Nowhere," by Jonathan Mahler, who lost their high-paying jobs when the New Economy tanked and have had trouble resigning themselves to the kinds of jobs that are left: selling pants for Jeff; substitute teaching in the public schools for Lou Casagrande, a former information-technology consultant (at $100,000 a year); and volunteering as a "networking" coordinator for Tom Pyle, who'd left the stressful life of banking ($200,000) for the calmer waters of the nonprofit sector ($100,000), only to be laid off within six months.

After more than a year holding out for the next big thing, their wallets are thin, their cars are falling apart, their self-esteem is wilted, and their marriages aren't in such great shape either: Jeff takes the Gap job only because his wife finally threatens to evict him if he doesn't start helping out with the rent. (Just between you and me, I suspect he could have done better but took the Gap job just to spite her.) It's all about masculinity, Mahler informs us. Women have been as likely to lose their jobs as men in the current climate, but "for most women, survival trumps ego; they simply adapt and find some job." I like that "simply." No cover story there.

But wait. Those $10-an-hour jobs, the ones we're supposed to pity the men for having lowered their masculine dignity to take, look kind of familiar, don't they? They're the "good jobs" women on welfare are encouraged to get, the ones that are supposed to transform them from mooching layabouts to respectable, economically self-sufficient, upright, and orderly citizens. (Of course, both Tom and his stay-at-home wife recoil at the possibility that she may have to get a job. I guess this is because, unlike poor single mothers, she's a "homemaker.")

What happened to all those homilies about personal responsibility and the dignity of a job—any job—that were trotted out to justify forcing welfare mothers to work off their checks at subminimum wage by cleaning toilets in public parks or scraping chewing gum off subway platforms? Somehow, those sermons don't apply to Mahler's guys, but only to those single mothers of small children who get up at dawn for long bus rides to jobs as waitresses or hotel maids or fast-food workers— jobs that one calls "menial" at the risk of being tarred as an elitist snob by welfare-reform enthusiasts. The point is not so much work—the exchange of labor for pay and benefits—but work experience: work as behavior modification. For Mahler's subjects, work is about masculine dignity, so a low-status job is worse than none. Poor women apparently have no dignity to be affronted.

Take the first job you can get and be glad you have it is the philosophy of welfare today. If you are poor and had the bad judgment to become a single mother, well, no education and training for you. The welfare reauthorization bill, approved by the House and soon to be voted on by the Senate, raises the percentage of welfare clients who must work from 50 to 70 percent and ups work requirements for single parents from twenty to forty hours a week. This is well above the norm for working mothers, which is thirty-one to thirty-five hours. A proposal by House Democrat Ben Cardin that education and training count toward that total was rejected along party lines. In New York City, where unemployment is 8.6 percent and half of welfare clients didn't graduate high school, Mayor Bloomberg vetoed a similar set of modifications from the City Council. (The Council overrode his veto, and he has threatened a legal challenge.)

Is there a middle-class person in America who doesn't understand the relation of education and skills to self-support in the twenty-first century? You'd almost think the people who write the welfare laws don't want poor women to earn a middle-class income—just to adopt the imaginary middle-class sexual values embodied in abstinence classes and marriage promotion schemes, which welfare reauthorization funds to the tune of $50 million and $300 million a year, respectively.

Maybe I lack sufficient regard for the male ego, but I found it hard to shed a tear for the men in Mahler's profile. They may have lost their dreams of financial glory, but this is not exactly *King Lear.* By the standards of normal life they're not doing so badly. They live in safe suburban neighborhoods, with food on the table and good schools for the kids. Indeed, Jeff's wife earns $80,000 a year, which puts the family in the top third of U.S. household incomes before he's sold a single pair of jeans. At the end of the piece, we learn that Lou and Tom have come to terms with reality and are planning to become public school teachers. This is hardly a tragedy. In fact, it will likely be the first really useful and important work either has ever done.

Zora Neale Hurston, a great writer who made quite a bit of money in her time, ended her days as a cleaning lady. That's what I call tragic. All over America, single mothers with nothing like the advantages or prospects of Jeff, Lou, and Tom are being told to sink or swim, and their children along with them. That's tragic too.

•◀ MAY 5, 2003 ▶•

Weapons of Mass Delusion?

Tom Friedman doesn't care if the United States ever finds weapons of mass destruction in Iraq. The recently discovered skull of a murdered Iraqi political prisoner is all the retroactive justification he needs for the preemptive war: "That skull, and the thousands more that will be unearthed, are enough for me," he wrote in his April 27 *New York Times* column. "Mr. Bush doesn't owe the world any explanation for missing chemical weapons (even if it turns out the White House hyped this issue)."

Nothing succeeds like success. Who cares about WMDs when you have Baghdad? Just the usual handful of liberal columnists, it seems— oh, and the rest of the world, which is less willing than Mr. Friedman to be hoodwinked in the interest of a higher cause. Here in America, we've already forgotten about the nuclear evidence that wasn't. When the proposition that aluminum tubes found in Iraq could have been used to refine uranium was debunked by UN atomic energy head Mohamed El-Baradei, and when the evidence Colin Powell presented that he said proved Iraq had imported uranium from Niger turned out to be based on forged documents, did the ubiquitous former CIA analyst Kenneth Pollack, whose *The Threatening Storm* specifically argued for war on the grounds that Saddam was developing nuclear weapons, say, "Oh well, never mind"? (Come to think of it, did Pollack, on his rounds as a TV commentator, ever point out that his book called for war *after* breaking Al Qaeda and cooling Israeli–Palestinian tensions?)

Bush himself said in his State of the Union address that the case for war was not so much Saddam Hussein's brutal doings as the threat he represented to the United States, and his neighbors, as warmonger and terrorist. So if it turns out that Saddam did not have significant stocks of biological or chemical weapons and had no dealings with Osama bin Laden—according to the London *Observer,* Tony Blair never believed he did—can we rewind the tape and get the Baghdad antiquities museum and the national library and all those dead people back?

Perhaps Saddam did have lots of WMDs, and perhaps the United States will find them. Not a day goes by, it seems, without a front-page announcement of their discovery that is retracted, on page B18, the next morning. Meanwhile, as David Corn reports, the hunt for WMDs is hardly proceeding with the seriousness and singlemindedness one might expect, given how impatient Bush was with poor Hans Blix. After all, if they are out there and we don't find them quick, then someone else—a Baath party loyalist, a renegade scientist, Al Qaeda—might get hold of them. Oh, but I'm forgetting—they're in Syria.

It's now sport to mock the antiwar movement for predicting that the invasion would be a catastrophe, with huge casualties on both sides, millions displaced, and the Middle East in flames. Fortunately, the worst did not happen. But the antiwar movement was right about the war being unnecessary for our own security: As the twenty-six-day "cakewalk" to Baghdad demonstrated, the moth-eaten Baathist regime, with its poorly equipped soldiers and unenthusiastic citizenry, was in no shape to threaten the United States or cause world turmoil. That should be properly acknowledged, discussed, and debated, not waved away, in the rush of victory, as a mere detail.

We're not supposed to compare Iraq to Vietnam—this is not, repeat, not, your father's quagmire!—but how's this for a similarity? If Saddam's dangerousness was a pretext, a way to win popular support by spreading fear, those insistent charges of WMD possession start looking rather like the manufactured Gulf of Tonkin incident. Is it okay for the government to lie as long as things go well?

As the administration begins the project of nation-building that Bush the candidate said he wanted to avoid as President, Iraqi "regime change" is presented as if it will be as easy a cakewalk as the war itself. The neoconservatives point to the encouraging examples of Japan and Germany post–World War II. But Afghanistan is a more relevant case, since it is a project of this very administration. There, a mere seventeen months after overthrowing the Taliban and installing the genial Hamid Karzai as head of a warlord-heavy central government, the United States no longer talks about turning Afghanistan into a modern country run on democratic principles. In Bush's initial proposed budget, he allotted no money for Afghanistan—none.

Iraq, we are told, is a different story: It has a large educated middle class and a modern infrastructure; it has all that oil. But it also has a lot of angry people. As soon as Iraqis could demonstrate, they carried placards that read, "No to Saddam, No to America, Yes to Islam." I'm just guessing, but those million Shiite pilgrims flogging themselves bloody on the road to Karbala might not be so enthusiastic about the Iraqi National Congress, or modern roles for women, or the values of the Enlightenment as interpreted by *The Weekly Standard*. One day Jay Garner says Iraqis will run their country themselves, the next day Donald Rumsfeld says that under no circumstances will Iraq become an Iranian-style Islamic fundamentalist state. So what happens if that's what the majority of Iraqis want?

It would be strange indeed if "regime change" means replacing tyranny with theocracy, but the pitiful number of Iraqi women involved in official gatherings to set up the transitional government is a bad sign. Meanwhile, the United States seems to be doing everything possible to infuriate and alienate the Iraqi people. In Faluja, near Baghdad, soldiers shot into a crowd of anti-American demonstrators, killing thirteen and wounding seventy-five. At the next day's demonstrations, they killed two more.

In a column from February 12, when he still had his doubts, Friedman compared invasion to having to buy what you bust at a pottery store: "We break Iraq, we own Iraq." If ownership turns out to be less exhilarating than the war looked on Fox, if it's expensive, dangerous, and unrewarding, will the American people hold the Bush administration accountable for saying "WMD" when they meant "regime change" all along? Or will we be too busy cakewalking our way to Damascus and Teheran?

Bah, Humbug

I wish it had been sex, maybe some of that hot "man on dog" action that Senator Rick Santorum is so keen on chatting about. But let me not be picky. Since we are talking about that thundering sultan of sanctimony Bill Bennett, high-stakes gambling will do quite nicely. In eleven books, including the mega-selling *Book of Virtues*, a PBS cartoon series on morality for kids, countless speeches at $50,000 a pop, a slew of op-eds, and more face time on TV than the man who squeezes the Charmin, Bennett has made himself our Cato, inveighing against everyone else's licentious, addicted, family-destroying ways. Abortion! he growled. Drugs! Rap! Adultery! Homosexuality! Divorce! Single moms! *The Simpsons!* To the wall with you, feminists, gay priests, and fornicating Democrats Bill Clinton, Jesse Jackson, and Gary Condit! To prison, not rehab, any of you who've so much as looked hopefully at a nickel bag of weed! He's expatiated upon the joys of teenage shotgun marriages and the selfishness of having fewer than "six or seven" kids. (Bennett himself married at thirty-eight and has two children—a hypocrisy tip-off right there, for those who were paying attention.)

Bashing moral laxity—and blaming it on liberals—was a popular and very profitable line of tripe that made Reagan's Education Secretary and Bush Senior's drug czar a millionaire many times over. Is it any wonder that honest sinners are rising as one to cheer now that *Newsweek* and *Washington Monthly* report that he plowed a staggering eight of those millions right back into the vice economy as fast as he could pull the handle of the $500 slot machines that were his favored mode of "relaxation"?

Bill Kristol, Jonah Goldberg, and other conservatives maintain that

Bennett has done nothing wrong. Gambling is, after all, legal, and Bennett says he never gambled "the milk money." Unfortunately, Bennett sandbagged his defenders by admitting that he had "done too much gambling" and vowing to quit. In any case, the legality defense won't wash. Except for drugs and, in some states, homosexuality and (nominally) adultery, most of the things Bennett inveighed against are legal. Complaining about that sorry fact was part of his shtick.

Bennett's point was never just that people ought to obey the law: Sure, drink yourself into a daily stupor, as long as you're not driving. No, *The Book of Virtues* evoked the old Aristotelian/Stoic/Christian/Early American civic values: piety, sobriety, temperance, honesty, prudence, self-control, setting an example. It's hard to imagine John Bunyan or George Washington giving Bennett a high five on his way to private rooms at various Las Vegas casinos, where he was such a loyal and lavish customer he was comped for limos, rooms, and Lord knows what else.

Bennett's defense that his family didn't suffer may be true, or it may be denial, but it misses the point. As Michael Kinsley observes in the *Washington Post,* Bennett has always argued that being good is a form of noblesse oblige; even minor vices indulged in by the privilege-cushioned elite corrupt those lower down the social scale, who have less to fall back on. Let Muffy toke up on some hydro at Harvard, and before you know it Charlene is on crack in the projects. Let same-sex love flourish, and by some mysterious process, it will wreak havoc on heterosexual marriage.

But gambling is a perfect example of a trickle-down vice: A multimillionaire can afford to lose an amount that would send most Americans to the poorhouse. By his own lights, Bennett has failed the truckers, waitresses, and retirees who, faced with continuous temptation and omnipresent opportunities to gamble, end up betting the Christmas money at Foxwoods or blowing the phone bill on the lotto.

"Pathological" or "problem" gambling is a serious social malady that, according to the National Council on Problem Gambling, affects some 6 million Americans. It destroys and impoverishes families and, like all obsessive behavior, makes practitioners and those who love them miserable. But don't take my word for it. Just ask the folks at Empower America, of which Bennett is chairman. Empower America opposes the expansion of legalized gambling and lists problem gambling as a leading indicator of America's cultural decline. In fact, widespread conservative disapproval of Bennett's open secret is part of why the story got leaked.

It's debatable whether decriminalizing marijuana would increase its use—and whether that would be so very awful. But there's no doubt that the widespread legalization of gambling, or "gaming," as the industry prefers we call it, has boosted it into the mainstream. Moreover, where you have gambling you also tend to find organized crime, prostitution, political corruption, and the illusion of a budgetary free lunch—as when legislators use lottery profits or gambling taxes to substitute for regular funding of education. As a pseudolibertarian tax on the poor, gambling is the perfect Republican revenue stream. Even as I write, George Pataki is proposing to cure New York's budget woes by installing 4,500 video lottery terminals—anything but raise taxes on the wealthy!

Bennett's defenders make much of the fact that he never condemned gambling and so was not actually a hypocrite. Leaving your own pet vice off a long, long list of sins, and then, when you are found out, exempting that vice as practiced by you but not as practiced by others—that's not exculpation from charges of hypocrisy, that's what hypocrisy *is*.

If Bennett were a jolly, modest fellow, full of love for fallen humanity and the first to admit he was just another sinner like the rest of us—if he were less quick to impute the worst motives to perfectly ordinary behavior, like having two kids; if he spent less time promoting rigid, puritanical morals and more time promoting, oh, kindness and tolerance and looking into your own heart and cutting other people some slack because you never really know what demons they're contending with—no one would be piling on now.

But then, with a message like that, no one would have heard of him in the first place. You don't get to play Christian on TV, or amass real political power along with your millions, by urging people not to throw the first stone, especially if they live in a glass house. Jesus tried that, and look what happened to him.

•◄ JUNE 2, 2003 ►•

White Lies

The radio went on in the middle of the night and there in my ear was the voice of a young man. It was a soothing voice, deferential, quizzical, NPR-ish, the voice boy journalists in the high-end media use when they are trying to get Nazis to talk about their childhoods. And yet there was a kind of suppressed glee in it, too—as if he had just gotten the perfect quote from Adolf Junior. Yes, the young man said ruefully, he knew people hated him; yes, he's become more religious. Well, naturally! This was Stephen Glass, the *New Republic* tale-spinner, pushing his autobiographical novel *The Fabulist,* and public contrition just goes with the territory. F. Scott Fitzgerald, who famously said there are no second acts in American lives, should only be alive to see how wrong he was.

There's one person besides his agent who should be overjoyed at Glass's splashy reemergence from obscurity, and that is Jayson Blair. Forced out at the *New York Times* on May 1 for a wide variety of journalistic sins—plagiarizing, making things up, getting things wrong, pretending to be eyewitness-reporting from Maryland and Texas while never actually leaving the city—Blair too has acknowledged that he was "troubled," and has an agent trying to secure a six-figure advance for a tell-all book. While no one judged Glass as a case of whiteboyism run amok, Blair, who is black, is now exhibit A for affirmative-action bashers: You see what happens when guilty liberals coddle the unqualified? Janet Cooke, the black journalist fired from the *Washington Post* after winning a Pulitzer for a fabrication, tends to come in for a mention at this point—never mind that she was canned twenty-two long years ago. Glass's reappearance is a timely reminder that liars and manipulators come in all colors of the rainbow.

Everyone is asking how these two were able to deceive so many for so long. But is it so mysterious? As many a woman has learned to her chagrin, pathological liars are brilliant at deception. They know how to make a story sparkle, they breezily proffer instant explanations for any little inconsistency, they're scheming all the time while you, their mark, are preoccupied with a hundred other things. Besides, you *want* to believe them—they're so charming, attentive, and flattering. According to numerous accounts, Blair was a champion sycophant to *Times* top editor Howell Raines and Gerald Boyd, his second-in-command; Glass was the quintessential young man in a hurry, smart and needy, someone in whom his editors could see their younger selves. As *George* editor Richard Blow, one of Glass's victims, confessed in *Salon,* these professional liars know how to play to your secret wishes and preconceptions. Glass's hilarious tales—young conservatives engaging in drug-fueled orgies, women stricken en masse with crushes on UPS men—played on the desire of his wonkish Beltway editors to feel superior and in-the-know.

As Blow acknowledges, to his credit, Glass pandered to his editors' tacit racism too. He wrote a piece for *Harper's* alleging that blacks spend tons of cash on phone psychics and one for *The New Republic* that told of his cabdriver being robbed by a black man. One of the fabrications that finally brought him down was an article for *George* alleging that Clinton adviser Vernon Jordan had Monicas of his own. It's interesting how often race and class prejudice show up in these discredited stories. Janet Cooke's Pulitzer was for a feature about an eight-year-old black heroin addict. Ruth Shalit, *The New Republic*'s star plagiarizer, attacked the *Washington Post* in an error-strewn piece for pandering to racial sensitivities. (Her editor, Andrew Sullivan, is now enjoying himself at the *Times*'s expense—but while the *Times* prostrated itself with a 14,000-word article detailing Blair's derelictions, *The New Republic* issued only pro forma regret.) Jay Forman's mostly invented *Slate* article on the obscure Florida sport of monkey-fishing in the mangroves played to stereotypes about backwoods southerners—they eat squirrels and sleep with their sisters, so why wouldn't they fish for monkeys too?

Blair now joins a lengthening list of disgraced journalists—don't forget Mike Barnicle (plagiarized), Patricia Smith (made up quotes and people), and my favorite ethical line-crosser, Bob Greene (slept with a high-schooler who interviewed him for her school paper). The *Times* has suspended Rick Bragg, a Raines protégé whose lavishly overwritten tales of southern life provoked many an eye-roll from acerbic New Yorkers, for excessive reliance on an uncredited volunteer stringer who did his actual reporting. Several other *Times* reporters are allegedly under investigation by management as well.

It sounds like management needs to take a look at itself, and not just about such common journalistic failings as borrowed phrases and embellished quotes. It's embarrassing to see *Times* brass flagellating themselves with tiny Blair corrections ("The sister of Corporal Gardner is named Cara, not Kara") while weighty issues of news content go unaddressed. For all their slapdash dishonesty, none of Blair's stories affected the course of any event. That cannot be said of the paper's relentless pushing of Whitewater, which helped stall a presidency but ended without a Clinton indictment, or its unfounded, life-destroying pursuit of Wen Ho Lee.

At the present moment, the question of whether Rick Bragg personally witnessed the "jumping mullet that belly-flop with a sharp clap into steel-gray water" is trivial compared with Judith Miller's credulous reports on Iraq. Here we have a Pulitzer-winning reporter who alleges that an unnamed Iraqi scientist has proof both of WMDs and of Saddam's connections with Al Qaeda and Syria. Miller got this fascinating scoop from her Army handlers—she never questioned him herself; indeed, she never even met him! She allowed the Army to vet her copy and determine the timing of its publication. Result: a front-page story that was trumpeted everywhere as the retroactive justification for war.

Where were the editors who should have reined in this administration-friendly flight of fancy? The person who put Miller's story on page one has more to answer for than the harried administrator who didn't notice that Blair's travel receipts were from a Starbucks in Brooklyn.

•⊣ JUNE 16, 2003 ⊢•

Blond Ambition

Hillary Clinton's autobiography comes out barely a week after Martha Stewart is indicted for obstruction of justice and fraud related to alleged insider trading, and you *still* don't believe in God? Two blond middle-aged icons of female preeminence, each virtually unique in the testosterone-drenched worlds of politics and business, are ruling the headlines and obsessing the talk shows at exactly the same moment—how likely is that? Obviously this is some kind of harmonic convergence intended to induce mass heart attacks at Fox News. It's not just the sheer excitement—"Hil: Wanted to Wring His Neck"! "Martha's Mug Shots"!—that's raising pulses. It's the fact that despite everything, millions of women insist on adoring them anyway.

I've written many a column criticizing Hillary Clinton for the rightward tilt of her politics—her support for welfare reform, capital punishment, "family values," and so on. I even made a catty remark about her hairband back in 1992, for which I'm truly sorry. Truth, moreover, compels me to admit that *Living History,* her mega-hyped memoir, has that unfortunate processed-cheese, as-told-to taste. It's the verbal equivalent of her Barbara Walters appearance: one long fixed, glazed smile under the pink lights. But none of that matters. People aren't lining up by the thousands to purchase signed copies because they want to get the real scoop on tax policy or even Travelgate. They want to know if she really believed Bill when he told her there was nothing to the Monica story, how she felt when she finally learned it was true, and why she stays with him. The answers to be found in her book are yes; she was really upset; and thanks to prayer and marriage counseling she was eventually able to move on.

Whether this is the whole truth is impossible for a stranger to know. Like Joe Klein, I tend to believe she really loved him—she writes in the book about her first impression of him as a "Viking" and lyrically describes his hands, his boundless energy, his fascinating conversation. I was ready to date him myself! She certainly wouldn't be the first smart, straitlaced woman who fell for a sexy charmer and ended up, as the joke goes, believing what he told her instead of what she saw. Nor, on the other hand, would she be the first wife who decided to live with what she couldn't change rather than throw away a relationship that was also a way of life. Or the first First Lady who put up a good front in public while quietly seething at home. I doubt the right-wingers going after Hillary for staying with Bill would have cheered if evidence of George Bush Senior's rumored infidelities had come to light and Barbara had abandoned him in his hour of need. Hillary must be the only woman the family-values crowd has ever castigated for sticking with her marriage. Just you try suggesting, though, that Pat Nixon was maybe not the most fulfilled woman in America, or that Laura Bush sometimes looks a little subdued, a little out of focus, and see how fast you get accused of being an East Coast elitist, slut, and traitor.

For the right, Hillary's book comes just in time. In the third year of the Bush administration, it was beginning to look like conservatives might finally have to acknowledge that Bill Clinton is not President anymore. Now they can sink into a nostalgic delirium—ah, for the days of Whitewater, Morgan Guaranty, Gennifer Flowers, Paula Jones, Vince Foster, and all the other horrors from which the Supreme Court rescued us in December 2000. Hillary's book is handy too in helping Bill Kristol and his fellow talking heads brush aside pesky questions about the shifting rationales for invading Iraq and those missing WMDs. Could Bush have been shading the truth? No, it was Bill Clinton who "lied to the American people." Right, and about something so very important, too! In right-wing mythology, if Hillary knew about Bill's women, she is an ambitious schemer; if she didn't, writes Jonathan Alter in *Newsweek*, she's not fit for higher office: "Blinders are understandable in a wife, but could be a concern in a future president." According to Alter, when Bush claimed an "imminent threat" from Iraq or said the "average" tax cut is $1,000 a year, "he is deceiving us, not himself," a pettier crime. So if there's one thing worse than lying to the American people, it's believing your husband is telling the truth.

One hears so much from people who hate Hillary, one forgets that millions think she's great, a self-made working wife and mother who actually managed to turn the routine subordinations—and, in her case, profound humiliations—of political wifehood into real power: from First Lady to senator! Martha Stewart offers the same contradictory blend of traditional femininity and modern feminism: She is a brilliant businesswoman, but she sells retro domesticity. Her fans seem to have no trouble integrating these two rather different visions of womanhood or believing that she's been singled out for prosecution as a woman while Ken Lay walks free. Marthatalks.com, a website she set up to mobilize support, has received 7 million hits and features fervent e-mails thanking her for introducing graciousness and beauty into harried and humdrum lives. And why not? Martha never tells women they should quit their jobs in order to make apple pie from their very own organic orchard. She doesn't say they're ruining their kids and ought to work harder at sex. She just tells them a lot of neat stuff about, oh, slipper chairs and how to take the thorns off roses.

Martha's reputation as a first-class bitch (on full view in Cybill Shepherd's portrayal in a recent NBC movie) hasn't put a dent in her cult, and that's only fair. This is a nation that reveres Donald Trump, for heaven's sake, who famously trashed his wife and has devoted his entire life to profiting off gambling and hideous buildings. Donald Trump, icon of manly capitalism, destroyed the beautiful Art Deco frieze on the Bonwit Teller building after promising to preserve it. That's a lot worse than $45,000 worth of insider trading, in my view. True, Trump is a man, and successful men have always been allowed to be mean and worse than mean; only women have to be sweet, kind, gentle, modest, sexually circumspect, and scrupulously honest 24/7 no matter what—even in the nasty worlds of politics and business.

Or they did until Hillary and Martha came along.

•◀ JUNE 30, 2003 ▶•

Lost Innocents

Every day, DNA testing overturns another man's rape or murder conviction. *The Exonerated,* a play drawn from the stories of innocent people released from death row, is an Off Broadway hit. We are learning that people confess to crimes they did not commit, that the most confident eyewitness testimony can be mistaken, that a state crime lab can be as sloppy as a greasy-spoon kitchen, that police officers lie. As *New York Times* columnist Bob Herbert reports, the state of Texas has released from prison all but two of the forty-six residents of Tulia—including 10 percent of the town's black population—who had been essentially framed by an undercover cop on drug charges. These and other high-profile reversals might almost make you believe the cliché that "the system works."

But then there is the case of Bernard Baran. Three years ago in this space I wrote about Baran, who, as a nineteen-year-old childcare worker in Pittsfield, Massachusetts, was the first to be convicted in the wave of mass-molestation daycare cases that swept the country in the 1980s. Ever since, I've hoped to follow up with the news that he too is free (he has been incarcerated since 1985, or just about half his life). After all, DNA isn't the only kind of forensic science that has moved ahead: The assumptions under which the daycare cases were prosecuted, the methods used to gather evidence, the expertise advanced by the prosecution, have all been pretty much exploded. Thanks to researchers like Elizabeth Loftus, Maggie Bruck, and Stephen Ceci, we know much more now about how to interview children, about the role that adult pressure, including the questions of anxious parents, can play in getting small kids to "disclose" things that never happened and sometimes to remember them as if they did. As uncovered by crusading journalists Debbie Nathan and Dorothy Rabinowitz, cases like that of the McMartin Preschool (the Buckeys), Wee Care (Margaret Kelly Michaels), and Fells Acre (the Amiraults) look in retrospect like bouts of collective insanity. It seems amazing now that anyone could believe that perversions of a Sadean extravagance—being tied to a tree on the front lawn while a teacher cut the leg off a squirrel, being forced to lick peanut butter off a teacher's genitals while she played the piano—could take place in busy spaces with no one the wiser and the children trooping cheerfully back the next day. *Capturing the Friedmans,* Andrew Jarecki's much-praised documentary about the case of Arnold and Jesse Friedman, raises these questions well: How likely is it that the Friedmans orchestrated group sessions of naked anal-penetration "leap frog" that one student "remembered" only under hypnosis?

Baran's case lacks the wilder elements of some other daycare cases—there were no tales of tunnels, spaceships, robots, or magic rooms. But in many ways it was typical. The Early Childhood Development Center was a well-run, well-staffed, respected facility in which parents were free to drop in anytime and in which privacy was minimal. The original complaint came from a troubled family—the mother and her boyfriend were drug addicts leading violent and chaotic lives, and "Peter," whose alleged complaint to his mother that his penis hurt set off the investigation, was an unruly, difficult child. Once the panic got going, the children were presumed to be "in denial" if they said nothing happened and truthful if they "disclosed." Against a gung-ho prosecutor riding a tide of national and local hysteria, Baran had the kind of legal counsel you get if all you can pay is the $500 your mother got from selling her car.

An important and unusual feature of Baran's case is that he is gay. "Peter's" family had complained to the ECDC about that, as had another family, whose daughter testified against Baran. Playing on the popular image of homosexuals as pedophiles (never mind that Baran was accused of molesting girls as well as boys), the prosecutor compared him to "a chocoholic in a candy store." To explain why "Peter" tested positive for gonorrhea of the throat but Baran tested negative, he suggested that Baran might have taken penicillin before being tested (Baran is allergic) and reminded the jury that male homosexuals and prostitutes had high rates of STDs. Unfortunately, that prosecutor, Dan Ford, is now a judge in western Massachusetts.

Would Baran be convicted today? As a not entirely sympathetic article in the *Boston Globe* (October 1, 2000) observed, there were two pieces of medical evidence against him, and both have been scientifically discredited: That particular gonorrhea test is now known to give many false positives, and the "notches" on one girl's hymen, presented as evidence of penetration, are now known to be normal features in some 60 percent of nonabused girls. Tellingly, moreover, no fresh cases of mass-molestation have made headlines in the past eight years. Rape, murder, assault, child abuse still happen all the time, but this particular crime does not. The acclaim for *Capturing the Friedmans,* and the publication of *No Crueler Tyrannies,* Dorothy Rabinowitz's exposé of the Amirault case and others, are perhaps signs that we are ready to see the panic in historical perspective. But is the justice system ready to do the right thing by the people convicted when the panic was at its height? Gerald Amirault is still in prison, and so is Bernard Baran.

His legal team—John Swomley, Pam Nicholson, and Harvey Silverglate—has been trying for more than two years to get from the district attorney, Gerard Downing of Berkshire County, records to which the court has agreed the defense is entitled and which, the lawyers believe, could exonerate Baran. There's been one delay after another. You would think the least the state of Massachusetts could do would be to turn over to the defense in an expeditious fashion materials the state's own courts have agreed it should have.

Bernard Baran is a working-class man with no money and no wealthy defenders. Gay groups won't touch the case—the stigma of pedophilia is too great. All he has is his family and a small band of supporters, led by Bob Chatelle and Jim D'Entremont. Three years ago, the generosity of *Nation* readers gave a huge boost to Baran's cause. If you would like to help now, you can send a donation to The Bernard Baran Justice Committee, PO Box 230783, Boston, MA 02123. To learn more, see www.freebaran.org.

•◄ JULY 14, 2003 ►•

Selling Dean Short

What did Howard Dean do to make the media so snarky about his primary run? Now that he has emerged as a major fund-raiser with flocks of enthusiastic supporters, a vigorous campaign staff, a bag full of Internet tricks, and respectable—and rising—poll numbers, the pundits and reporters have to go through the motions of taking him seriously. In a single August week he was on the cover of *Time* and *Newsweek* and had a major story in *U.S. News & World Report*. But aside from some curiously cheerful coverage in the *Wall Street Journal,* they obviously don't like him. He's "brusque," "testy," the "ex-Governor of a speck of a state," and "a shrill Northeasterner," Karen Tumulty wrote in *Time.* "It's hard to imagine Dean's glorious season ending without disappointment," adds John Cloud in his profile in the same issue, in which he draws a labored and precious similarity between Dean and George W. Bush (both come from rich Republican families, both went to Yale, partied hearty, speak Spanish—never mind that Dean went to medical school while George II relied on his father's cronies to set him up in the oil business). "The Doctor Is In—In Your Face!" warns *U.S. News.* Over at *Newsweek* ("Destiny or Disaster?"), Jonathan Alter also finds "the diminutive family doctor" "brusque" and says he "strutted like a little Napoleon onto the floor of the usually genteel Vermont State Senate."

A little Napoleon? Is that the problem—Dean is short? (He's 5' 8".) In order to run for President one must not only be white, a man, mar-ried, religious, and southern—not to mention whatever the opposite of brusque may be—one must be tall as well? No wonder I love this man! Every time the press pooh-poohs his chances, every time they gloat over some trivial misstatement, every time they make fun of Vermont and describe his supporters as "Birkenstocked" "Deanyboppers," I think about the free ride the media give Bush, who says more false and foolish things in an afternoon than Dean has said in a lifetime, who is unmaking everything good about this country from Head Start to habeas corpus, who is stacking the government with faith healers and fanatics, and my fingers itch to write Dean another check.

So what if on *Meet the Press* Dean gave ballpark answers to Tim Russert's gotcha questions about the number of soldiers in Iraq? Compared with the President he's a Talleyrand reborn. On July 14, Bush explained why the United States invaded Iraq as follows: "The larger point is, and the fundamental question is: Did Saddam Hussein have a weapons program? And the answer is: absolutely. And we gave him a chance to allow the inspectors in, and he wouldn't let them in. And therefore, after a reasonable request, we decided to remove him from power." Eat your heart out, Hans Blix! The President of the United States can bizarrely declare that weapons inspectors never entered Iraq, and that's not a news story. He's "likable," he's tall—he's not a Democrat.

Dean opposes the war on Iraq, wants to rescind the Bush tax cuts, and has a plan for quasi-universal healthcare coverage. But he's not particularly progressive, despite the Democratic Leadership Council's accusation that he is on the "far left," "McGovern-Mondale" wing of the party and will lead it straight to hell. In the 1990s, he was a darling of the DLC, and he governed Vermont as a budget-balancing centrist ("I was a triangulator before Clinton was a triangulator," he recently told the *New York Times Magazine*). If you want a great platform on everything from single-payer health insurance (yes) to the death penalty (no), Dennis Kucinich is definitely your man. Indeed, some pundits predict that when Dean's lefty supporters discover Dean's center-right positions on such issues as Israel and welfare, his campaign will fizzle. "The guy they think Dean is, Dennis is," Jeff Cohen, Kucinich's ebullient communications director, told me, predicting an exodus of progressives from Dean to Kucinich as the truth comes out. (Presumably despite the fact that Kucinich is a whole inch shorter.)

Maybe so. But I've talked to quite a few Dean supporters, including mainstream Democrats, lapsed voters, flaming leftists, Naderites, gay activists, civil libertarians, anti–death penalty lawyers, pro–single payer health professionals, and even a surprising number of *Nation* staffers. I have yet to find one who mistakes Dean for Eugene Debs, or even for Paul Wellstone, whose line about belonging to the "democratic wing of the Democratic Party" Dean likes to borrow. They've gone for Dean because, alone among the major Democratic contenders, he has taken Bush on in an aggressive and forthright way, because he's calling the craven Democratic Party to account, and because they think he can win. "I have no illusions that Dean is a true progressive," said one young graduate student who describes himself as a leftist, "but I don't care. I just want to beat Bush. If Dean has the momentum, I say go for it." That word "momentum" comes up a lot.

Right now, Dean is the only viable candidate who speaks to the anger, fear, and loathing a large number of ordinary citizens feel about the direction Bush has taken the country, while the mainstream media blandly kowtow and the Democratic Party twiddles its thumbs. He has gone out and actually asked for the help of these citizens, rather than taking them for granted. That is why 70,000 people have sent him money, and why 84,000 have shown up to work for him, and why tens of thousands of volunteers wrote personal letters to Iowa and New Hampshire Democrats and independents urging them to support Dean. His willingness to challenge Bush without looking over his shoulder at the last undecided voter in Ohio is the big story—not whether he signed Vermont's civil-union legislation in a private ceremony to avoid publicity, or even whether he insisted on balancing Vermont's budget at the expense of worthy social programs.

What the media see as progressive self-delusion is actually the opposite: a bare-knuckled pragmatism born from the debacle of the 2000 elections. If Kucinich can capture the public's imagination, great. If Kerry acquires more backbone and fire, fine. Right now, though, it looks like Howard Dean is Ralph Nader's gift to the Democratic Party.

●◀ SEPTEMBER 1, 2003 ▶●

Stacked Decalogue

The 5,300-pound hunk of granite carved with the Ten Command-ments has been rolled out of Alabama chief justice Roy Moore's Montgomery courtroom to gather moss in an unspecified back room. According to a Gallup poll, 77 percent of Americans think the rock should have been allowed to remain; many are hopping mad at Alabama attorney general William Pryor, only yesterday the darling of the reli-gious right and the object of an ongoing Senate filibuster against his nomination to an appellate court, because Pryor reluctantly agreed to do his job and enforce a federal court order to have the monument re-moved. As *New York Times* columnist Nicholas Kristof loves to remind his readers, Americans are big believers—the virgin birth (83 percent), creationism (48 percent), the devil (68 percent). Forty-seven percent think the Antichrist is on earth *right now.* How many of these devotees, though, have actually read the Ten Commandments lately? There's a rea-son the laws inscribed on those stone tablets are often represented by Roman numerals or squiggles. As a vague wave in the direction of law and order, the Decalogue pops up in thousands of public places, includ-ing the Supreme Court building, where Moses shares a frieze with Ham-murabi and Justinian. Spelled out in all their ancient splendor, though, the commandments are a decidedly odd set of directives to be looming, physically or spiritually, over an American courtroom.

Consider Commandment One: God identifies himself as God—as if you didn't know! Who else crashes about with thunder and lightning? He reminds the Jews that he brought them out of Egypt and orders that "thou shalt have no other gods before me." What does that mean, ex-actly? No other gods, period, or no other gods come first? No other gods because they don't exist, or no other gods because they are minor and inferior and God doesn't like them? His need for constant reassurance is one of God's more perplexing characteristics. If you had created the universe and everything in it down to the seven-day week, would you care if people believed in you? Wouldn't it be enough that you knew you existed? Why can't God give anonymously? So what if people give Baal or Ishtar the credit?

In any case, God's status anxiety has precious little to do with the civil and criminal codes of the state of Alabama, where worshiping Baal and Ishtar is legal. Commandments Two, Three, and Four continue God's preoccupation with himself. No graven images, indeed, no "likeness" of anything in nature, to which he holds the copyright; no taking his name in vain; no work on the Sabbath. Representational art and sculpture, swearing a blue streak, and working on Saturday (or, in Alabama, Sunday) are all legal; nor does the law require that we honor our fathers and mothers as enjoined in the Fifth Commandment, despite God's barely veiled threat of death and/or exile if we sass them. Adultery is legal (well, actually, not in Alabama), as is coveting your neighbor's house, wife, servants, livestock—or husband, a possibility God seems either not to have considered or not to have minded. In fact, the only activities banned by the Ten Commandments that are also crimes under American law are murder, theft, and perjury. But those are illegal (I'm guessing) under just about every civil and religious code. Even Baal and Ishtar presumably took a dim view of them.

What sets the Ten Commandments apart is not content but style: that gloomy, vengeful, obsessive, insecure authorial voice, alternately vulnerable (he confesses he's "jealous") and dissociated (he talks about himself in the third person, like an American celebrity). As elsewhere in the Bible, God looks constantly over his shoulder at the competition, threatens to visit the sins of the father on generations yet unborn, raves against those who hate him. He is equally disturbed by killing and cursing, and is incredibly possessive (I made that tree! No copying!). Granted we all know people like this, but would you want them presiding over your trial?

When you consider that God could have commanded anything he wanted—anything!—the Ten have got to rank as one of the great missed moral opportunities of all time. How different history would have been had he clearly and unmistakably forbidden war, tyranny, taking over other people's countries, slavery, exploitation of workers, cruelty to children, wife-beating, stoning, treating women—or anyone—as chattel or inferior beings. It's not as if God had nothing more to say. The minute he's through with the Decalogue, he gives Moses a long list of legal minutiae that are even less edifying: what happens if you buy a Hebrew slave and give him a wife who has children (he goes free after six years, but you keep the rest of the family); what should happen if a man sells his daughter as a "maidservant" and her master decides he doesn't fancy her after all (he can give her to his son). God enjoins us to kill witches, Sabbath violators, disrespectful children, and people who have sex with animals, but not masters who beat their slaves to death, especially if the death takes place a day or two after the beating, because the slave is the master's "money." No wonder the good white Christians of Alabama believed the Bible permitted slavery! It does! After several chapters in this vein, with much tedious discussion of oxen and more inveighing against other gods and their benighted followers, God finally settles down to the subject closest to his heart: the precise mode in which he would like to be worshiped. He drones on for pages and pages about the tabernacle, the ark, and the ephod, like a demented Bronze Age interior decorator—*golden* candlesticks, mind you, and *ten* linen curtains twenty-eight cubits long and four cubits wide, and loops around the edges, and *eleven* goat-hair curtains, maybe a little wider, and loops around their edges too. He specifies down to the last beryl the ostentatious getup he wants his priests to wear and what animals they should sacrifice and when, and which parts of the burnt offering he likes best (the fat around the tail and liver—well, that's everyone's favorite, isn't it?); he even gives recipes for incense and priestly perfume.

Has anyone checked out Judge Moore's aftershave?

●◄ SEPTEMBER 22, 2003 ►●

Governor Groper?

What was the lowest point in Arnold Schwarzenegger and Maria Shriver's appearance on *Oprah*? Was it when the three of them chortled and beamed about how exciting it was for Arnold to learn about "all those issues" he'll have to deal with as governor ("Like, are they at your house to—teaching you stuff every night?" Ms. Winfrey asked)—and the audience applauded? Or was it when Schwarzenegger compared his refusal to participate in more than one debate to the way he had skipped over the Mr. Venice Beach contest and gone straight for the Mr. Olympia title—and the audience applauded? Hurray for the candidate with no experience, no information, and no knowledge! Bravo for the candidate who won't stoop to defending his platform—or even explain what it is!

The purpose of this hour-long infomercial—but why, Oprah, why?—was to give Schwarzenegger a chance to debunk his image as a male chauvinist boor with Oprah's huge, mostly female audience. Who knows, maybe it worked. First there was Maria, glamorous, lean as a whippet, her diamond cross sparkling against her black long-sleeved sweater, enthusiastically proclaiming how much she loved him, how ardently he supported her career (he was "one of the most gracious, supportive women—I mean man—man I've ever met") and how peeved she was by suggestions that as a Kennedy female she had been "bred to look the other way" while her husband pawed, cavorted, and harassed his way through life. Those stories were all lies. Then Arnold bounded out, looking tanned and relaxed, and the three sat around like the old showbiz troupers and friends they are and laughed about the cup of coffee Arnold makes Maria every morning, and the children, who do their own laundry and are being brought up to be, says Maria, "kind, polite, you know, grateful" (grateful? *Achtung!*), and the crazy things people did back in the 1970s, when Arnold told *Oui* magazine that he took part in a gangbang of a "black girl" at Gold's Gym. Except maybe he didn't: "The idea was always to say things, as I said, over the top so you get the headlines because bodybuilding, like I said, had no reputation yet." He was just pretending to be a macho jerk for the good of the sport. See?

As of this writing the California recall has been postponed, which is supposed to hurt Schwarzenegger, because it allows people more time to find out how conservative and obnoxious and ignorant he is. (I know, I know, I say that like it's a bad thing.) But it also allows him more time to win over women, who favor his Democratic rival Cruz Bustamante. The media seem determined to defuse the sexism issue. On CNN, Howie Kurtz pooh-poohed the *Oui* interview as "celebrity gossip," and his guest, William Bastone, of TheSmokingGun.com barely demurred, even though Bastone broke the story. The day after the *Oprah* appearance, the *Los Angeles Times* ran a front-page article pointing out how often in his career Schwarzenegger has noted that a woman is "smart" or mentioned brains as a good thing for a woman to have. As he says in the July *Esquire*, "When you see a blonde with great tits and a great ass, you say to yourself, hey, she must be stupid or must have nothing else to offer. . . . But then again there is the one that is as smart as her breasts look, great as her face looks, beautiful as her whole body looks gorgeous, you know, so people are shocked."

Now just imagine for a moment that a Democratic politician had told a soft-core men's magazine in 1977 about gangbanging a "black girl"—and when asked about it in 2003 said he didn't remember a thing about the interview or the incident itself, but also said he made the whole thing up to get attention. Would that story have been relegated to the bin of youthful escapades by Fox, CNN, the *New York Post,* Peggy Noonan, Ann Coulter, Bill O'Reilly, and the rest? Or would we be hearing a lot about "character" and the "I was lying" defense? Suppose that same Democrat told *Playboy* in 1988 he didn't allow his wife or mother (?!) to wear pants in public. And suppose that in 2000, two British television journalists accused that Democrat, now fifty-three, well past the youthful-escapade phase, of groping them, and publicly declared themselves disgusted and offended? Let's say that he told *Entertainment Weekly* this past July how much fun it was to push Kristanna Loken's head into a toilet in *Terminator 3* ("I wanted to have something floating in there"). Let's say papers in Britain were reporting all this and more—from feeling up women in the presence of his wife to heavy use of illegal steroids to rumors of an extramarital affair with a sixteen-year-old actress—wouldn't we be hearing about it night and day?

And if that Democrat was a woman? Forget it! A rich, egocentric, freaky Hollywood diva whose naked photos were plastered all over cyberspace, who waves away questions about her program ("Details, details!") would have no credibility in the first place. Angelina Jolie for governor of the fifth-largest economy in the world? Are you out of your mind? But even if she were a Rhodes scholar, a four-star general, and a churchgoing mother of six, that woman would be finished the minute the media turned up so much as the femur or tibia of a sexual skeleton among the power suits in her closet. Wherever that "black girl" is today, you can bet it's not politics. What's good for the groper is not good for the groupie.

The explanation for the political and gender double standard can't be something as simple as the media being mostly owned by conservatives and mostly written, edited, produced, and spoken by men—can it? (Fun fact: There are actually fewer female newspaper executives or top editors today than five years ago.) After all, there is Oprah—the queen of go-girl empowerment, the anti–Howard Stern, the woman who brought Toni Morrison to the masses—and Oprah thinks Arnold Schwarzenegger is a prince among men. Celebrity is thicker than sisterhood. Now that she has jumped into the California recall, the *New York Times* rightly called on Oprah to invite all the major candidates onto her show. The people who really need a platform, though, are the women like the activists of Code Pink who follow Schwarzenegger around with their "Arnold, You're Terminated" banner—the women who think humiliating, insulting, and harassing women is something worth talking about.

•◀ OCTOBER 6, 2003 ▶•

After You, My Dear Alphonse

What's the matter with conservatives? Why can't they relax and be happy? They have the White House, both houses of Congress, the majority of governorships, and more money than God. They rule talk radio and the TV political chat shows, and they get plenty of space in the papers; for all the talk about the liberal media, nine out of the fourteen most widely syndicated columnists are conservatives. Even the National Endowment for the Arts, that direct-mail bonanza of yore, is headed by a Republican now. Never mind whether conservatives deserve to run the country and dominate the discourse; the fact is, for the moment, they do.

What I want to know is, Why can't they just admit it, throw a big party, and dance on the table with lampshades on their heads? Why are they always claiming to be excluded and silenced because most English professors are Democrats? Why must they reprosecute Alger Hiss whenever Susan Sarandon gives a speech or Al Franken goes after Bill O'Reilly? If I were a conservative, I would think of those liberal professors spending their lives grading papers on *The Scarlet Letter* and I would pour myself a martini. I would *pay* Susan Sarandon to say soulful and sincere things about peace, I would hire Al Franken and sneak him on O'Reilly's show as a practical joke. And if some Democratic dinosaur lifted his head out of the congressional tarpits to orate about the missing WMDs, or unemployment, or the two and a half million people who lost their health insurance this year, I'd nod my head sagely and let him rant on. Poor fellow. Saddam Hussein was his best friend, after Stalin died. No wonder he's upset.

For some reason, right-wingers do not take this calm and broad-minded view. Maybe they didn't get enough love in their childhoods, or maybe they're in more trouble than we know. In any case, they've taken to lecturing the opposition on manners whenever it shows signs of life. Ted Kennedy says the Iraq war was "a fraud made up in Texas" and Bush complains that he's "uncivil." "Not civil," Condoleezza Rice agrees, "not helpful." Well, *excuuuse* me! In *National Review,* Byron York obsesses about anti-Bush websites and the "one long bellow of rage" that is . . . MoveOn.org? David Brooks, the *New York Times*'s new conservative op-ed columnist, mourns the passing of the culture wars, which were about ideas, and wrings his hands over the "vitriol" of the new "presidency wars," which are just about hating Bush as "illegitimate . . . ruthless, dishonest and corrupt." Exhibit A: Jonathan Chait's eloquent, shrewd, and not at all vicious *New Republic* essay on why he hates President Bush (among other things, his triumph is an affront to meritocratic principles—well, it is!). Even Ann Coulter is worried that "the country is trapped in a political discourse that resembles professional wrestling." Gee, is this the same Ann Coulter who wrote that Timothy McVeigh should have driven his truck into the *New York Times* headquarters, and whose bestselling polemic *Treason* argues that liberals are Commie-loving traitors who hate America? The Prozac must be working.

As Brooks, at least, acknowledges, the right is in a weak position when it claims to be shocked, shocked by liberal speech today. Remember when Newt Gingrich blamed Susan Smith's drowning her children on Democrats? ("How a mother can kill her two children, 14 months and 3 years, in hopes that her boyfriend would like her is just a sign of how sick the system is, and I think people want to change. The only way you get change is to vote Republican.") Never mind that Smith had been molested as a young girl by her stepfather, a South Carolina Republican Party activist with close ties to Pat Robertson's Christian Coalition. Remember when Gingrich called the Democratic Party "the enemy of normal Americans," and Dan Burton, chairman of the House Reform Committee, called President Clinton a "scumbag"? (Committee spokesperson Will Dwyer defended this epithet as "straight talk.") During the Clinton years you could turn on the TV and watch Jerry Falwell hawking videos "proving" that Vince Foster was murdered—a view promoted repeatedly by the *Wall Street Journal* editorial page and even entertained by Brooks' *Times* colleague William Safire. (And Foster's was only one of the many murders the President was supposed to have arranged.) You could hear Rush Limbaugh declare, "Bill Clinton may be the most effective practitioner of class warfare since Lenin"—Bill Clinton, the best friend Wall Street ever had!

Ancient history? It was only two years ago that Richard Lessner of the Family Research Council asked in a press release, "What do Saddam Hussein and Senate Majority Leader Tom Daschle have in common?" Answer: "Neither man wants America to drill for oil in Alaska's Arctic National Wildlife Refuge." Just this September, Tom DeLay accused Ted Kennedy of "extremist appeasement," charged that "national Democrat leaders this year have crossed a line and now fully embrace their hostile, isolationist extreme," and called opposition to the Miguel Estrada nomination "a political hate crime." (You'll notice—a small but telling point—DeLay continues the Gingrich-era intentionally rude substitution of "Democrat" for "Democratic.") Coulter's *Treason* sits on the bookshelves alongside right-wing ravings with titles like *Bias, The No-Spin Zone,* and *Useful Idiots* (in which Mona Charen cites yours truly as "demonstrating the reliable theme of America-loathing that informs much leftist thinking" because I didn't want to fly the flag after 9/11). Very high-minded, very rational!

Well, they wanted state power, and thanks to the Supreme Court Five, they got it. But unfortunately, running the country turns out to be harder than it looked when Bill Clinton was killing off Hillary's lovers between Cabinet meetings. He made it seem so easy! Now unemployment is way up, the government's awash in red ink, Iraq is a mess. So everything has to be someone else's fault—mean liberals who really, really want to win in 2004; Osama-loving pranksters who forward e-mail jokes about the President's IQ; Bill and Hillary, still magically pulling the strings three years after leaving the White House, having thoughtfully arranged for 9/11 before they departed.

They can dish it out, but they sure can't take it.

•◄ OCTOBER 20, 2003 ►•

Is the Pope Crazy?

There are many things to be said against condoms, and most people reading this have probably said them all. But at least they work. Not perfectly—they slip, they break, they require more forethought and finesse and cooperation and trust than is easy to bring to sex every single time, and, a major drawback in this fallen world, they place women's safety in the hands of men. But for birth control they are a whole lot better than the rhythm method or prayer or nothing, and for protection from sexually transmitted diseases they are all we have. This is not exactly a controversial statement. People have been using condoms as a barrier against disease as long as rubber has been around (indeed, before—as readers of James Boswell's journals know). You could ask a thousand doctors—ten thousand doctors—before you'd find one who said, "Condoms? Don't bother."

But what do doctors know? Or the Centers for Disease Control, or the World Health Organization, or the American Foundation for AIDS Research (Amfar)? These days, the experts on condoms are politicians, preachers, and priests, and the word from above is: Condoms don't work. That is what students are being taught in the abstinence-only sex ed favored by the religious right and funded by the Bush administration—$117 million of your annual tax dollars at work. The theory is that even mentioning condoms, much less admitting that they dramatically reduce the chances of pregnancy or HIV infection, sends a "mixed message" about the value of total abstinence until marriage. How absurd—it's like saying that seat belts send a mixed message about the speed limit or vitamin pills send a mixed message about vegetables. Anti-condom propaganda can backfire too: True, some kids may be scared away from sex, although probably not until marriage; others, though, hear only a reason to throw caution to the winds. According to a 2002 Human Rights Watch report on abstinence-only sex ed in Texas, a condoms-don't-work ad campaign led sexually active teens to have unprotected sex: "My boyfriend says they don't work. He heard it on the radio." Why is the Bush administration giving horny teenage boys an excuse to be sexually selfish? You might as well have high school teachers telling them using a condom during sex is like taking a shower in a raincoat.

Now it seems the Vatican is joining fundamentalist Protestants to spread the word against condoms around the globe. "To talk of condoms as 'safe sex' is a form of Russian roulette," said Alfonso Lopez Trujillo, head of the Vatican's office on the family. On a BBC *Panorama* program, "Sex and the Holy City," Lopez Trujillo explained, "The AIDS virus is roughly 450 times smaller than the spermatozoon. The spermatozoon can easily pass through the 'net' that is formed by the condom." That latex has holes or pores through which HIV (or sperm) can pass is a total canard. A National Institutes of Health panel that included anti-condom advocates examined the effectiveness of condoms from just about every perspective, including strength and porosity; according to its report, released in July 2001, latex condoms are impermeable to even the smallest pathogen. Among STDs, HIV is actually the one condoms work best against. "We're all a bit stunned by Lopez Trujillo's lack of respect for scientific consensus," Dr. Judith Auerbach of Amfar, who sat on the NIH panel, told me. "Where do his numbers come from?" Is Lopez Trujillo, who even suggests putting warnings on condoms like those on cigarettes, a loose cannon such as can be found in even the best regulated bureaucracies? According to "Sex and the Holy City," in Africa, where HIV infects millions—20 percent in Kenya, 40 percent in Botswana, 34 percent in Zimbabwe—Catholic clergy, who oppose condoms as they do all contraception, are actively promoting the myth that condoms don't prevent transmission of the virus and may even spread it. The *Guardian* quotes the archbishop of Nairobi, Raphael Ndingi Nzeki, as saying: "AIDS . . . has grown so fast because of the availability of condoms." Thus is a decade of painstaking work to mainstream and normalize condom use undone by the conscious promotion of an urban legend.

When the Nobel Prize for Peace was awarded to Shirin Ebadi, the first ever to a Muslim woman, an Iranian and a crusader for women's rights, not everyone was thrilled. What about Pope John Paul II, now celebrating the twenty-fifth anniversary of his election, and possibly near death? "This . . . was his year," wrote David Brooks in his *New York Times* column, a hymn of praise for the pope as the defender of "the whole and the indivisible dignity of each person." A few pages over, Peter Steinfels said much the same in his religion column: "Is there any other leader who has so reshaped the political world for the better and done it peacefully?" More knowledgeable people than I can debate how much credit the pope should get for the fall of communism—I always thought it was Ronald Reagan with an unintentional assist from Gorbachev plus the internal collapse of the system itself. With the crucial exception of Poland, the countries in the old Soviet bloc aren't even Roman Catholic, or are so only partially. Whatever his contribution to that historic set of events, though, the pope is on the wrong side of history now. Women's equality, sexual rights for all, the struggle of the individual against authoritarian religion, and of course the global AIDS epidemic—the pope has been a disaster on all these crucial issues of our new century. It's all very well for David Brooks to mock those who critique the pope for his "unfashionable views on abortion," as if 78,000 women a year dying in illegal procedures around the world was just something to chat about over brie and chablis. But add it up: a priesthood as male as the Kuwaiti electorate—even altar girls may be banned soon, according to one recent news story—no divorce, no abortion, no contraception, no condom use even within a faithful marriage to prevent a deadly infection.

It's bad enough to argue that condoms are against God's will while millions die. But to maintain, falsely, that they are ineffective in order to discourage their use is truly immoral. If not insane.

•◄ NOVEMBER 3, 2003 ►•

There They Go Again

Why is it that "think pieces" about women and work and kids and marriage always leave one suspecting that the minute these corporate-lawyers-turned-stay-at-home-moms hang up the phone on the reporter, they rip off their rubber masks, reveal themselves as space aliens, and pour themselves an enormous martini? Lisa Belkin's confused, myopic *New York Times Magazine* cover story, "The Opt-Out Revolution," is the latest version of that journalistic evergreen, "The Death of Feminism," in which privileged white women quit their high-powered jobs to find "balance" and "sanity" raising their kids, volunteering, and hanging out at Starbucks. "Don't make me look like some 1950s' Stepford wife," one interviewee pleads, but the photographer couldn't resist. On the cover a thin, elegant, blandly expressionless young woman sits cross-legged with her toddler next to the glowing ladder she is no longer climbing. Inside, sleekly groomed Atlanta book clubbers stand or sit as stiffly as androids. Why are we supposed to see these socially conservative women, whose husbands earn more in a year than most households earn in five or even ten, as representative, much less as bellwethers of social change? Because they went to Princeton, as Belkin did? Princeton always gets the preppies.

Belkin's thesis is that "women" are turning away from demanding careers because they realize that there's more to life than work-work-work. As Joan Walsh points out in her witty riposte in *Salon,* Belkin hedges her argument with the sort of qualifiers editors tend to insist on: Yes there's discrimination, yes Princeton isn't Everycollege, yes black women (they get a whole parenthesis to themselves) are working more, not less. But none of the caveats seem to matter as she states her central conclusion: "Why don't women run the world? Maybe it's because they don't want to." Any woman who has ever been passed over for a deserved promotion in favor of a less qualified, but maybe louder, schmoozier man can just leave the room quietly, please.

Belkin, who is married to a pediatric cardiologist, cites herself as an example of happily downsized ambitions; once she dreamed of running the *New York Times,* now she enjoys mothering while writing a biweekly column from home. Interestingly, her interviewees tell a darker story. Several describe being pushed out of their workplace after they had children. A TV reporter saw her hours grow longer—from fifty to sixty hours a week—after her son was born; a lawyer with a major firm exhausted herself as a new mother preparing for a big trial, only to have the judge postpone it so he could go fishing for two weeks. Neither woman could get a part-time contract—it was "all or nothing." They didn't want to go back home, they wanted normal hours or, failing that, part-time jobs at decent salaries with real opportunities for advancement. If quitting was a "choice," it was a very constrained one.

Do Belkin's subjects represent a trend? There has indeed been a small decline in the percentage of married mothers who work, from 59 percent in 1998 to 55 percent in 2000. But Heidi Hartmann, MacArthur-winning economist and founder of the Institute for Women's Policy Research, calls this a "blip" connected to the weakening economy. When the job market sours, people with options tend to leave the workforce because their conditions of employment deteriorate and they can't advance or get a better job; others simply give up on finding work. (Meanwhile, single mothers are working more than ever, a fact Belkin overlooks, and far from all are poor: The number of unmarried professional women who have babies or adopt is exploding.) In the early 1990s, the percentage of married mothers in the workforce also went down, and this decline was also trumpeted as a major turning point, a free decision by women who'd come to their senses (remember The New Traditionalism?). But that was just a blip too: When the economy heated up again, women went back to work. The long-term trend, Hartmann points out, is for married women to work more, not less; for women to work more the better educated they are; for women to work more the more they earn. On the other hand, women married to rich men have always been less committed to work than comparable women married to less rich men: They don't need the money, and being a rich man's wife is already a kind of job. Why look to them as honing the cutting edge of history? Social change is made by people who can't live with the status quo, not by the most protected and comfortable.

Belkin's idea of feminism is a caricature of the actual women's movement. "The women's movement was largely about grabbing a fair share of power—making equal money, standing at the helm in the macho realms of business and government and law," she writes. But feminism was never about shoulder pads and power suits, or taking "only the shortest of maternity leaves," or "becoming a man." Feminism is about changing the ground rules, not just entering the game. Feminists, in fact, are the ones who first put forward the idea of balance between work and family—for both sexes—of a more humane and flexible and less hierarchical workplace, of childcare as a task for both parents and for society as a whole. Belkin puts these ideas forward as the antidote to feminism, when they are, in fact, what feminism is.

Belkin ends on a note of hope: By quitting, elite women will force employers to offer better terms. Since most of the women see their time at home as temporary, a brief hiatus, one hopes she's right. But why would the workplace that wouldn't accommodate them as new mothers accommodate them several years later when their skills are rustier and their résumés dustier? Whether her subjects get the deals they want will largely depend on forces outside their control: where their husbands' jobs take the family, how tight the labor market is. In today's bad economy, companies are cutting "family-friendly" policies—not an encouraging sign.

The best thing these women could do for themselves would be to organize a new, muscular, inclusive women's movement that would fight for a fairer deal for working mothers in their jobs, at home and in government policy. True, that would be feminism, the dreaded and despised. But it just might work.

Adam and Steve—
Together at Last

Will someone please explain to me how permitting gays and lesbians to marry threatens the institution of marriage? Now that the Massachusetts Supreme Court has declared gay marriage a constitutional right, opponents really have to get their arguments in line. The most popular theory, advanced by David Blankenhorn, Jean Bethke Elshtain, and other social conservatives is that under the tulle and orange blossom, marriage is all about procreation. There's some truth to this as a practical matter—couples often live together, tying the knot only when baby's on the way. But whether or not marriage is the best framework for child-rearing, having children isn't a marital requirement. As many have pointed out, the law permits marriage to the infertile, the elderly, the impotent, and those with no wish to procreate; it allows married couples to use birth control, to get sterilized, to be celibate. There's something creepily authoritarian and insulting about reducing marriage to procreation, as if intimacy mattered less than biological fitness. It's not a view that anyone outside a right-wing think tank, a Catholic marriage tribunal, or an ultra-Orthodox rabbi's court is likely to find persuasive.

So scratch procreation. How about: Marriage is the way women domesticate men. This theory, a favorite of right-wing writer George Gilder, has some statistical support—married men are much less likely than singles to kill people, crash the car, take drugs, commit suicide—although it overlooks such husbandly failings as domestic violence, child abuse, infidelity, and abandonment. If a man rapes his wife instead of his date, it probably won't show up on a police blotter, but has civilization moved forward? Of course, this view of marriage as a barbarian-adoption program doesn't explain why women should undertake it—as is obvious from the state of the world, they haven't been too successful at it, anyway. (Maybe men should civilize men—bring on the Fab Five from *Queer Eye*!) Nor does it explain why marriage should be restricted to heterosexual couples. The gay men and lesbians who want to marry don't impinge on the male-improvement project one way or the other. Surely not even Gilder believes that a heterosexual pothead with plans for murder and suicide would be reformed by marrying a lesbian?

What about the argument from history? According to this, marriage has been around forever and has stood the test of time. Actually, though, marriage as we understand it—voluntary, monogamous, legally egalitarian, based on love, involving adults only—is a pretty recent phenomenon. For much of human history, polygyny was the rule—read your Old Testament—and in much of Africa and the Muslim world, it still is. Arranged marriages, forced marriages, child marriages, marriages predicated on the subjugation of women—gay marriage is like a fairy-tale romance compared with most chapters of the history of wedlock.

The trouble with these and other arguments against gay marriage is that they overlook how loose, flexible, individualized, and easily dissolved the bonds of marriage already are. Virtually any man and woman can marry, no matter how ill assorted or little acquainted. An eighty-year-old can marry an eighteen-year-old; a john can marry a prostitute; two terminally ill patients can marry each other from their hospital beds. You can get married by proxy, like medieval royalty, and not see each other in the flesh for years. Whatever may have been the case in the past, what undergirds marriage in most people's minds today is not some sociobiological theory about reproduction or male socialization. Nor is it the enormous bundle of privileges society awards to married people. It's love, commitment, stability. Speaking just for myself, I don't like marriage. I prefer the old-fashioned ideal of monogamous free love, not that it worked out particularly well in my case. As a social mechanism, moreover, marriage seems to me a deeply unfair way of distributing social goods like health insurance and retirement checks, things everyone needs. Why should one's marital status determine how much you pay the doctor, or whether you eat cat food in old age, or whether a child gets a government check if a parent dies? Still, as long as marriage is here, how can it be right to deny it to those who want it? In fact, you would think that, given how many heterosexuals are happy to live in sin, social conservatives would welcome maritally minded gays with open arms. Gays already have the baby—they can adopt in many states, and lesbians can give birth in all of them—so why deprive them of the marital bathwater?

At bottom, the objections to gay marriage are based on religious prejudice: The marriage of man and woman is "sacred," and opening it to same-sexers violates its sacral nature. That is why so many people can live with civil unions but draw the line at marriage—spiritual union. In fact, polls show a striking correlation of religiosity, especially evangelical Protestantism, with opposition to gay marriage and with belief in homosexuality as a choice, the famous "gay lifestyle." For these people gay marriage is wrong because it lets gays and lesbians avoid turning themselves into the straights God wants them to be. As a matter of law, however, marriage is not about Adam and Eve versus Adam and Steve. It's not about what God blesses, it's about what the government permits. People may think "marriage" is a word wholly owned by religion, but actually it's wholly owned by the state. No matter how big your church wedding, you still have to get a marriage license from City Hall. And just as divorced people can marry even if the Catholic Church considers it bigamy, and Muslim and Mormon men can only marry one woman even if their holy books tell them they can wed all the girls in Apartment 3G, two men or two women should be able to marry, even if religions oppose it and it makes some heterosexuals, raised in those religions, uncomfortable.

Gay marriage—it's not about sex, it's about separation of church and state.

•◀ DECEMBER 15, 2003 ▶•

Good News for Women

There was plenty of gloomy news for women in 2003. American women make just under 80 cents on the male dollar for full-time, year-round work. We lost Carolyn Heilbrun, Carol Shields, Rachel Corrie, Nina Simone, and Martha Griffiths. Russia tightened its abortion laws; in Slovakia, Romani women were sterilized without their permission; Iraqi women were freed from Saddam but confined to their houses by crime and Islamic fundamentalists. The *Globe* ran a slutty cover photo of Kobe Bryant's accuser. The *New York Times* reported that women are having painful and potentially crippling surgery on their toes in order to fit into their Manolos and Jimmy Choos, while in China, where short people are subject to major discrimination, they are undergoing excruciating operations to lengthen their legs. What's the matter with people? Don't answer that.

Still, it's the end of the year, so let's break out the champagne for good news around the world for women in 2003—accomplishments, activism, bold deeds, and grounds for hope.

1. Shirin Ebadi won the Nobel Peace Prize. The Iranian feminist and human-rights crusader is the first Muslim woman to receive this honor. The ayatollahs are furious!

2. Hormone replacement therapy was further debunked. Instead of protecting you from Alzheimer's, it doubles your risk. The unmasking of HRT is a major triumph for the women's health movement, which has claimed for decades that its supposed benefits are drug-industry hype.

You can read all about it in Barbara Seaman's devastating exposé, *The Greatest Experiment Ever Performed on Women: Exploding the Estrogen Myth.*

3. Antiwar activism got a feminist edge. The Lysistrata Project saw 1,029 productions of Aristophanes' hilarious, bawdy comedy performed all over the world on March 3. Code Pink took on Bush—and Schwarzenegger—with nervy humor.

4. Barbara Ransby's moving and invaluable *Ella Baker and the Black Freedom Movement: A Radical Democratic Vision* illuminated a behind-the-scenes heroine of the civil rights struggle. As Ransby showed, there are other, more egalitarian, ways to move forward than by playing follow the leader.

5. A Department of Education commission rejected energetic efforts to water down Title IX, the main legal vehicle promoting equality for women's athletics in schools; the Supreme Court didn't overturn affirmative action.

6. Some movies had leading female characters who were not wives, girlfriends, prostitutes, or assassins: *Whale Rider, Bend It Like Beckham, Sylvia, Mona Lisa Smile.* Sofia Coppola's *Lost in Translation* got raves. Older women were beautiful and sexy in *Swimming Pool,* starring the ever-fabulous Charlotte Rampling, and in *Something's Gotta Give,* where fifty-seven-year-old Diane Keaton gets to choose between grumpy-old-man Jack Nicholson and boy toy Keanu Reeves.

7. One in four people in Ireland saw *The Magdalene Sisters,* the movie that exposed the lifelong virtual consignment to hard labor in convent laundries of Irish girls who fell afoul of the church's harsh double standard of sexual morality by, for example, being raped.

8. Afghan women set the gold standard for courage with major conferences in Kandahar and Kabul to push for women's rights in the new constitution. At the *loya jirga,* twenty-five-year-old delegate Malalai Joya

electrified the world when she accused the mujahedeen, who control the assembly, of destroying the country in the early 1990s.

9. In *Lawrence v. Texas,* the Supreme Court struck down sodomy laws criminalizing gay sex. The Massachusetts Supreme Court, headed by a woman, ruled that the state constitution required that gays should be able to marry.

10. Amina Lawal, condemned to death by stoning by a Nigerian Sharia court for having sex out of wedlock, was set free on appeal.

11. Prodded by an ACLU lawsuit, Michigan stopped drug-testing welfare recipients (only 7.8 percent came up positive, by the way—the same as at your office) as well as applicants.

12. Jessica Lynch showed herself a real heroine by refusing to go along with the propaganda parade.

13. Seventy-eight-year-old Essie Mae Washington-Williams confirmed longstanding rumors that she is the daughter of racist senator Strom Thurmond and his family's sixteen-year-old black maid, Carrie Butler. That Strom died at one hundred, reputation intact, definitely proves that God does not exist.

14. In New York, the U.S. Court of Appeals for the Second Circuit upheld the 2001 ruling in *Nicholson v. Scoppetta* that child services can't take away the children of battered women.

15. Louise Glück, who has written poems that are burned into my brain, became Poet Laureate, only the ninth woman to hold the post in the past sixty-six years.

16. Desperately poor women in Nigeria's oil-rich Niger delta staged militant demonstrations—including stripping—against Shell, demanding that the company employ locals and share the wealth with the community. They won!

17. An FDA panel gave the thumbs-up to making emergency contraception an over-the-counter drug. Teen pregnancy, still too high, has hit a historic low.

18. Under heavy attack from women, DaimlerChrysler abandoned its sponsorship of the Lingerie Bowl, a pay-per-view Super Bowl halftime event involving models playing full-contact football in their underwear. Turns out women buy cars too.

19. Lieutenant General William "Jerry" Boykin, who thinks Allah is an idol and that God put Bush in the White House, quoted his ex-wife as follows: "I don't love you anymore, you're a religious fanatic, and I'm leaving you."

20. The Dixie Chicks survived. Pro-war crowds stomped on their records, Clear Channel refused to give them airplay, and Christopher Hitchens called them "f**king fat slags." But they're still singing to sold-out crowds, and they're still great.

> Hoping you are the same,
> Happy New Year!

•◄ JANUARY 12, 2004 ►•

Lost in Space

A while back, in a column calling for more arts funding, I observed that a lot more people are interested in classical music, ballet, theater, and museums than are interested in space exploration, so the NEA should get at least as much money as NASA. Who cares, I blithely asked, what color rocks Mars has? Lots of *Nation* readers, as it turned out, and a number of staffers too. I had no idea. Now that George W. Bush is proposing to establish a long-term base on the moon as early as 2015 and eventually to send humans to Mars, I won't repeat the mistake of assuming that everyone shares my lack of enthusiasm for astronautery and outer space. According to a somewhat confusing AP-Ipsos poll, 48 percent (disproportionately men, but you knew that) favor Bush's proposals for space exploration and 48 percent oppose it, although only 38 percent support sending people, which the proposal involves (57 percent prefer using robots). Fifty-five percent oppose it when given the option of spending the money on education and healthcare, and two-thirds of Democrats oppose it when it is identified as a "Bush administration" plan. But let's not quibble—space is probably fascinating once you get into it, like Wagner or *The Lord of the Rings* or football. Someday, it might even be interesting to know if there was ever life on Mars— although it would also be interesting to know who put those statues on Easter Island, or why so often you can tell who's calling by the way the telephone rings.

Life is full of mysteries, I'm trying to say, and space is such an expensive one! Estimates of Bush's proposals run into the hundreds of billions of dollars over the next several decades. If you care about the deficit, as conservatives claimed they did until Bush created a huge one through tax cuts for the rich, it's hard to justify. Even if the immediate amount turns out to be much smaller—Bush has proposed only $1 billion in new funding over the next five years, leaving the big bills for his successor—does it really makes sense to spend a significant sum to satisfy an idle curiosity when we can spend the money solving some other, equally daunting, scientific challenge that would actually make people happier, healthier, and better able to fulfill their capabilities in their brief time on earth? I'm all for boldly going forth and expressing the human spirit—why can't we do that by solving the enormous scientific and technological challenges posed by global warming? Because that would involve admitting that global warming is happening? And is caused by human activity? In the January 13 *New York Times* Science section, the front page that carried Kenneth Chang's article championing the idea of a moon base also carried an ominous article detailing rising temperatures in the Alaskan tundra, which is now frozen for only 100 days a year; thirty years ago it was 200. Of the photographs in that section, which ones represent a phenomenon that is more likely to affect humanity first—the grim ones comparing the robust summer polar ice cap of 1979 with its moth-eaten 2003 self, or the lovely ones of planets and nebulae and galaxies illustrating the story on mapping the cosmos? Space isn't going anywhere—we can always study it later. Earth, however, may be going down the tubes a lot faster than we imagine. Those billions would fund a lot of environment-friendly innovation.

As for science, fighting AIDS is science. "We can put a cowboy on Mars," quips my colleague Richard Kim, "or we can treat everyone on the planet with AIDS for the next generation. Three hundred billion dollars would pay for AIDS drugs at the generic prices cited in Bush's State of the Union address ($300 per year, per person) for all 40 million people with HIV for the next twenty-five years." Reproductive health is science. According to the January *Lancet,* half a million women die every year from pregnancy-related causes, 99 percent of them in underdeveloped countries; it's one of the most neglected health problems in the world today. Delivering quality care adapted to the circumstances of impoverished and often illiterate people living in isolated villages and farms, training a local healthcare force and paying it enough to stay put instead of fleeing to jobs in wealthier places, insuring women the human rights that undergird safe maternity, whether freedom from forced child marriage or access to family planning—that seems to me as urgent as setting up house on the moon.

Education is science—you could fund a lot of schools in poor countries, where 43 percent of boys and 48 percent of girls aren't even getting a primary education; you could buy a lot of books and maps and lab equipment and train a lot of teachers and create, in the next generation, a lot more scientists—let *them* go to the moon! We say we're so upset about the spread of Islamic fundamentalism—yet we stand by while rich Saudis set up Wahhabi *madrassah*s all over the Muslim world and invite poor parents to send their kids for free. These youngsters could be learning astronomy instead of memorizing the Koran. We could put our Mars money where our mouth is.

I actually believe in science. I believe we are clever enough to think our way out of the problems we make for ourselves. We need to think big—on contraception, medicine, pollution, energy, food, water. Indeed, one of the worst aspects of the Bush administration is its contempt for science. Thanks to Bush, creationist tracts are being sold in national parks—did you know that the Grand Canyon is only a few thousand years old, like the rest of the world? And faith healers like David Hager, who thinks Jesus will cure your PMS, sit on FDA advisory panels. Bush policies disregard serious research—on the effectiveness of condoms to prevent HIV, on the ineffectiveness of abstinence-only sex education—and shun the promise of stem-cell research, all in obedience to the crabbed sexual taboos of the right.

Besides, doesn't the moon belong to everyone, not just NASA, not just the United States? Must lovers and lonely people, from Newfoundland to Bangladesh, look up at night and think: There's the moon, round and silvery and full of Republicans?

●◀ FEBRUARY 2, 2004 ▶●

Judy, Judy, Judy

Iused to think we should get rid of First Ladies. Plenty of countries manage without a national wife: Cherie Blair aside (and how long would Britain's answer to Hillary have lasted over here?), can you name the spouse of the man who leads France, Germany, China, Canada, or Russia? And no, "Mrs. Putin" doesn't count as a correct answer. Is Lula married? What about Ariel Sharon? Is there a Mrs. General Musharraf ready with a nice cup of tea when her man comes home after walking the nuclear weapons? Do you care? The ongoing public inquest into Dr. Judith Steinberg, *aka* Judy Dean, makes me see that we need First Ladies. Without them, American women might actually believe that they are liberated, that modern marriage is an equal partnership, that the work they are trained for and paid to do is important whether or not they are married, and that it is socially acceptable for adult women in the year 2004 to possess distinct personalities—even quirks! Without First Ladies, a woman might imagine that whether she keeps or changes her name is a private, personal choice, the way the young post-post-feminists always insist it is when they write those annoying articles explaining why they are now calling themselves Mrs. My Husband.

The attack on Dr. Judy began on the front page of the *New York Times* (you know, the ultraliberal paper) with a January 13 feature by Jodi Wilgoren, full of catty remarks about her "sensible slipper flats and no makeup or earrings" and fatuous observations from such academic eminences as Myra Gutin, "who has taught a course on first ladies at Rider University in New Jersey for 20 years." It seems that Dr. Steinberg "fits nowhere" in Professor Gutin's categorizations. Given that she counts Pat Nixon as an "emerging spokeswoman," maybe that's not such a bad thing. "The doctors Dean seem to be in need of some tips on togetherness and building a healthy political marriage," opined Maureen Dowd, a single woman who, even if she weds tomorrow, will be in a nursing home by the time she's been married for twenty-three years like the Deans. Tina Brown, another goddess of the hearth, compared Dr. Judy to mad Mrs. Rochester in *Jane Eyre.* On ABC News's *Primetime,* Diane Sawyer put both Deans on the grill, with, according to Alexander Stille, who counted for the *L.A. Times,* ninety negative questions out of a total of ninety-six. Blinking and nodding like a kindly nurse coaxing a lunatic off a window ledge, Sawyer acted as if she wanted to understand Dr. Judy's bizarre behavior: She keeps her maiden name professionally (just like, um, Diane Sawyer, *aka* Mrs. Mike Nichols); she doesn't follow the day-to-day of politics (like, what, 90 percent of Americans?); she *enjoyed* getting a rhododendron from Howard for her birthday. Throughout this sexist inquisition, Dr. Steinberg remained as gentle as a fawn, polite and unassuming—herself. "I'm not a very 'thing' person," she said when Sawyer pressed too close on that all-important rhododendron. She allowed as how she was not too interested in clothes—whereupon Sawyer cut to a photo of Laura Bush, smiling placidly in a red ball gown.

I don't think Dr. Judy is weird at all. She's leading a normal, modern, middle-class-professional life. She has been married forever. She has two children. She likes camping and bike riding and picnics. She volunteers. She has work she loves, as a community physician—not, you'll note, as a cold-hearted, status-obsessed selfish careerist user, as professional women are always accused of being. (Let's also note that she is not someone who was ever, even once, during her husband's twelve-year stint as governor of Vermont, accused of using her marriage to advance a friend or enrich herself or obtain special perks and privileges.) And here's another secret: Not too many women in long marriages want to spend their lives gazing rapturously at their husband for the benefit of the camera every time he opens his mouth. Vermonters liked Judy Dean—they had no problem with her low-key, independent style. But, then, if you listen to the press, you know Vermonters—they're weird, too.

I have no idea why Judith Steinberg hasn't slogged through the snow for her husband. Maybe she's nervous in public. Maybe she's busy. ("It's not something I can say, 'Oh, you take over for a month,'" she explained to Diane Sawyer. Imagine that, Tina, Diane, Maureen—a job where if you don't show up, it matters!) Maybe, like lots of Democrats, she's waiting to see if the Dean campaign has legs. It's possible she and her husband didn't understand they had left the real world for Mediaville, where it's always 1955, and thought it was no big deal if she kept working in Shelburne instead of being marched around Iowa in a power suit with a big bottle of Valium in her purse. Here's something I do know, though: Every day, this woman, about whom nobody who knows her has a mean word to say, gets up and does one of the most valuable things a human being can do on this earth. She takes care of sick people. Ordinary local people, not media princesses and princes. Is that the problem? If Judy Steinberg were a cosmetic surgeon or a diet doctor or held Botox parties after office hours, if her patients were famous, or the friends of the famous, if she could dish on the phone about Arnold Schwarzenegger and Martha Stewart, would the media cat pack think Judy Steinberg was cool?

Granted, rightly or wrongly, the media are going to take a look at the wives of the candidates, so you can argue that the Deans should have been prepared, especially given the media's dislike of Howard. This, after all, is the same media that managed to make a major scandal out of the Scream, a moment of campaign exuberance of zero importance (especially when compared with—for example!—Bush's inability to speak two consecutive unscripted sentences that are not gibberish, his refusal to read newspapers, and the fact that much of the world thinks he's a dangerous moron). But actually, it's only when a wife has her own identity that her choices are scrutinized. If Dr. Judith Steinberg was simply Judy Dean, if she spent her life doing nothing so important it couldn't be dropped to follow her husband as he followed his star, no one would question her priorities. No one thought less of Barbara Bush because she dropped out of college to get married, like those Wellesley girls in *Mona Lisa Smile*. No one reprimands Laura Bush for abandoning her career as a librarian and spending her life as her husband's den mother. No one asks Hadassah Lieberman or Elizabeth Edwards or Gertie Clark how come they have so much free time on their hands that they can saddle up with their husbands' campaign for months, or why, if they care so much about politics, they aren't running for office themselves.

Don't you wish, just once, the questioners and pontificators would turn it around? After all, if a woman were running for President, would they expect her doctor husband to abandon his ailing patients and his teenaged son to soften her image? *Au contraire,* they would regard such a man as a pussy-whipped wimp, a loser, very possibly even . . . weird. When Bob Dole said he'd give money to John McCain, his wife Elizabeth's rival in her brief presidential campaign in 2000, nobody called him a self-centered, disengaged, mean husband, or made much of the fact that his wife had knocked herself out for him when he ran in 1996.

What if the media tried on for size the notion that having an independent wife says something *good* about a candidate? For example, maybe, if his wife is not at his beck and call, he won't assume the sun rises because he wants to get up. Maybe, if his wife has her own goals in life, her own path to tread, he won't think women were put on earth to further his ambitions. Maybe, if he and his wife are true partners—which is not the same as her pouring herself into his career and his being genuinely grateful, the best-case scenario of the traditional political marriage—he may even see women as equals. Why isn't it the candidates who use their wives to further their careers with plastic smiles and cheery waves who have to squirm on *Primetime*?

Dean's poor showing in Iowa and second-place finish in New Hampshire suggest that media mud sticks. In a race with many candidates, in which the top contenders each have their pluses and minuses but are also rather close to one another politically, perception matters. Dean too "angry"? Something off about the marriage? Mrs. Dean a fruitcake? Oh, you heard that too? A lot of Democratic primary voters are looking not for the candidate they themselves like best but for the one with the best shot at beating Bush. If a candidate starts looking wounded, however unfair the attack, forget him—on to the next. The process feels a bit like rifling through the sale racks at Bloomingdale's when you have to find a fancy dress for a party given by strangers—no, no, maybe, hmmm, oh all right—but who knows, maybe out of all this second-guessing the strongest candidate, with the broadest appeal and the best organization, will ultimately emerge.

Right now, John Kerry may look like that man. But consider this: Before Dr. Judy, it was Teresa Heinz Kerry in the headlights of the *New York Times* front page. She was, John Tierney suggested, too opinionated, not fixated enough on her husband, unable to connect with the voters, off in her own world. You know, weird. There was that pesky name problem, too: Teresa Heinz? Teresa Kerry? Such a puzzle.

●◀ FEBRUARY 16, 2004 ▶●

Kristof to the Rescue?

This morning I got an e-mail from Feminist Majority asking me to e-mail the President protesting the Iraqi Governing Council's approval of Resolution 137, which would abolish current family law and allow Sharia to take its place. This depressing development has not been widely reported, but I already knew about it thanks to MADRE, the women's international human-rights organization. No sooner had I dispatched my message than up popped Amnesty International, alerting me to the work being done to end sexual violence around the world by V-Day, Eve Ensler's feminist activist organization. Then it was MADRE again, with news of an Islamic fundamentalist death threat against Iraqi feminist Yanar Mohammed. My snail mailbox is the same story: news and appeals from Equality Now, which uses letter-writing campaigns and legal action to combat injustices around the world, from female genital mutilation and honor killings to the imprisonment of Nepalese women who've had abortions; the Global Fund for Women, which sponsors a wide variety of pro-woman projects in 160 countries; Network of East/West Women, which supports women's rights activists in the former Soviet bloc; the women's desks of Amnesty International and Human Rights Watch; and many more.

I'm reminded of these good people because the *New York Times*'s Nicholas Kristof is once again accusing American feminists of ignoring Third World women and girls. Last spring, he discovered obstetric fistula in Africa—the tear between the birth canal and the lower intestine that can happen during protracted labor and that, unless corrected, condemns a woman to a lifetime of physical misery and social ostracism. Kristof profiled Addis Ababa Fistula Hospital in Ethiopia and wondered why "most feminist organizations in the West have never shown interest in these women." Perhaps, he wrote, "the issue doesn't galvanize women's groups because fistulas relate to a traditional child-bearing role." Right, we all know that feminists only care about aborting babies, not delivering them safely. The *Times* got a lot of letters (and published some, including one from me) pointing out that feminists, in fact, were behind numerous efforts to combat fistula and other maternity-related health problems in Africa, including the work of the UNFPA, praised by Kristof, whose funding was eliminated by the White House to please its right-wing Christian base.

You'd think he'd learn. But no. Now Kristof is complaining that American women's groups such as NOW and Feminist Majority don't care about sexual slavery and the trafficking of women and children for commercial sex. In a series of columns, he describes his efforts to "buy the freedom" of two Cambodian teenage prostitutes living in a sleazy brothel in Poipet and to get them home to their families. Evangelical Christians, he argues, care about girls like these; feminists are too busy "saving Title IX and electing more women to the Senate," he observed in a *Times* online forum. Right, why should American women care about equal opportunities and electing to office people who think contraception is as important as Viagra? Never mind that putting more *feminists* in the Senate—not more "women"—would mean more help for the very causes Kristof supports!

To tell you the truth, I thought those columns were a little weird— there's such a long tradition of privileged men rescuing individual prostitutes as a kind of whirlwind adventure. You would never know from the five columns he wrote about young Srey Neth and Srey Mom that anyone in Cambodia thought selling your daughter to a brothel was anything but wonderful. I wish he had given us the voices of some Cambodian activists—for starters, the Cambodian Women's Crisis Center and the Cambodian League for the Promotion and Defense of Human Rights (LICADHO)—both of which are skeptical about brothel raids and rescues, which often dump traumatized girls on local NGOs that lack the resources to care for them. Instead he called Donna Hughes— a professor at Rhode Island University who publishes in *National Review, The Weekly Standard,* and *FrontPage Magazine,* and whose opposition to all forms of prostitution is so monolithic that she has written against the Thai government's policy of promoting and enforcing condom use in brothels to prevent transmission of AIDS—and gave her space to ventilate against American feminists.

Just for fun, I called Kim Gandy, head of NOW, something Kristof forgot to do. "We're basically a national organization with a domestic agenda," she told me. "I mean, that's what our mission is. If we had more money, we could do a lot more." Still, NOW had, along with Equality Now, Feminist Majority, and other groups, lobbied for passage of the Trafficking Victims Protection Act, passed in 2000 under President Clinton, which established legal rights for trafficking victims in the United States and mandated cuts in aid to governments involved in the sex trade. Over at Feminist Majority, Ellie Smeal was peeved as well. They'd spent hours, she told me, informing Kristof's assistant about their organization's work on sex trafficking—beyond lobbying for the trafficking bill, the Feminist Majority's Center for Women and Policing holds regular conferences on implementation for law-enforcement officials. "You could say that on every issue, we could do more," she said. "But 'complacent'? 'Shamefully lackadaisical'? I don't think that's fair." Jessica Neuwirth and Taina Bien-Aimé of Equality Now also met with Kristof, to little avail. "It's great that he brought the issue to greater public attention, and we hope he'll stay with it," Neuwirth said. "But I don't think he appreciates how stretched women's organizations are."

You can see the narrative in the process of creation: Third World women are victims; American men are saviors. Right-wing Christians care about Third World women; feminists only care about themselves. Meanwhile, Equality Now fights the good fight on "spit and a nickel," as Bien-Aimé says, and gets ignored.

As my daughter used to say when she was small and the grownups were talking, "What do you have to do to get some attention around here?"

•◄ MARCH 1, 2004 ►•

Toothpaste, Cough Drops, Aspirin, Contraception

For a moment it looked as if the FDA was going to do the right thing. It was going to go with medical science and make emergency contraception available over the counter, so that women who've had unprotected sex would have ready access to a postcoital method that prevents pregnancy 89 percent of the time. This was, after all, the overwhelming recommendation of its own advisory committee (of twenty-seven members, only three voted against OTC status, all professionally undistinguished Bush appointees from the Christian right: David Hager, the notorious promoter of prayer as the cure for PMS and denier of birth control to unmarried women; and Susan Crockett and Joseph Stanford, who won't prescribe it, period).

It makes sense. After all, emergency contraception, also known as the morning-after pill and marketed as Plan B and Preven, is only a quadruple helping of certain birth control pills. Women in the know have been dosing themselves this way for years; the FDA found it safe and effective in 1999. Emergency contraception (EC) is available over the counter or directly from a pharmacist in some seventeen countries, including the United Kingdom, France, Switzerland, Scandinavia, Canada, and Portugal. The current system in the United States, in which women have to find a doctor or clinic and a pharmacy that stocks EC ideally within twenty-four hours (EC works for seventy-two hours, but less effectively as time goes on), is clearly too cumbersome. In a few states—California and Washington, for example—pharmacists can dispense it directly, which is better, but still an unnecessary complication.

You would think that anti-choicers would leap to embrace emergency contraception, which, according to the Alan Guttmacher Institute, already prevents 51,000 abortions a year, making it a significant, if little-noted, factor in the decline in abortion. This is the Bush administration, though, in which science and women's rights and the actual, factual lessening of the need for abortion are all less important than "values"—i.e., the narrow ideology of the Christian right. In December, forty-four congressional Republicans sent a letter to the FDA advisory committee urging its members to reject OTC status: EC "stacked casually on shelves next to toothpaste and cough drops" would allow "our schoolchildren" easy access to a drug that, according to Jesse Helms, is an "abortifacient." After the committee endorsed it, forty-nine congressional Republicans sent another letter, this time expressing alarm at "the impact this decision will have on the sexual behavior of adolescents." On February 16, FDA head Mark McClellan (brother of Bush press secretary Scott McClellan) postponed the agency's decision; now he's leaving to take charge of Medicare, and EC risks being delayed again by future appointees.

Years ago, pundits scoffed when pro-choicers argued that antis would target birth-control too if they could. EC primarily works by preventing ovulation and fertilization, but like the birth control pill, it may also prevent the implantation of a fertilized egg in the womb. As Gloria Feldt, head of Planned Parenthood, pointed out when I spoke to her by phone, "anti-choice people are trying to redefine pregnancy to begin at fertilization rather than implantation," which is the medical definition of pregnancy, and EC is the wedge. If EC is a "human pesticide," so are the pill, the patch, injectables. If "schoolchildren" ought not purchase EC without parental supervision or knowledge, nor should they be able to obtain those forms of contraception without parental permission, as current law allows. And if being able to purchase EC like "aspirin or hairspray" promotes promiscuity—studies suggest, by the way, that it will not—the same can be alleged of birth control in general. In fact, contraception has always been attacked as promoting loose morals among women (curiously, "schoolchildren" excepted, one hears less about the fact that condoms promote loose morals among men—why not make them available only by prescription, too?).

Recently a pharmacist and two assistants at an Eckerts drugstore in Denton, Texas, refused to fill an EC prescription for a teenage rape victim (they were fired). In Virginia, state legislator Robert Marshall, who last year was able to prevent James Madison University from filling EC prescriptions, is noisily seeking to extend the ban to all the state's public colleges and universities. EC, he claims, turns young women into "chemical Love Canals for frat house playboys." Instead of the natural love canals God meant them to be? This spurious concern for women's health is the cousin of the argument that abortion should be banned because it is "traumatic" for women—a line that has persuaded the state legislature of South Dakota to pass a flagrantly unconstitutional ban on all abortions and which Norma McCorvey, Roe of *Roe v. Wade,* is pushing in her ridiculous attempt to get the decision overturned on the grounds that she has changed her mind—about an abortion she never had.

Doctors and clinics are beginning to offer prescriptions for women in advance of need, which is great. But women can be proactive too. At a recent demonstration in New York City, women symbolically handed EC pills to others, declaring their willingness to break the law to put the drug in the hands of any woman who needs it (it is illegal to give a prescription medication to someone for whom it has not been prescribed). Any woman with the right kind of birth control pills can package her own EC and share it; years ago, journalist Debbie Nathan would walk into Mexico from her home in El Paso, buy birth-control pills for two dollars a cycle, and make EC necklaces with foil, glitter, and charms. Until women can pick up EC along with, yes, "aspirin or hairspray," that ingenuity and boldness is just what we need.

•◀ MARCH 15, 2004 ▶•

The Protocols of Mel Gibson

My friends had one question for me after I saw Mel Gibson's *The Passion of the Christ*: Is it anti-Semitic? It's a testament to Gibson's public-relations genius that this is an open question. In the endless run-up to opening day, Gibson drove assorted Jewish spokespeople so wild with his absurd claims of persecution that pooh-poohing charges of anti-Semitism became a badge of professional cool. Who wants to sound like Abraham Foxman, choleric head of the Anti-Defamation League? Except for David Denby, whose scathing review in *The New Yorker* should have set the tone, and of course the indefatigable Frank Rich, whose intestines Gibson has said he wants on a stick, early high-end reviewers like the *New York Times*'s A. O. Scott and *Newsweek*'s David Ansen have given Gibson a pass on a movie that could safely be shown at the Leni Riefenstahl Memorial Film Festival.

You'd think it was impolite to make anything of the fact that Gibson's father is a Holocaust denier who claims the European Jews simply moved to Australia. True, we don't choose our parents, but Mel Gibson has not only not dissociated himself from his father's views but indirectly affirmed them ("The man never lied to me in his life," he told Peggy Noonan in *Reader's Digest*; pressed to affirm that the Holocaust was real, he replied that many people died in World War II and some were Jews—the classic Holocaust-revisionist two-step). Nor would it do to dwell on the "traditional" (i.e., ultra right-wing) Catholicism Gibson practices, which specifically rejects the reforms of Vatican II, presumably including its repudiation of the belief that "the Jews" are collectively responsible for the death of Christ.

So how anti-Semitic is *The Passion*? Gibson claims that there are good Jews and bad Jews in the movie, as in the Gospels. This is true, but disingenuous. In *The Passion,* the high priest Caiaphas and his faction are not just bad, they fit neatly into ancient Christian stereotypes. They are rich, arrogant, and gaudily dressed; they plot and scheme and bribe; they cleverly manipulate the brutal but straightforward Romans; they are gratuitously "cruel" and "hard-hearted," to quote Anne Catherine Emmerich, the nineteenth-century German nun whose visions of the Passion Gibson relied on for some of the more disgusting tortures he in- flicts on Jesus. Physically, they are anti-Semitic cartoons: The priests have big noses and gnarly faces, lumpish bodies, yellow teeth; Herod Antipas and his court are a bizarre collection of oily-haired, epicene per- verts. The "good Jews" look like Italian movie stars (Magdalene actually *is* an Italian movie star, the lovely Monica Bellucci); Mary, who would have been around fifty and appeared seventy, could pass for a ripe thirty- five. These visual characterizations follow not just the Oberammergau Passion Play that Hitler found so touching but a long tradition of Chris- tian New Testament iconography in which the villains look Semitic and the heroes, although equally Jewish, look Northern European.

Gibson claims he's only telling the story as written in the Gospels, which he calls eyewitness accounts (historians say no). That the film is entirely in Aramaic and Latin underscores this bid for authenticity: "It is as it was," as his publicist falsely claimed the pope had said. Thus Gib- son, the literalist, presents himself as bending over backward to placate the you-know-who by removing from the subtitles (but not the sound- track) the line from Matthew in which the crowd condemns itself: "Let his blood be on us and our children." Yet when called on his inaccura- cies and distortions, Gibson claims artistic license. Thus, Pontius Pilate is upright and sensitive; too bad for Josephus, the first-century historian who described him as savage and corrupt. Most improbably, the temple priests tell their Roman overlord what to do. The Bible's brief mention of Jesus' flogging—one sentence in three Gospels, nothing in one—be- comes a ten-minute homoerotic sadistic extravaganza that no human being could have survived, as if the point of the Passion was to show how tough Christ was.

Gibson adds considerably to the Gospels in ways that emphasize Jewish villainy. The Gospels contain no scene in which the Jewish guards who arrest Jesus whip him with chains, throw him over a bridge and dangle him over the water, choking, for fun; or in which Caiaphas and his most Fagin-resembling sidekick show up to watch Christ's scourging by the Romans; or in which Satan (played by a woman, for a nice touch of misogyny) flits among and merges with the crowd as it shouts, "Crucify him! Crucify him!" Why does Gibson dress Mary and Magdalene in what look like nun's habits, if not to turn these two Jewish women into good Catholics *avant la lettre*? And why does he show an earthquake splitting the temple interior as Christ expires (in the Bible, a curtain is torn), if not to justify as God's vengeance the historical destruction of the temple by the Romans a few decades later and all the sufferings of the Jewish people since?

It's a mystery to me why the United States Conference of Catholic Bishops has given this crude and kitschy film a thumbs-up ("deeply personal work of devotional art . . . the Jewish people are at no time blamed collectively for Jesus' death"). Gibson has violated just about every precept of the conference's own 1988 "criteria" for the portrayal of Jews in dramatizations of the Passion (no bloodthirsty Jews, no rabble, no use of Scripture that reinforces negative stereotypes of Jews, etc.). Even stranger is the enthusiasm for the film among Protestant evangelicals and fundamentalists, who seem not to realize how specifically Catholic Gibson's theology is. A generation ago, "Bible-believing" Protestants would have been up in arms over, among other "popish heresies," the quasi-divine role given to Mary and the reverence for Christ's blood (in one extrabiblical scene, Mary on her knees mops the floor where he has been scourged, using some towels given to her by Pilate's kind and thoughtful wife). Do evangelicals not have theology anymore—anything goes as long as it's "conservative" and puts Jesus on top?

The Passion is nondenominational bigotry. Jesus wept.

●◄ MARCH 29, 2004 ►●

Pull Over, NASCAR Dads

Single women under sixty-five—those separated, widowed, divorced, or never married—represent at least 24 percent of the voting-age population and a whopping 46 percent of voting-age women. According to an influential study by the Democratic pollsters Stan Greenberg and Celinda Lake, they tend to be progressive and to lean Democratic. Indeed, if the nation's 45 million single women voted at the same rate as married women—52 percent versus 68 percent—there would be 6 million more voters in the electorate, and Gore would be in the White House today. Had they turned out at the same rate as other voters in Florida in 2000, there would have been an additional 202,640 votes cast in that state—and no razor-thin 537-vote margin. Party leaders like Ann Lewis, national chair of the DNC's Women's Vote Center, want the Democratic Party to cultivate single women and connect them with the polling booth; Page Gardner and Christina Desser have founded "Women's Voices. Women Vote" (www.wvwv.org), to reach out and register them. You've probably read about attempts to woo these "*Sex and the City* voters" in one of the dozens of nearly identical articles that have come out since Greenberg and Lake's study was released in December.

It's about time! The silly nickname aside—most unmarried women live for a month on what Carrie, Miranda, Samantha, or Charlotte spend on lunch and taxis—single women are a natural constituency for the Democratic Party. They tend to be pro-choice, anti-gun, socially liberal, and supporters of "big government." Single women's main issues are, theoretically, Democratic strong suits: healthcare, employment, education. Certainly it makes more sense to cultivate them than the other

demographic superstars pollsters have come up with: the suburban soccer moms who were supposed to save the party's bacon in the late 1990s
but have since morphed into security moms, keen on defense; or the
NASCAR dads—blue-collar white men from rural and southern parts,
who tend to be conservative, live in "red" states, and are drawn to the
racial-gender politics of the Republican Party. (Whatever happened to
the waitress mom? I kind of liked her.)

The focus on single women is good in another way. For years we've
been hearing that the problem with the Democratic Party is that it's too
liberal, too limp-wristed, insufficiently attentive to religious voters, and—
especially—too pro-choice. *The American Prospect*'s Michael Tomasky
recently suggested that Democratic intransigence on abortion rights was
alienating religious swing voters. Why not court them, he suggested, if
not by naming an anti-choicer as the vice presidential candidate, then
by having an anti-choice speaker at the convention? Well, perhaps because that would demoralize the legions of feminist activists already
knocking themselves out for Kerry and blur the party's message: Support for abortion rights is one of the few sharp differences between the
national parties (state legislatures swarm with anti-choice Dems), one
that motivates more people than it turns off. I can't tell you how many
progressive women I know who voted for Gore instead of Nader specifically, and sometimes solely, because of the threat to legal abortion posed
by a Bush victory. Why is it that Republicans understand so clearly that
they have to keep the base happy, while the Democrats seem to delight
in insulting theirs in order to court some temperamental sliver of voters
who don't like them very much? Which are there more of? So-called
progressive pro-lifers who care so much about forcing pregnant women
to bear children that they would pull the lever for Bush, maker of dishonest war and champion of death row? Or women and men who want
abortion to be legal and who fear the encroachments of sectarian religion on private life?

But there are problems with the single-women idea. For one, this is
not a coherent demographic: There may be more single women than
blacks, Jews, and Hispanics put together, but that does not mean a
Wellesley student, a welfare mother, and a fifty-five-year-old divorced
bookkeeper have much in common. There is no NAACP for unmarried

women, no equivalent of the pride, identity, and agenda that mark those powerful ethnicities, and no single-woman politician who campaigns around that status. Indeed, being unmarried is more often something a female politician needs to manage carefully or risk accusations of lesbianism, man-hating, oddness, or social failure. Then, too, single women are disproportionately young, mobile, struggling, and/or very, very poor—all categories that are less likely to register, vote, or want to vote. The qualities associated with marriage—being older, more socially and financially stable, living in one place, owning one's home, belonging to the PTA—are the same qualities that knit one into voting. Single women are less likely to see themselves as part of the classes politics is for, the classes that actually can get something from politicians. "They don't believe politicians care about what they have to say," WVWV codirector Chris Desser told the *Christian Science Monitor.* That might sound cynical, but it may well be true.

The trouble with going after single women, those fans of progressive change, is that one has to offer them something progressive. Pay equity, for example, comes in at the top of polls of women's concerns—yet in the primary debates, Carol Moseley Braun was the only candidate who made an issue of it. Or take healthcare: Why doesn't Kerry's plan cover all of the 44 million Americans—disproportionately female Americans, by the way—now without health insurance? Education? Do the Dems really talk about fixing the public schools in ways that would affect single mothers? Tom Geoghegan, Mark Dudzik, and Adolph Reed have all suggested in these pages that the Democrats mobilize young voters by proposing to make college free. It's a great idea, but nobody picked up on it. One could easily come up with similar lures for the votes of single women—a federal living wage, universal public preschool and after-school (don't forget, singles with kids don't have the luxury of staying home with them), heck, free birth control. It will be interesting to see if the Democratic campaign to sign up these voters involves offering them things they want or just telling them that they want what's on offer.

•◀ April 12, 2004 ▶•

Pregnant and Dangerous

The good news is that Utah has dropped murder charges against Melissa Rowland, who rejected her doctors' advice to undergo an immediate cesarean section and gave birth to a stillborn boy and a girl who tested positive for cocaine. The bad news is that she has accepted a plea to two counts of child endangerment for using drugs during pregnancy and faces a possible five-year sentence. Whatever one calls it, this is what we've come to in America: Failure to produce a live, healthy, non-drug-exposed baby can land you in prison.

Stillbirth is a tragedy. Drug use during pregnancy is a terrible idea. But should they be crimes as well? Admittedly, Melissa Rowland is not exactly a poster child for pregnant women's rights. Early news reports, which are all most people have heard, made her sound frivolous and vain: She refused the operation, we were told, because she thought the scar might diminish her sex life (she denies having said this and points out that her two older children were born by C-section, as, finally, were the twins). In the public eye, Rowland is a monster mother: sexual, selfish, whimsical, like Susan Smith, who drowned her kids supposedly to win back a wealthy boyfriend, or the anonymous women whose newborns are found frozen to death in dumpsters.

The truth is, Rowland is a deeply troubled woman: mentally ill, estranged from her family, sometimes homeless. She was confined to a mental hospital at twelve, bore twins at fourteen, has tried to kill herself twice; four years ago her daughter was placed in foster care after Rowland was convicted of child abuse for punching her in a supermarket. Her boyfriend, father of the second set of twins, abandoned her before the birth (although the two took the drugs together, he was never charged with anything). A supporter, Lorna Vogt of the Utah Progressive Network, says Rowland told her that the reason she was in Utah in the first place was that she had been brought to Salt Lake City from Florida by an adoption agency to deliver the babies and give them up. (Utah has lax adoption laws, and apparently this practice is not uncommon.) Rowland also said she was living in a hotel room on a $100 weekly allowance from the agency and was treated with hostility by doctors and nurses—who called the police when she left the hospital instead of instantly submitting to surgery. In other words, Rowland lacked everything a pregnant woman should have: support, security, understanding, respect. That she is said to have described C-section as "being gutted from breastbone to pubic bone" suggests to me that she was terrified.

Assistant DA Langdon Fisher says the prosecutors dropped the murder charge because Rowland was mentally ill. Maybe. But perhaps they were also affected by the unexpected storm of controversy. "They went after a vulnerable woman because she was an easy target," Vogt told me. "They thought they'd make some headlines." And so they did. Pregnant drug users don't get much sympathy from the public, but the specter of women forced under the knife against their will, compelled by law to risk their lives and health despite their own judgment, is one many women can relate to. As Lynn Paltrow of the National Advocates for Pregnant Women (NAPW) points out, doctors are often wrong about the need for C-sections, as you might expect in the country with the highest rate of cesareans in the world—nearly one in four births, twice the proportion recommended by the World Health Organization. Granted, Rowland may not have had this statistic at her fingertips, but the point at issue in the murder charge remained whether pregnant women are people or vessels: Can they decide what is done to their bodies, what risks to take, or not? And what's next? Will women who miscarry or whose babies are born dead or sickly be jailed for smoking or drinking during pregnancy? For failing to follow doctor's orders on diet or bed rest? For choosing a home birth?

Now for the moment those slippery-slope arguments have been set aside, and we are back with what is becoming an American tradition: arresting poor women for illegal drug use during pregnancy. For the past eight years, South Carolina has been charging women, mostly poor and black, with child abuse if they deliver babies who test positive for illegal drugs; the Supreme Court recently refused to hear the appeal of Regina McKnight, who is serving twelve years in maximum security for "homicide by child abuse" after delivering a stillborn baby who tested positive for cocaine. If you think what happens to a poor black drug user with an IQ of 72 doesn't apply to you, think again: In its 1997 decision in *Cornelia Witner v. State of South Carolina,* the state Supreme Court decreed that *anything* a pregnant woman does after viability that causes "potential harm" to the fetus is child abuse—anything.

The prosecutor denied that the murder charges against Rowland had anything to do with abortion politics. NAPW's Paltrow, who argued the McKnight case, agrees: This is about the rights of pregnant women to decide on their medical care. Still, it is hard not to connect Rowland's case with the ongoing spate of antiabortion legislation and the disrespect for women's decision-making powers it fosters. The resistance of anti-choicers to health exceptions on abortion restrictions says it all. Recently in a challenge to the "partial-birth abortion" ban brought by the Center for Reproductive Rights, Dr. Watson Bowes testified in support of the ban that he opposed all abortions unless the chance that a woman would die was greater than 50 percent.

Melissa Rowland's case is one that never should have happened. Instead of arranging her auto-da-fé, whether for murder or child endangerment, the state of Utah should be asking itself how it can improve services for poor, pregnant, mentally ill substance abusers—and maybe take a look at adoption agency practices, too. When doctors and nurses take the time to know their patients and treat them with empathy and respect, patients usually follow their advice. It's good that Utah has decided that when doctor and patient disagree, the last word has to be hers, even though sometimes she will be wrong, as sometimes the doctor is wrong. After all, it's her body—for now.

•◀ April 26, 2004 ▶•

Down and Out in Texas

Did you know that since January 1, women in Texas have not been able to obtain abortions from the sixteenth week of pregnancy on? This blackout on women's rights and health is happening not because abortions after the fourth month were declared illegal—far from it. In theory, all that has changed is a bureaucratic regulation included in a bundle of antiabortion legislation, HB15. Most of the provisions in HB15, which sailed through the Republican-dominated state legislature, are familiar: There's a twenty-four-hour waiting period and a requirement that clinics offer a flower-decorated pamphlet called *A Woman's Right to Know*, which suggests a link between abortion and breast cancer, stresses the possibility of psychological damage, and gives the death rate for abortions performed at various stages of pregnancy. The bill also requires providers to photocopy patients' IDs and keep them on file.

The killer provision, though, is the one that has received the least press coverage. Beginning with the sixteenth week of pregnancy, abortions can no longer take place in clinics—they must now be performed in a hospital or an ambulatory surgical center. The catch is, Texas hospitals, many of which are Catholic, do almost no abortions, and of the state's 273 surgicenters not one performs the procedure or plans to take it on. For a clinic to qualify as a surgical center it would have to meet hundreds of architectural specifications at a cost of well over a million dollars. "There's nothing about these abortions that requires these regulations," says Sarah Wheat, director of public affairs at TARAL, the state's NARAL affiliate. "They were presented as necessary for women's health, but women's health organizations opposed them."

What happens when the only facilities that can legally provide abortions after sixteen weeks won't, and the only facilities that want to provide them are legally barred from doing so? Thousands of Texas girls and women suffer. The law is written so tightly—no exceptions, even to save the woman's life—that clinics have no wiggle room, says Amy Hagstrom Miller, who owns the Whole Woman's Health Clinic in Austin and another in McAllen, near the Mexican border. In fact, many clinics have stopped doing abortions after fourteen weeks just to be on the safe side. Miller has been referring three or four women a week to clinics in Louisiana, Arkansas, and Kansas. (Paradoxically, HB15 has meant plenty of work for Wichita's Dr. George Tiller, whom anti-choicers consider the Antichrist.) "Anyone I refer is at least eight hours away from an out-of-state clinic. It's a real burden on them. The majority don't make the trip—it's too expensive." Even if the two clinics now considering an upgrade manage to pull it off, the state is so huge that most women will be left in the cold.

The vast majority of women who terminate their pregnancies do so quickly: 88 percent of abortions are performed before the twelfth week; 96 percent before the sixteenth week. Most who wait that long are young, poor, or both: teens in denial about what's happening to their bodies, women trapped in abusive situations, rural women without transportation, women who spend the first trimester chasing the money to pay for the procedure even as delay drives up the price. These women have little political power and get little sympathy from those who do. Along with the stealthy nature of the regulation, that helps explain the lack of furor over what is a ban in all but name. Another Chicana tenth-grader has a baby; who gets all worked up about that? Even the most privileged woman, though, can have a wanted pregnancy that goes terribly wrong. Amniocentesis, still the main method for detecting genetic defects, yields its results well after the Texas cutoff date. Think about it: You get the worst news about your baby a doctor can give—it has Tay-Sachs disease, say, which means it will die, horribly, by age three—and the state of Texas shrugs its shoulders. Or you find that your health or even your life is suddenly at risk—and the state of Texas washes its hands of you. Recently, Miller says, she got a call from a woman who had aborted a much-wanted pregnancy because the fetus had defects incompatible with life. What would happen to her today, the caller wondered? Would she have to go through a whole pregnancy in order to deliver a dying baby? How is "life" served by that?

HB15 is a flagrant violation of *Roe v. Wade,* which allows states to regulate second-trimester abortions only to protect women's health; if ever there was an "undue burden" on women's ability to access abortion, this is it. Eventually, it may be thrown out in court—but how many girls and women will have been forced to bear children by then? How many will have injured their health and risked, perhaps even lost, their lives? There's a bigger agenda here too: Around the nation, anti-choicers are proposing bills that contradict *Roe* in hopes of providing the Supreme Court with an occasion to overturn it down the road, when George W. Bush has had his chance to alter the balance of the Court.

Texas is a conservative state, where the religious right is strong. In Austin, Planned Parenthood had to become its own contractor on building a new clinic when local contractors boycotted the project. In Denton, an Eckerd pharmacist refused to fill a rape victim's prescription for emergency contraception, and a CVS pharmacist refused to refill a prescription for ordinary birth-control pills. Waco recently made the news when locals organized a boycott of Girl Scout cookies to protest the scouts' endorsement of Planned Parenthood sex-ed programs. But Texas is also a big, rich, modern state: Houston and Dallas are the fourth- and eighth-largest cities in the country. If abortion access can be denied across the board in Texas, where will it happen next? Utah, for one, is moving in that direction: A law just enacted by the legislature cuts off state funding to any agency (including hospitals) that performs an abortion except in cases of rape, incest, or "permanent, irreparable and grave damage" to the woman. As a result, Salt Lake City's University Hospital has announced that it will no longer terminate pregnancies involving fatal fetal deformities.

•◄ May 10, 2004 ►•

Show and Tell in Abu Ghraib

What are the thousand words, I wonder, that are worth the pictures of grinning U.S. soldiers sexually humiliating Iraqi prisoners in Abu Ghraib prison? An essay by Michael Ignatieff about human rights as the justification for war? An article by Samuel Huntington on the superiority of Western values? A rousing column by Tom Friedman calling on America to make Iraq a modern democratic state? Maybe Bernard Lewis could write up a talk about Islamic paranoia, or perhaps Alan Dershowitz could reprise in an op-ed his argument that torture can be morally permissible—a view that found a ready, even gleeful, hearing, I seem to remember, in journalistic circles after 9/11.

It's one thing, though, for writers to euphemize about "rough treatment" and propose scenarios in which there is one man in custody who can prevent World War III—and another to look at those pictures. Who are those soldiers, looking so much like frat boys and mean girls on steroids, how did they come up with their pornographic tableaux, and what were they thinking when they took their snapshots? True, Saddam's men tortured with impunity while our thugs will be brought to account (although maybe not those on contract—apparently even wartime atrocities are being outsourced now). Six supervisors have already been severely reprimanded and a seventh has received a "letter of admonishment." When you consider that Lieutenant William Calley spent just three days in prison for presiding over the mass slaughter of men, women, and children at My Lai in March 1968, a blot on one's résumé for overseeing prisoner abuse seems about on target. It was war. Things happen. And they take time to process: Maybe there were good reasons why the Army took no action for months after first learning of the abuse, why General Richard Myers hadn't read the report although it was completed in February, why he asked *60 Minutes II* to postpone showing the photos, why Donald Rumsfeld took six days to comment, and why George W. Bush's early reaction was a peeved and childish "I didn't like it one bit." (Compare that with his comment in the State of the Union address on torture and rape under Saddam Hussein: "If this is not evil, then evil has no meaning.")

The fact is, whatever the reason or excuse, however unrepresentative those photos are ever shown to be—and whatever punishment is eventually meted out to the perpetrators—the United States has just lost its last remaining rationale for the misbegotten invasion of Iraq. The WMDs are missing, the nuclear weapons never existed (even the "nuclear weapons program" has been dead since 1991); you don't hear much anymore about Saddam having been behind 9/11, although thanks to the media's slavish channeling of White House propaganda, 70 percent of Americans will probably go to their graves believing him Osama's best friend. Now the rescue of the Iraqi people from tyranny and brutality is turning out to be another fantasy. The humanitarian argument persuaded a lot of people—good people—to give this war the benefit of the doubt. Does anyone still think Iraqis are about to shower their invaders with roses and sweetmeats?

The Administration will do everything it can to portray Abu Ghraib as, in Rumsfeld's words, "an exceptional, isolated" case. That seems unlikely: Human-rights groups report many more instances of unlawful detention, torture, and abuse, and there are at least ten pending investigations of prisoner deaths that we know of. Perhaps Western observers should have been less skeptical of reports that women inmates were raped and had pleaded to be saved, in smuggled leaflets. It is hard to believe human rights was one of the Coalition Provisional Authority's primary concerns, considering that it has permitted private companies to hire for security work Serbian mercenaries and confessed members of South African pro-apartheid death squads.

The pictures and stories have naturally caused a furor around the world. Not only are they grotesque in themselves, they reinforce the preexisting impression of Americans as racist, cruel, and frivolous. They are bound to alienate—further alienate—Iraqis who hoped that the invasion would lead to secular democracy and a normal life and who fear Islamic rule. Abroad, if not here at home, they underscore how stupid and wrong the invasion of Iraq was in the first place, how predictably the "war of choice" that was going to be a cakewalk has become a brutal and corrupt occupation, justified by a doctrine of American exceptionalism that nobody but Americans believes.

In the United States that doctrine still burns bright. What, Americans commit atrocities? Our boys? Our *girls*? For having the courage to speak out in 1971 against rampant wartime atrocities in Vietnam—his finest hour—John Kerry has been demonized as a traitor, a defamer of servicemen who is unfit to serve as commander in chief. Tim Russert helped launch this line of attack on *Meet the Press* in April, when he offered Kerry the opportunity to distance himself from testimony that has been "discredited." Now, Swift Boat Veterans for Truth, a hastily formed group with close ties to the Bush administration and big-time Republican donors, is leading the charge, and cable TV commentators are debating the "questions" these GOP hacks have raised about Kerry's patriotism. This, mere weeks after the *Toledo Blade* won a Pulitzer for its series on Tiger Force's vicious rampage across the Central Highlands of Vietnam in 1967—a months-long fiesta of murder, torture, rape, and mutilation. The commander in chief who avoided active service and has made such a mess of Iraq is honored as manly and decisive; the man who volunteered to serve and then protested a war few would defend today gets labeled a prevaricating shirker, unqualified to lead.

The big winners, as with so many steps taken by this administration for our supposed protection—Guantánamo, the confinement of José Padilla and Yaser Esam Hamdi, the harassment and deportation of law-abiding Muslims—are Islamists and Al Qaeda. To their ideological bag of tricks, already bulging with religion, nationalism, misogyny, ethnic pride, and antimodernism, they can now add the defense of civil liberties, human rights, and the Geneva Conventions. Clash of civilizations, anyone?

•◄ MAY 24, 2004 ►•

Desperately Seeking
Health Insurance

As crises go, medical insurance is not a very sexy one. It's not that no one talks about the 43.6 million uninsured, skyrocketing drug costs, emergency rooms crammed with patients in search of routine care, or the 18,000 Americans who, according to the Institute of Medicine, die each year for lack of care. Every politician has a stump speech and a plan—usually a rather complicated one. (Insert your Kerry joke here if you must, but give the man credit—at least he'll cover most people.) The simple solution would be a single-payer system like Canada's, a mantra the left has been humming for decades, but where's the big, irate, energetic movement for it? Health coverage doesn't seem to bring out the fire-breathers, like, oh, gay marriage or "partial-birth" abortion or whether "under God" belongs in the Pledge of Allegiance.

Why is that? Maybe we've been living this way so long that we've just accepted it, like the housing crisis. Maybe the kinds of people who are uninsured are the sort voters are all too used to ignoring. Maybe people don't want to pay for universal coverage (even though they tell pollsters they're willing). And maybe the political classes, who have good coverage and money and tend to live in places with lots of specialists and state-of-the-art hospitals, fear they'd have to stand in line under a Canadian-style system, as the *New York Times* is always warning them they would.

While wonks debate, the crisis deepens. Dr. Michele Barry, who directs tropical medicine at Yale Medical School, sent me notes on three patients she saw within a single week recently at Yale–New Haven Hospital:

Mr. N. An Italian-American man in his early 50s who moved from Florida to New Haven to let his wife die up near her family in Maine. He went 250,000 dollars in debt trying to self-pay for care for his wife, who was diagnosed with cervical cancer over a year ago. He was admitted to my service with hyperkalemia [high potassium] due to using expensive medicines he could get for free from pharmaceutical donations—these were inappropriate for his kidney problems, which were caused by diabetes. He could not even afford the long-acting insulin we wanted to give him. His reply to my telling him he might die if we didn't treat his potassium was: "Doc, maybe that's for the better."

Mr. M. A 38-year-old auto mechanic who was admitted in narcotic withdrawal. A year ago, he was the victim of a freak accident when a clutch released and a car rolled back into him. He developed back pain which subsequently caused him to seek several neurosurgical opinions, but nothing was done because he couldn't afford follow-up appointments. He became addicted to the OxyContin the doctors prescribed. Unemployed, disabled, and out of money due to medical costs of imaging and doctors, he lost his home and was forced to move to a motel and file for bankruptcy. He came into the hospital when he could not afford his motel room or any more narcotics and thus started to withdraw.

Ms. W. A 40-year-old black woman from North Carolina who came into my service with hypertensive emergency (escalating blood pressure) and heart failure. She had stopped taking any blood pressure medicines in order to save for her husband's kidney transplant. Due to her prolonged non-treatment, she developed irreversible heart damage.

As these tragic stories show, health insurance is about more than treating an immediate illness. Lack of insurance can precipitate an avalanche of trouble: job loss, debt, bankruptcy, more illness, inappropriate charity treatment that worsens the original problem, prescription-drug addiction, homelessness. The crisis doesn't even have to be yours: Mr. N.'s diabetes and Ms. W.'s hypertension—common, manageable conditions—became life-threatening because they skimped on their own medicine to help a spouse with an even bigger problem. In the case of Mr. N.'s wife, her fatal illness was itself possibly related to lack of preventive care because she didn't have health insurance: Cervical cancer is usually curable if caught early on by regular Pap smears.

Critics complain about the cost of universal coverage, but if you think of those 43.6 million uninsured as embedded in families, you have to count the privations endured by everyone in them as part of the true cost of the status quo. More money for a parent's doctor means less for the children's dentist—or summer camp, or college fund. Untreated or inadequately treated illness means stress and anxiety for the whole family. When a patient goes bankrupt, like Mr. M.—and healthcare costs are involved in 50 percent of bankruptcies, which have risen 400 percent in the past twenty-five years—the whole family suffers. Conservatives are always worrying about divorce—what about divorce as triggered by the financial and emotional stresses of uninsured illness? Maybe universal coverage could be sold as a family value.

Dr. Barry, who moves mountains for her patients, is doing all that one doctor can do. She was able to arrange donated drugs for Ms. W. and Mr. N., as a temporary stopgap. But what will happen to them down the road? As for Mr. M., she writes, "We gave him a long-acting morphine compound—not OxyContin!—for his pain and are trying to find him a surgeon who will accept state insurance. Not one orthopedic in our area does this. He was last seen living in a shelter in town."

•◀ JUNE 21, 2004 ▶•

Sex and the Stepford Wife

A s numerous reviewers of the overblown and over-remade remake of *The Stepford Wives* have pointed out, men do not really want to be married to robots. In particular, it is probably safe to say, they do not want to be married to robots who wear pastel flowered dresses and floppy garden-party hats and who wax ecstatic over cupcakes and Christmas crafts—even if they fetch drinks like Rover and don see-through lingerie for a lunchtime quickie. Indeed, in none of its versions—Ira Levin's slender novel, the 1975 scary movie, or the new comic rendition—does the plot of *The Stepford Wives* make a lot of sense. Why would men go to all the trouble of killing their uppity feminist wives and replacing them with pliant androids when they could just divorce them and marry twenty-five-year-olds? Or hire a housekeeper and have girlfriends?

A lot of cultural change has gone over the dam since 1975. By today's standards the original heroine, Joanna Eberhart, a mildly spirited amateur photographer, would be a slacker. In the remake, Joanna (Nicole Kidman) is the brilliant, tightly wound head of a TV network who specializes in battle-of-the-sexes reality shows (*I Can Do Better*) in which the women always win. In the original, the men were cold and sinister; in the new version, they're nebbishes who need to be constantly drilled in masculine prerogatives by the head of the Men's Association (Christopher Walken). Time has changed Stepford too, the Connecticut suburb to which Joanna's junior-executive husband (Matthew Broderick) whisks her away to save their marriage after a career crash gives her a nervous breakdown. The town has morphed from staid and comfortable to hard-right and rich. It's lost its one black family and gained a token pair of homosexuals.

It's all downhill after the setup. Paul Rudnick, who wrote the script, is a very funny man in the classic gay style—the movie has enough camp for all the Boy Scouts in America—but the story makes no sense. Basically, Rudnick wants to have his cupcakes and eat them too: Thus, men *are* sexist weaklings and housewives *are* servile bimbos and ambitious women *are* obnoxious but will either mellow through love or turn the tables on men because They Can Do Better—take your pick. The movie is such a confused satire of its original premises—this time, the ultimate villain is an ultratraditional *woman*—that the characters seem to utter all their lines as if they are speaking in air quotes.

Commentators have bridled at the implication that men are hustling resistant women into suburban purdah: Today, women stay home because they want to. "Look at the fringe benefits," Stephanie Zacharek writes in *Salon*, "a giant, comfortable house in Connecticut, the freedom to watch your children grow up instead of rushing off to work every day, enough money to feed and clothe them well—sure doesn't look bad to me." (Children are barely more visible than blacks in Stepford, but let that pass.) Domestic goddesshood is definitely back, and, if only as a fantasy, a lot of women are buying it: It wasn't men who made Martha Stewart a multimillionaire. On the Upper West Side of Manhattan, where I live and where the standard feminine garb has for decades been strictly Hot Sicilian Widow, the display windows this season are full of frilly getups straight out of a Stepford shoppe (if you'd rather be a doll than an automaton, Mattel is bringing out a line of Barbie clothes for real-life women).

As a plot the story may be silly, but as a metaphor it's powerful. There's a reason "Stepford wife" has entered the American lexicon. It expresses, dramatically and succinctly, two compelling and in some ways competing explanations for women's subjection within marriage: Men insist on it, and women—other women—insist on it. In the 1970s, when feminism was new, both these truths were obvious. Now, they are obscure: Women have learned to describe everything they do, no matter how apparently conformist, submissive, self-destructive, or humiliating, as a personal choice that cannot be criticized because personal choice is what feminism is all about. Women have become incredibly clever at explaining these choices in ways that barely mention social pressures or male desires. How many bright little essays have I read by young brides who insist that giving up their names is just the sensible, logical, mature, modern, *feminist* thing to do, the very proof of their marriage's egalitarianism? Probably they actually believe this. And yet, were it not for those social and masculine pressures, it is difficult to imagine that women would make some of the "personal" choices they now truculently defend.

After all, you have to wonder, as Catherine Orenstein did in a much-discussed *New York Times* op-ed, if women are free to be whatever they want, why are they still so obsessed with fitting narrow and rigid definitions of beauty? Feminism was supposed to send those to the trash can along with girdles and white gloves. Who would have thought in 1975 that thirty years later women would be tottering about in excruciating high heels—and having their little toes cut off to fit into them? Or injecting their faces with botulism toxin and undergoing plastic surgery at ever younger ages? Even teenagers are getting breast implants—11,326 girls eighteen and under had them in 2003, nearly triple the previous year's figure. Just try, though, to find a female in a plastic surgeon's waiting room who'll admit that breast augmentation has anything to do with pleasing men. Oh no, that expensive and painful operation, with its attendant, well-publicized dangers, is all about curing a tragic disease (micromastia, *aka* small breasts), finding clothes that fit, or boosting her self-esteem. But why does her self-esteem hinge on having big breasts in the first place? Forget self-esteem, what about self-respect? Why can't she feel good about herself by accomplishing something—climbing a mountain, painting a picture, reading a book? That's what real self-esteem comes from. In fact, according to several studies, women with breast implants are three times as likely to kill themselves as other women, even the flat-chested.

Of course, the critics are literally right: There is no town like Stepford, even in deepest Connecticut. But it still exists where it always did: in our heads.

●◀ JULY 5, 2004 ▶●

Let's Not Devalue Ourselves

It says something about the iron grip of the culture wars on our politics that no less a liberal than John Kerry—with his 100 percent ratings from NARAL, Human Rights Campaign, the AFL-CIO, and the NAACP—recently claimed that he represents "conservative values." There may even be a sense in which that's true. "Values" is one of those bland, spongy, good-for-you words that are the verbal equivalent of tofu: It means whatever you want it to mean. As for "conservative," in certain key states that's a synonym for "not a crazy hippie," and by that definition Kerry undoubtedly qualifies. Values, even conservative values, don't have to mean the three G's (God, guns, and gays) or the four A's (antiabortion, abstinence, antifeminism, and anti–affirmative action), either.

In any case, the reason Kerry's so concerned about values has a lot to do with the unfairness of the Electoral College, which awards outrageously disproportionate political power to rural conservative states with fewer voters than, say, the enlightened borough of Brooklyn. Through one of those ironies with which history is so replete, the Electoral College, intended by the Founding Fathers to insure that the President was chosen by the ruling elite, has become an antidemocratic mechanism of quite another kind, giving unequal weight to votes based merely on the state in which they are cast. (How unequal? A vote from Wyoming counts almost four times as much as a vote from California.) In a country that actually practiced the principle of one person, one vote, the political landscape would be markedly different. Every vote in a presidential election would be campaigned for—the Texas liberal and the Massachusetts right-winger—and candidates would have to address the issues important to the largest number of people instead of pampering the vanity of tiny demographic slivers favored by geography. Candidates would have to wrestle with the fact that most Americans are not family farmers, that 43 percent seldom or never go to church, that one in four is nonwhite. We wouldn't obsess over swing voters in Ohio—what, they still haven't made up their minds? they've had four years!—and Thomas Frank's fascinating analysis of the growth of the right in the so-called heartland, *What's the Matter with Kansas?* would be a curiosity, not required reading.

Given the current system—which will never change, because the small states would have to approve a constitutional amendment, and why would they do that?—Kansas matters, and Kansans care about values. As political currency, "values" may be, as Frank argues, counterfeit coinage in which working-class and lower-middle-class red-staters are paid to forgo their economic and social interests in favor of the pleasures of moral superiority over the Sodom and Gomorrah that are the blue states. (Illusory moral superiority, I might add, when you consider that rates of divorce, teen pregnancy, and out-of-wedlock childbearing are higher in the Bible Belt than in the latté-sipping, sushi-nibbling Northeast.)

The usual Democratic response in the values debate is either to change the subject—"It's the economy, stupid"—or concede the high ground. Thus, Randall Balmer, professor of religion at Barnard and an evangelical Christian, urged Kerry in a recent *Nation* piece to stress his personal opposition to abortion and his commitment to making abortion, as Clinton put it, "safe, legal, and rare." This may be the only time in *The Nation's* 139-year history that a candidate followed its advice—interviewed on *Larry King Live,* Kerry not only said abortion should be "rare, but safe and legal"; he said he wanted to talk about "morality, responsibility, adoption, and other choices." In other words, anti-choicers are right: Abortion is bad, women are insufficiently thoughtful about it, and they should feel even worse about choosing abortion than they already do. This from the man who hopes to win the single-woman vote!

It is a mistake to give the right a monopoly on values by agreeing with them in a half-baked, yes-but, wishy-washy way. Sure, abortion should be rare—but it should be rare thanks to birth control and support for women and children, not because women guilt-trip themselves into continuing crisis pregnancies. It's not a satisfying answer, either, to change the subject, as when Kerry said that "good-paying jobs" is a Democratic value. People need to hear about those good jobs, but they also need to hear about a social vision that isn't just about their own immediate self-interest.

We liberals and progressives and leftists have our own noble principles, our own beautiful abstract words. We should take our stand on them. Fairness is a liberal value. Equality is a liberal value. Education is a liberal value. Honesty in government, public service for modest remuneration, safeguarding public resources and the land—these are all values we share. Liberty is a liberal value, trusting people to make their own decisions, letting people speak their minds even if their views are unpopular. So is social solidarity, the belief that we should share the nation's enormous wealth so that everyone can live decently. The truth is, most of the good things about this country have been fought for by liberals (indeed, by leftists and, dare one say it, Communists)—women's rights, civil liberties, the end of legal segregation, freedom of religion, the social safety net, unions, workers' rights, consumer protection, international cooperation, resistance to corporate domination—and resisted by conservatives. If conservatives had carried the day, blacks would still be in the back of the bus, women would be barefoot and pregnant, medical care would be on a cash-only basis, there'd be mouse feet in your breakfast cereal, and workers would still be sleeping next to their machines.

Of course, it won't be easy for Kerry to make these points, even if he wants to. For one thing, it's hard to run as an economic populist when corporate donors are paying your bills. For another, a lot of those precious swing voters have strong conservative views—it's often a mistake to think people who disagree with you really don't, deep down. For a third, there's Iraq, a subject on which Kerry has yet to present a clear and coherent position.

Still, in the war over values, we needn't be shy. Liberty, Equality, Fraternity—it has a certain ring to it, don't you think?

•◄ AUGUST 16, 2004 ►•

Bush Bashers and the Bashers Who Bash Them

For well over a decade now, right-wingers and Republicans have heaped insult, lies, and slander on liberals and Democrats, who responded for the most part by becoming starchy, self-doubting, and depressed. To complain was to be labeled elitist and fuddy-duddy: Rush and Ann and Bill and Sean say liberals are traitors and hate America? They're populist entertainers! Jerry Falwell hawked a video accusing Bill Clinton of murder? Shut up and finish your latte. It took ages, not to mention a suspect election and a suspect war, but suddenly, everywhere you look, Democrats and liberals are fighting back.

The prissy and thin-lipped are cracking jokes, policy wonks are gabbing on Air America, voters once proud of being as unherdable as cats leap aboard the projects of MoveOn.org and write checks to long-shot red-state candidates because Howard Dean says it's a good idea. Do some of these newborn activists feel an intense personal dislike of Bush and all his works? Think he's a blithering idiot? Quiver with rage and loathing when they watch him flash that arrogant sneer and speak in that weird lurching way, as if he's on the edge of blanking out totally? Sure. Probably some of them even enjoy seeing his features merged with an ape's on smirkingchimp.com. But so what? This is America, where pundits have for years reassured us politics is a down-and-dirty contact sport with no room for girly-men.

Bush hatred wasn't supposed to happen. Liberals were supposed to be lofty and wistful and clueless, even as their enemies slimed them into irrelevance. They were supposed to say things like "Have you no sense of decency, sir?"—not cram into movie theaters to laugh hysterically at the president sitting in that classroom reading "The Pet Goat." Something must be wrong with these Bush-haters, with their "No More Years" bumper stickers and their obsessional blogs. Could they be insane? "Monomaniacal," as Tucker Carlson put it on *Crossfire*: "Their hatred has become the focus of their lives. It's actually a clinical description."

In the *New York Times Book Review*, Leon Wieseltier uses his review of Nicholson Baker's thin, sensationalistic novella *Checkpoint*, about a man holed up in a hotel with fantasies of assassinating the President, to deliver a long, sanctimonious lecture to the anti-Bush crowd: "The virulence that calls itself critical thinking, the merry diabolization of other opinions and the other people who hold them, the confusion of rightness with righteousness, the preference for aspersion to argument, the view that the strongest statement is the truest statement—these deformations of political discourse now thrive in the houses of liberalism too. The radicalism of the right has hectored into being a radicalism of the left. The Bush-loving mob is being met with a Bush-hating mob. . . . American liberalism, in sum, may be losing its head." Wieseltier sees "signs of the degradation . . . everywhere": Janet Malcolm wrote a letter to the *Times* in which she claimed the present moment is "as fearful as the period after Munich"; an anti-Bush anthology is decorated with anagrams like "The Republicans: Plan butcheries?"; MoveOn publishes an ad—a "huge" ad—that reads "The communists had *Pravda*. Republicans have Fox." Liberalism, it would seem, is supposed to consist of constantly reminding ourselves that we do not live in a murderous, totalitarian regime. Things could be worse! This too shall pass!

Actually, I too bridle when people start talking about Hitler. It sounds naïve and overwrought. If the Republicans really were Nazis, you wouldn't be holding this magazine in your hands. And I don't like the endless theme of Bush's stupidity, either—it's mostly a way for the marginalized to feel culturally superior. I don't even believe that Bush is so dumb—he seems to have plenty of political cunning and skill, and that's a kind of intelligence, albeit not the kind that has much relation to making good policy decisions in a complex and dangerous world. On the *Times* op-ed page, Dahlia Lithwick made some good points about the impulse to portray Bush as a child: It insults people who voted for him in 2000 and whom we hope are persuadable this time, and it lets him off the hook, since children aren't responsible for the damage they cause.

And yet there is a schoolmasterish quality to all this finger-wagging. What are we talking about here? Some over-the-top e-mails? Whoopi Goldberg's off-color jokes? Nicholson Baker's novel has the obsessive-compulsive, look-at-me creepiness of all his fiction, but surely it's *L.A. Times* book reviewer P. J. O'Rourke who has the problem when he compares its characters' dismay at suburban sprawl to the hatred of humanity that fuels Robespierre and Pol Pot. Is it anti-humanity to wish for more trees? Imagining characters named "Ann Coulter" and "Bill O'Reilly" up in that hotel room, he writes, "Hmmm, they don't appear to be discussing whether to kill Bill Clinton." Well, maybe not in the novel in O'Rourke's head—but in real life, Nicholson Baker's would-be assassin doesn't exist, while Ann Coulter has called for the murder of Islamic heads of state, the invasion of their countries, the forced conversion of their citizens to Christianity, the execution of liberals, and a terrorist attack on the *New York Times*. Hilarious, I know.

It's really a stretch to suggest that the newly awakened anti-Bush advocates are just the lefty equivalent of the hard-right disinformation machine. Al Franken is no Bill O'Reilly. The *New York Times* editorial page equates MoveOn PAC's ads with those of the Swift Boat Veterans for Truth, and it's true both are funded through gaps in campaign-finance laws, and both attack the enemy candidate on his war record. But the Swift Boat vets' charges are a mess of smears and lies with Karl Rove's fingerprints all over them, while MoveOn's ads raise genuine questions about Bush's service record that have never been answered.

One group protesting at the Republican convention is planning to hand out 3,000 fortune cookies with messages like "Do not change horses midstream unless horse lies to you and stream is on fire," and lists of ways Bush has mispronounced "Abu Ghraib." You can be sure the Republicans will portray these mild jabs as demonic howls of rage and fury.

Where's their sense of humor?

•◄ SEPTEMBER 13, 2004 ►•

Mary Cheney, Mary Cheney

Reservists mutiny in Iraq, old people keel over standing in line for flu shots, and all sorts of cats leap out of Bush's bag of secrets: According to Ron Suskind's revelatory *New York Times Magazine* cover story, the President himself recently told a closed Republican meeting that if elected he would "move quickly" to privatize Social Security, lavish funds on faith-based initiatives, and more. The debates, which were supposed to seal Kerry's doom as a garrulous dandy, actually showed that he'd make a pretty good President: confident, serious, knowledgeable, affable. Who cares about his windsurfing now? The President's performance—sluggish and sullen in the first debate, prickly and evasive in the second and third—was so disgraceful that even on the *National Review* website there was wailing and gnashing of teeth. He couldn't recall a single mistake he'd made in four years? Most people would have no problem thinking of a mistake they'd made that week.

Thank God for Mary Cheney. Without her, right-wing pundits would be stuck with David Brooks's truly embarrassing "Bush is heart, Kerry is head" line—vote for Bush, he cares less about the facts! Defending the honor of Mary Cheney has to be more fun than that: How dare John Kerry, that cad, that lowlife, that poltroon, mention on national TV that the Vice President's older daughter is a . . . lesbian? Writes Brooks, "He will say or do anything to further his career." Was Kerry's remark "spontaneous—and unpleasant" (Robert Novak) or "McCarthyite" and evidence of Kerry's "cheap, cold, calculating cynicism" (William Kristol)? As I write, the phony scandal is in full swing. Pundits preen, shock jocks rant, closet Republican Ed Koch waxed so wroth he practically gave himself a heart attack on New York 1. We're back in the world of soaps and scandal and sex: Maybe Zell Miller will challenge Kerry to a duel!

In the media spin world, it doesn't matter that Dick Cheney has spoken publicly about his gay daughter or that she attended the Republican convention with her girlfriend and was even shown with her on TV. It doesn't matter that Mary Cheney, currently managing her father's campaign office, has not only been out of the closet for a decade, she's a kind of professional gay conservative—faced with a national boycott during the 1990s due to its antigay policies, Coors hired her to spruce up its image among gay beer drinkers. No one is asking why this grown-up woman is not speaking for herself: to reinforce the damsel-in-distress motif? to keep from screaming at her parents? (Mom! Dad! Stop looking so mournful!) All that matters is the instaquiz: Was Kerry "offensive"? Two-thirds of those polled say yes. Probably they'd be offended if he said Sappho herself was a lesbian, because being a lesbian is shameful and perverted and just . . . not . . . something you talk about.

Thus are positions reversed: Kerry, the gay-friendly candidate, becomes the victimizer of innocent daughters, and Bush, who supports a constitutional amendment banning gay marriage and who relies on homophobia to excite his fundamentalist base, becomes the generous protector. But if there's nothing immoral about being gay, and if Mary Cheney has herself made her sexual orientation public, what did Kerry do that was so monstrous?

Here's what I find offensive: Kristol and William Safire comparing Kerry to Joseph McCarthy. Republicans, Safire writes, "have in mind a TV spot using an old film clip of a Boston lawyer named Welch at a congressional hearing, saying 'Have you no sense of decency, sir, at long last? Have you left no sense of decency?'" Who knew Safire, that old Nixonian, held McCarthy in such low esteem! Let's see: McCarthy destroyed lives with dubious accusations of secret Communist affiliations, something he regarded as evil. Kerry mentioned Mary Cheney's sexual orientation, which is a fact, is not a secret, and is not a bad thing in Kerry's eyes. The analogy only makes sense if Kristol and Safire think homosexuality is as bad as communism—or communism is not as bad as they thought.

The Mary Cheney gaffe is a bit like Paul Wellstone's memorial service, or for that matter the "Dean scream"—a blip, a nothing, a wisp that the Republican wind machine wants to whip into a tornado of hysterical outrage. And because so much of the media are frivolous and lazy, it can. The tactic doesn't work for long—don't you feel silly now, Minnesotans, for voting Republican because of a eulogy? and does anyone today think Howard Dean is crazy?—but it doesn't need to. It only needs to push the right buttons—propriety, prudishness, politeness—for a few crucial days.

Every minute people are focusing on what John Kerry said about Mary Cheney is a minute they're not talking about Iraq, or Guantánamo, that swamp of injustice and torture, or the plain basic fact that Bush, who lost the popular vote, has used his four years in the White House to turn the country over to lobbyists, ideologues, and charlatans. It's a minute they're looking at Kerry's character and not at Bush's. It means they're not demanding action on the mushrooming scandal of vote suppression and fraud in Bush's favor, and not just in Florida either—the intimidation of black voters, the trashing of Democratic registration forms by GOP-contracted firms and their rejection by state authorities on flimsy pretexts, those paperless electronic voting machines. (Penny Venetis and Frank Askin of the Rutgers Constitutional Litigation Clinic just filed a magnificent brief challenging the use of such machines in New Jersey.)

Finally, as Richard Kim points out on www.thenation.com, defending Mary Cheney lets Republicans look concerned for a gay person while preserving their basic homophobic agenda. If they cared so much about gay women, they would rebuke Oklahoma Senate candidate Tom Coburn for nuttily claiming that lesbianism is so rampant at some local schools that girls are only permitted to go to the bathroom one at a time. They would reject support from fundamentalist ministers who talk about "biblical" punishment for gays. Bush himself would scorn to win the White House if it meant defacing the Constitution with prejudice.

But then, as Brooks might put it, this is a man who will say or do anything to further his career.

•◀ NOVEMBER 8, 2004 ▶•

Mourn

Please. Just right now, don't say, "Don't mourn, organize" or "Pray for the dead but fight like hell for the living." Don't explain Kerry's loss with Harry Truman's quip that voters will always choose the real Republican over the fake Republican. Don't let's talk about Eugene Debs and Fighting Bob La Follette and how important it is to lose and lose and lose until you win. It all seems a bit inadequate, a bit quaint and this-land-is-your-landish, the left's commitment to doing more of what we've been doing, only harder.

I also don't want to hear carping criticisms of John Kerry. Given that he is a fallible mortal, he was a pretty good candidate. Sure, he made mistakes—not responding instantly to the Swift Boat liars, wearing that silly goose-hunting getup, letting Bush get away with saying drugs from Canada will kill you—but Bush committed his share of gaffes as well. Any candidate does. Think back to the actual human beings running in the primaries: Who would have done better in the real-world mix of competing claims and hard choices and twenty-four-hour spin? Dennis Kucinich? Al Sharpton? I admired Howard Dean, but face it, the Republican attack machine would have shredded him in a week.

The Kerry campaign may have been a broth with too many cooks, but it did a lot of things right. It raised a ton of money from small and first-time donors instead of relying on big donors, as the Democrats have tended to do for the last decade. It had fantastic labor support. It had MoveOn, America Coming Together, and the other 527s, which mobilized intensity, creativity, time, and cash and evoked a surge of grassroots progressive activism like nothing in living memory. Hundreds of thousands of people—Democrats, leftists, Greens, independents,

Deaniacs, even a few stray Republicans—knocked themselves out regis-
tering voters, phone-banking, going door to door; for many, like me,
this was the first time they'd volunteered for a presidential campaign.
Kerry had the energy of millions, black and white, enraged by Florida
2000, by Iraq, by Bush's governing from the hard right without anything resembling a mandate—people who were willing to stand in long
lines in the hot sun or November chill for however many hours it took
to cast their ballot. Kerry may not have displayed passion, but his supporters had plenty to spare.

It's an article of faith among progressives that moving to the left
wins votes, and I have written many columns in witness to the creed.
But what if it isn't true? What if it wins fewer votes than being a liar and
a bigot? One leftist intellectual I saw at an election-night party suggested
to me that Kerry shot himself in the foot when he didn't throw Abu
Ghraib in Bush's face and proclaim that as President he would never permit torture. I would have wept with joy to hear that speech, but where
is the evidence that significant numbers of voters not already committed
to Kerry—let alone voters who supported Bush—were outraged by Abu
Ghraib? Did I miss the demonstrations, the sit-ins, the teach-ins, the
lying down in traffic by swing voters and nonvoters to force the Bush
administration to account for this outrageous crime against humanity?

Similarly, some were impatient with Kerry's "nuanced" position on
gay marriage, but is there any reason on God's earth to believe there are
lots of gay-friendly swing voters or nonvoters out there just waiting for
a candidate who wants to let Mary Cheney wed Rosie O'Donnell?
Everything we know—the passage of all eleven state bans on gay marriage, for example, some of which go so far as to ban civil unions as
well—suggests that Kerry understood quite well where the people were.

Okay, you say, that's one of those pesky newfangled cultural-elite issues that alienate the heartland, which yearns for the old-time religion
of "economic populism." Kerry's health insurance plan wasn't perfect, it
wasn't single-payer, but it would have insured all children and about half
the adults currently uninsured—26.7 million people!—and it would
have been paid for by canceling Bush's tax cuts for the wealthiest Americans, something populists should go for. No sale. His plan to help
young people pay for college wasn't perfect either, but it was a lot better

than what young people are getting now. Result: Young people constituted only a little more than their usual pathetic proportion of the total vote. And this is *after* the best efforts of P Diddy, Christina Aguilera, Eminem, and virtually every other pop icon except Britney Spears.

The logic of the "Left Is More" position seems to be this: What people really want is a Debs or La Follette who will smite the corporations, turn swords into plowshares, share the wealth, and banish John Ashcroft to a cabin in the Ozarks. But since the Democratic Party denies them their first choice, they will—naturally!—pick a hard-right warmaker of staggering incompetence and no regard for either the Constitution or the needs of the people. Better that than settle for a liberal centrist who would only raise the minimum wage by two dollars. In other words, these proto-progressives will consciously choose the greater evil out of what—spite? pride? I scorn your half-measures, sir! Keep your small change!

This makes no sense to me as an explanation of the recent election. It doesn't explain, for example, why Republicans gained in both House and Senate. It doesn't explain why Californians rejected a referendum to amend their three-strikes law so that twice-convicted felons wouldn't get twenty-five years for shoplifting, or why Arizonans voted solidly to bar undocumented aliens from obtaining a wide range of essential public services and to require public servants to report them if they try. It doesn't explain why the Kansas school board is once again a chorus line of creationists.

Maybe this time the voters chose what they actually want: nationalism, preemptive war, order not justice, "safety" through torture, backlash against women and gays, a gulf between haves and have-nots, government largesse for their churches, and a my-way-or-the-highway President.

Where, I wonder, does that leave us?

•◀ NOVEMBER 22, 2004 ▶•

Earthly Rewards for the Christian Voter

Sitting alone in a classroom at a Catholic all-boys high school this weekend (don't ask), I passed the time by browsing through the health textbooks stacked on the window sill. Sure enough: no discussion of contraception (condoms are mentioned, but not described, in connection with people who have HIV); abortion, still legal here in the United States, isn't even listed in the glossary. Sex itself is discussed only in the vaguest terms, with emphasis on how to avoid it. This wasn't a special Catholic-boy textbook, either—*Health: Skills for Wellness* is one of the bestselling health texts in the country.

Think about that when you read that "moral values" voters will get no payback for helping Bush to victory. Tom Frank, whose much-discussed *What's the Matter with Kansas?* is a colorful guide to the wing nuts of the Sunflower State, is the chief exponent of this view. Year after year, says Frank, working-class voters fall for fire-breathing crusaders who promise to crack down on abortion, gay rights, porn, Darwin, and so on, but once in office all they do is cut the taxes of rich people and shovel favors to corporations. Not only do these right-wing radicals vote against their own economic interests, Frank argues, they're suckers, too.

Has the Christian right really so little to show for its self-sacrifice? "John Kerry's defeat notwithstanding," Frank Rich argued in his *New York Times* column recently, "it's blue America, not red, that is inexorably winning the culture war, and by a landslide." So you might think if you watch a lot of TV, where, as Rich often points out, hedonism, vulgarity, and excess flourish more lavishly with each passing season—and nowhere more so than on Fox, the right's own network. It's probably true that when humongous amounts of corporate money unite with the national longing for wardrobe malfunctions of every kind, the mores of small-town Kansas don't stand much of a chance.

It may also be true that the radical right will never achieve its stated legal goals—the overturning of *Roe v. Wade,* passage of the Human Life Amendment, a constitutional amendment forbidding gay marriage, the reinstatement of prayer and Bible reading in the schools—much less such dystopian dreams as making Christianity the national religion, abolishing public schools, and banning the Pill and divorce. But that's like saying the left got nothing from FDR because it didn't get socialism. The fact is, anyone who thinks the GOP is stiffing its "moral values" backers hasn't been paying attention: George Bush, for one, has been paying them back for the past four years. He's promoted a raft of anti-choice legislation—including the Partial-Birth Abortion Ban, the Un-born Victims of Violence Act, and a law making it easier for health professionals to deny women abortions and even birth control for "reasons of conscience." He's packed the federal bench with anti-choice reactionaries, and he's seeded the federal bureaucracy and the government's international agencies with hard-line social conservatives like the faith-healing Dr. David Hager of the FDA reproductive health panel. These people wield immense power over regulations and funding and the flow of information. It did not take a Senate majority to keep emergency contraception from being sold over the counter; all it took was compliant Mark McClellan, willing to overlook the recommendation of his own expert panel and the overwhelming weight of medical opinion.

Bush has flat-funded Title X, which pays for birth control for poor women, while heaping federal dollars on abstinence-until-marriage programs, $138 million in fiscal 2004 and a requested $272 million for the next year. He's appointed delegates to UN conferences who have done their best to wreck global consensus on reproductive health, the rights of women and children, and AIDS. Fully one-third of the $15 billion budget for his international AIDS initiative goes to abstinence-only programs, cutting out established workers in the field in favor of Christian groups with zero experience. Even though his faith-based initiative tanked, Christian entrepreneurs—pastors, counselors, creators of "educational" materials, inspirational speakers, anti-sex impresarios—have gotten loads of federal money, with more to come. As a bonus, if you visit the Parks Department gift shop at the Grand Canyon, you can now buy *Grand Canyon: A Different View,* a creationist volume that claims that the earth couldn't possibly be more than a few thousand years old.

The cultural right may eventually find itself stymied at the federal level—although it may also luck out with Bush's upcoming Supreme Court appointments, and with such Talibanesque new senators as Tom Coburn, who wants to execute abortion providers, and Jim De Mint, who doesn't want gays or unmarried mothers teaching school. Most of government happens in the states, though, and in some the right is doing quite well. Eleven states passed gay-marriage bans. Four states— Georgia, Ohio, Pennsylvania, and Wisconsin—are poised to require that evolution be taught as an unproven hypothesis, with Kansas, where creationists just won back control of the school board, probably to follow. Florida is the proud home of a faith-based prison. In Mississippi, women who want abortions must be told, falsely, that there's a link between abortion and breast cancer. In Texas, due to a little-noted regulatory change reported in this space last spring, there is now exactly one clinic where a woman can get an abortion after sixteen weeks. I could go on and on. Some of these victories for the radical right may seem minor, or bizarre, or symbolic, but they add up.

I too believe that in the long run equality and tolerance and liberal sexual mores will win out over repressive Christian "moral values." After all, civil union, which no one had even heard of a few years ago, is now supported by two-thirds of the population. But before the tables turn on the Christian right, how many biology classes will be clouded with creationist nonsense? How many young people will suffer STDs and HIV and pregnancy because they learned in school that condoms "don't work"—or didn't hear about them at all? How many women will carry disastrous pregnancies to term? It's not much comfort that Pat Robertson can't ban *Trading Spouses.*

•◄ DECEMBER 6, 2004 ►•

Stop Crying, Start Working

How long did it take Republicans to write their thank-you note to the Christian right? About five minutes. On November 21, Congress passed a $388 billion spending bill that permits any health provider—not just doctors and nurses, who can already opt out in forty-five states, but health insurers, HMOs, public or private hospitals, clinics, pharmacists—to refuse to be involved in abortion, up to and including informing a woman where to get one. Your employer can now deny you abortion coverage! Coming up soon: the Child Custody Protection Act, which would make it illegal for anyone but a parent or guardian to take an underage girl across state lines for an abortion, thus making parental notification and consent laws impossible to get around; the grotesque Unborn Child Pain Awareness Act, which would require doctors to offer women aborting after twenty weeks pain medication for their fetuses; the Post-Abortion Depression Research and Care Act; and lots more. Measures like these make abortion harder to get: Arrangements take longer, travel becomes more burdensome, the clinic date gets pushed later, and the cost goes up—from around $350 for a first-trimester procedure to $1,000 or more after twelve weeks.

Most readers know this already, but did you know there's something you can do? If you've been racking your brains for an activist project to replace obsessively monitoring the Electoral College Vote Predictor, here is one that could make a real difference as former Texas Air National Guard pilot George W. Bush swoops us into the wild blue fundamentalist yonder: Get involved with your local abortion fund. If none exists in your area—there are 102 around the country—start one yourself.

Abortion funds help low-income women obtain a crucial medical service, but they also help clinics fulfill their mission of egalitarian feminist healthcare. Barbara Ehrenreich recently reminded *Nation* readers of the network of storefront services the left created in the 1960s and 1970s—neighborhood clinics, legal centers, preschools, coffeehouses near military bases. The country is dotted with abortion clinics—Aradia Women's Health Clinic in Seattle, Red River Women's Clinic in Fargo, the Concord Feminist Health Center in New Hampshire—that follow that model, reaching into the community and connecting the services they provide with the political organizing that keeps those services available.

To get you started, here's a handy guide from Jennifer Baumgardner, the author with Amy Richards of *Grassroots: A Field Guide to Feminist Activism* (forthcoming January 2005) and longtime supporter of the New York Abortion Access Fund:

1. *Assess need.* The first thing you should do is call your own local clinic, identify yourself as a pro-choice activist, and ask whether they need a fund. Even if there is a fund in place, it is highly unlikely that a clinic would not have a need for money. Patients show up all the time further along in their pregnancy than they thought, which requires more money. The New York City clinic that I work with has to raise around $1,500 in additional funds each week so that women can get their procedures. Their biggest single source of money is the New York Abortion Access Fund, which grants around $20,000 annually. Fargo, North Dakota, has a small local fund but it "could definitely use some big donations or people who want to organize fundraisers," says Tammi Kromenaker, director of Red River Women's Clinic, the only clinic in the state. At present, the clinic gets about $5,000 from the local fund and ends up asking patients to turn to the Hersey Fund in neighboring Minnesota.

2. *Find partners.* Whether you're creating a fund from scratch or organizing fundraisers for one that already exists, you are going to need help. Enlist friends, call the women's center at a local university, contact the local chapter of NOW, put up flyers in coffee shops ("Interested in abortion rights? We're going to start a fund—come to X place at Y time!").

3. *Formalize.* Contact the National Network of Abortion Funds (www. nnaf.org). E-mail info@nnaf.org or call 413-559-5645 and ask for their three-ring notebook called "Building an Abortion Fund." It details everything from how to run your organization to how to get tax-exempt status. Don't worry if you haven't done this sort of thing before. "The women and men who start these funds are all ages and range from Ivy League students to a social worker in a farm community," says Shawn Towey of NNAF.

4. *Raise the dough.* There are infinite creative ways to raise money— from grant-writing to art auctions—but start with letters and events. Letters can end up being formalized into a direct-mail campaign in which you buy a mailing list and have a letter with a brochure and return envelope for donations. Start personal, though, by writing to friends, relatives, and anyone else in your address book you think might be interested in supporting you or your cause. I wrote a heartfelt letter to pro-choice friends of my mother's, hoping they wouldn't be offended by my plea for money, and made $1,000 for an abortion documentary. For an event, you will use that same circle of donors, but invite them to your house—or that of a fabulous friend—for wine and cheese. About an hour into it, give a brief talk about the fund. Have a basket at the door and ask for $20 (or more) from each mini-philanthropist.

5. *Repeat step 4 as necessary.*

While you are mulling over Jennifer's advice, get in practice by making a donation to the Emma Goldman Clinic in Iowa City. Last year the clinic, which charges on a sliding scale in order to make quality reproductive healthcare available to all, was able to subsidize $230,000 worth of patient services. This year, it's having trouble meeting that goal, because it incurred heavy legal expenses to get an injunction against an antiabortion extremist who threatened murder and because it faces a big insurance rise (reason: It's an abortion clinic). To make a donation, go to www.emmagoldman.com or call 800-848-7684. You'll be helping women and supporting feminist activism—and in a red state, too.

•◀ DECEMBER 20, 2004 ▶•

Bittersweet Bomblets

I was listening to *Morning Edition* on December 30, and up came one of those end-of-the-year heart-warmers that's supposed to make you feel there's hope for this old world yet. It seems that a nine-year-old Iraqi boy, Saleh Khalaf, came across a cluster bomb and "because it was round and smooth" he picked it up and it blew off all of one hand and most of another, opened up his abdomen, took out his left eye, and horribly scarred his face. His sixteen-year-old brother was killed. Fortunately, and this is the point of the story, he was treated, "against protocol," in a U.S. Army hospital and flown with his father for further treatment in Oakland, where he was showered with help by a generous local couple and is now learning English and American expressions like "hold your horses." Recently his mother and sisters were permitted to join him in California. "I'm happy now," says Saleh.

Spunky child, loving family, wonderful doctors, heroically kind and generous benefactors. No wonder the reporter, Luke Burbank, got a bit emotional ("the moment you meet [Saleh] you have the overwhelming urge to protect him"). But wait a minute. What was that bit about a cluster bomb? Time was, cluster bombs got at least a sentence to themselves, even in a heart-warmer—a definition, a mini-history of their infamous usage against civilian populations, maybe even a quote from one of the many organizations that have tried to ban them under the Geneva Conventions. You know, *cluster bombs.* Remember how during the Soviet occupation of Afghanistan we read about village children blown apart by Soviet bomblets said to be brightly colored and to look like toys? Those were cluster bombs. It wasn't the Soviets, though, who dropped that "round and smooth" mini-bomb alongside the road where Saleh found it. It was the United States.

So this is what we've come to: We celebrate the rescue of one child and gloss over the inconvenient fact that it was our weapons that maimed him for life. The boy who lives cancels out the brother who died, the moral heroism of his befrienders cancels out the moral turpitude of our government, excuses ourselves, and lets us bask in poignant uplift. Over at NPR, it's a driveway moment.

Sometimes I think America is becoming another place, unrecognizable. David Harvey, the great geographer, tells the story of a friend who returned to the United States last spring after seven years away and could not believe the transformation. "It was as if everyone had been sprinkled with idiot dust!" Some kind of mysterious national dumbdown would explain the ease with which the Republicans have managed to get so many people agitated about the nonexistent Social Security crisis—at 82 percent, ranked way above poverty and homelessness (71 percent) and racial justice (47 percent) in a list of urgent issues in a recent poll—or about gay marriage, whose threat to heterosexual unions nobody so far has been able to articulate. Mass mental deterioration would explain too how so many Americans still believe the discredited premises of the Iraq War—Saddam Hussein had WMDs, was Osama's best friend, was behind 9/11. But even as a joke it doesn't explain the way we have come to accept as normal, or at least plausible, things that would have shocked us to our core only a little while ago. Michelle Malkin, a far-right frother, writes a book defending the internment of the Japanese in World War II, and before you know it Daniel Pipes, Middle East scholar and frequent op-ed commentator, is citing Malkin to support his proposals for racial profiling of Muslims. And he's got lots of company—in a recent poll, almost half of respondents agreed that the civil liberties of Muslims should be curtailed. Pipes's proposals, in turn, seem mild compared with the plans being floated by the Pentagon and the CIA for lifetime detention of terrorist suspects—without charges, without lawyers, in a network of secret prisons around the globe. Kafkaesque doesn't begin to describe it—at least Joseph K. had an attorney and the prisoner of "In the Penal Colony" got a sentence.

As I write, the Senate is preparing to take up the nomination of Alberto Gonzales to replace John Ashcroft as Attorney General. Despicable as Ashcroft proved to be, and much as the Senate should have foreseen that and rejected him, he had not at the time of his nomination been responsible for memos justifying torture. He hadn't argued that the President stood above the law and could pretty much do whatever he wanted. He had not been in the center of months and months of revelations about the horrific doings at Abu Ghraib, in detention centers in Afghanistan, or, even as you are reading this, Guantánamo. How can it be that the smart money is on Gonzales being confirmed? That Charles Schumer, a popular blue-state Democrat with a war chest bigger than Alexander the Great's, is already talking sagely about the presumption that the President gets the Cabinet members he wants?

If only the problem *was* stupidity. But Chuck Schumer, Daniel Pipes, the people at *Morning Edition,* are all very smart. Even Michelle Malkin is probably not actually dumb. And anyway, you don't need a high IQ or a Ph.D. to believe in law and human rights and the Golden Rule. The problem is fear. The media are afraid of looking too "liberal," intellectuals are afraid of being called "anti-American"—and they will be if they challenge too vigorously the crimes being committed in America's name—Democrats are afraid of having their remaining bits of turf plowed under and sown with salt by the Republicans, the left is afraid of looking too "secular" and not "supporting the troops," and ordinary people are afraid of being blown up by the terrorist next door.

Fear dust. That's what it is. Fear dust.

•◄ JANUARY 24, 2005 ►•

Jesus to the Rescue?

Can a dose of Christianity stiffen the Democrats' spine, win back Kansas, and bring people power to the anemic left? In the wake of the 2004 election, quite a few powerful liberals are wondering if they can frame their politics as "faith" the way the right has so effectively done. One of the people the Democrats have invited to tell them how to go about this is the evangelical Protestant activist Jim Wallis, a founder of the antipoverty group Call to Renewal and editor of the magazine *Sojourners*. Wallis, an early supporter of Bush's faith-based initiative, is on a roll. In late November he appeared with Al Sharpton, Jerry Falwell, and the Reverend Richard Land on the notorious all-male "values" debate on *Meet the Press*. His new book, *God's Politics*, currently hovers at the top of the Amazon list.

I admit I approached the book with a bit of an edge, having just seen the new film version of *The Merchant of Venice*, in which the callous anti-Semitism of the Venetian smart set is rendered with unusual vividness. This led me to further gloomy instances, from the Crusades and the Salem witch trials to the Magdalene laundries and the anti-evolution policies of the Dover, Pennsylvania, school board. After all, the case for Christianizing progressive politics is not just about quoting the Bible more, or framing healthcare as a religious value. It's about lowering the wall between church and state, giving churches more power, more rights, and more taxpayer money. The argument in favor often boils down to majority rule—most Americans claim to be devout Christians—but that's actually the argument against it. Look what Christians did when they had the chance! Preventing religious wars and godly tyranny was the original purpose behind the Founding Fathers' ban on the establishment of religion, and subsequent history has hardly out-moded their wisdom.

Wallis draws a sharp line between the God-on-our-side Christianity responsible for countless evils and the social-justice kind he favors. Yet the triumphalism and self-righteousness he condemns in the former crops up throughout *God's Politics*: "religion" and "faith" are usually syn-onyms for Christianity, and Christianity mostly means evangelical Protestantism. Evangelicals get most of the credit for everything good in U.S. history, from women's suffrage to the civil rights movement. This would surprise skeptics like Elizabeth Cady Stanton, who spent her life battling scriptural arguments for male supremacy, and the secular Jews and leftists who made up so much of the civil rights movement's white base. And what about the opponents of women's rights and racial inte-gration? Weren't a lot of *them* evangelicals too? At times Wallis seems to be in a kind of denial: If it's wrong, it isn't truly evangelical, therefore evangelicalism is purely good. Today's robust evangelical right is the fault of—wait for it—"secular fundamentalists"! Blame it on the ACLU.

Wallis's God calls on Christians to fight racism, poverty, war, and vi-olence. What's wrong with mustering support for these worthy goals by presenting them in the language spoken by so many Americans? The trouble is, the other side does that too. You can find anything you want in the Bible—well, almost anything. Thus, the more insistently people bring Christianity into politics, the more political argument becomes a matter of Christian hermeneutics. Does God say gays should be executed or married? "Spare the rod" or "suffer the little children"? I don't see how we benefit as a society from translating politics into theology. We are left with the same debates and a diminished range of ways in which to think about them. And, of course, a diminished number of voices—because if you're not a believer, you're out of the discussion. In this sense, Wallis's evangelicalism is as much a power play as Pat Robertson's.

And Wallis is as much a power player. By a remarkable act of prov-idence, God's politics turn out to be curiously tailored to the current cri-sis of the Democratic Party. God, like many of the black, Hispanic, Catholic, and working-class voters who voted for Bush in 2004, is an economic progressive and a family-values conservative. He doesn't like "pornography," divorce, abortion, or gay marriage (civil unions are okay). It's interesting that in his earlier book *The Soul of Politics* Wallis cited numerous women theologians, while *God's Politics* mentions not one. Perhaps this is because the liberationist theologians he wrote about in *The Soul of Politics* are mostly very strong feminists who think women are capable of making moral decisions about childbearing and that abortion can be one such decision. Wallis constantly accuses "the left" of resisting "moral" arguments. I would say it is he who resists fully engaging moral arguments that differ from his own.

The fact is, "seamless garment" Catholicism aside, the denominations that share his liberal views are pro-choice—most of the mainline Protestant churches, to say nothing of Reform and Conservative Judaism. (Just recently, more than 2,250 religious leaders from more than thirty-five faith traditions endorsed a strongly worded pro-choice statement from the Religious Institute on Sexual Morality, Justice, and Healing.) No wonder Wallis would rather talk about something else. Fortunately, God shares his priorities: Wallis often points out that the Bible mentions poverty thousands of times and abortion only a few. I'm not sure what this tells us—first we eradicate poverty and *then* we force women to have babies against their will? But in any case, Wallis is wrong: The Bible doesn't mention abortion even once. Wallis cites the text anti-choicers commonly use to justify their position: "For it was you who formed my inward parts; you knit me together in my mother's womb" (Psalms 139:13). Say what? Nothing about abortion there, pro or con. Nobody who wasn't sure that somewhere in the Bible there *must* be a proof text against terminating a pregnancy would read that meaning into these words.

That so many Christians are firmly persuaded that the Bible condemns abortion suggests that God's politics tend to be the politics of the people who claim to speak for him. Since these men, and now women, have been arguing for centuries without reaching agreement on even the simplest matters, the rest of us are entitled to wonder if perhaps they are reading the wrong book.

•◄ FEBRUARY 7, 2005 ►•

Summers of Our Discontent

As the saying goes, behind every successful woman is a man who is surprised. Harvard president Larry Summers apparently is that man. A distinguished economist who was Treasury Secretary under Clinton, Summers caused a firestorm on January 14, when, speaking from notes at a conference on academic diversity, he argued that tenured women are rare in math and science for three reasons, which he listed in descending order of importance. One, women choose family commitments over the eighty-hour weeks achievement in those fields requires; two, fewer women than men have the necessary genetic gifts; and three, women are discriminated against. Following standard economic theory, Summers largely discounted discrimination: A first-rate woman rejected by one university would surely be snapped up by a rival. We're back to women's lack of commitment and brainpower.

On campus, Summers has lost big—he has had to apologize, appoint a committee, and endure many a hairy eyeball from the faculty, and complaints from furious alumnae like me. In the press, he's done much better: Provocative thinker brought down by PC feminist mob! Women *are* dumber! Steven Pinker says so! The *New York Times* even ran a supportive op-ed by Charles Murray without identifying him as the coauthor of *The Bell Curve,* the discredited farrago of racist claptrap. While much was made of MIT biologist Nancy Hopkins walking out of his talk—what about free speech, what about Truth?—we heard little about how Summers, who says he only wanted to spark a discussion, has refused to release his remarks. The bold challenger of campus orthodoxy apparently doesn't want the world to know what he actually said.

Do men have an innate edge in math and science? Perhaps someday we will live in a world free of the gender bias and stereotyping we know exists today both in and out of the classroom, and we will be able to answer that question, if anyone is still asking it. But we know we don't live in a bias-free world now: Girls are steered away from math and science from the moment they are born. The interesting fact is that, thanks partly to antidiscrimination laws that have forced open closed doors, they have steadily increased their performance nonetheless. Most of my Radcliffe classmates remember being firmly discouraged from anything to do with numbers or labs; one was flatly told that women couldn't be physicians—at her Harvard med school interview. Today women obtain 48 percent of B.A.s in math, 57 percent in biology and agricultural science, half of all places in med school, and they are steadily increasing their numbers as finalists in the Intel high school science contest (fifteen out of forty this year, and three out of four in New York City).

Every gain women have made in the past 200 years has been in the face of experts insisting they couldn't do it and didn't really want to. Biology, now trotted out to "prove" women's incapacity for math and science, used to "prove" that they shouldn't go to college at all. As women progress, the proponents of innate inferiority simply adapt their arguments to explain why further advancement is unlikely. But how can we know that in 2005, any more than we knew it in 1905? I'd like to hear those experts explain this instead: The number of tenure offers to women at Harvard has gone down in each of Summers's three years as president, from nine in thirty-six tenures to three in thirty-two. (The year before his arrival, it was thirteen women out of thirty-six.) Surely women's genes have not deteriorated since 2001?

Whatever they may be in theory, in the workplace, biological incapacity and natural preference are the counters used to defend against accusations of discrimination. Summers argues that competition makes discrimination irrational; that wouldn't hold, though, if an entire field is pervaded with discrimination, if there's a consensus that women don't belong there, and if female candidates are judged more harshly by all potential employers. It also doesn't work if the threat of competition isn't so credible: It will be a long time before the Ivies feel the heat from Northwestern, which has improved its profile by hiring the first-rate women they foolishly let go. The history of women and minorities in the workplace shows that vigorous enforcement of antidiscrimination law is what drives progress. Moreover, the competition argument can be turned against Summers: After all, given its prestige and wealth, Harvard could "compete" for women with any university on the planet. So why doesn't it?

This brings us to that eighty-hour week and women's domestic "choices." It's a truism that career ladders are based on the traditional male life plan—he knocks himself out in his twenties and thirties while his wife raises the kids, mends his socks, and types his papers. If women had been included from the start, the ladder would look rather different— careers might peak later, taking a semester off to have a baby would not blot your copybook, women would not be expected to do huge amounts of academic service work and then be blamed at tenure time for not publishing more. By treating this work culture as fixed, and women as the problem, Summers lets academia off the hook. Yet Harvard, with its $23 billion endowment, doesn't even offer free daycare to grad students.

There's a ton of research on all the subjects raised by Summers—the socialization of girls; conscious and unconscious gender bias in teaching, hiring, and promotion; what makes talented females, like Intel finalists, drop out of science at every stage; what makes motherhood so hard to combine with a career. We are past the day when brilliant women could be expected to sit quietly while a powerful man parades his ignorance of that scholarship and of their experience. It is not "provocative" when the president of Harvard justifies his university's lamentable record by recalling that his toddler daughter treated toy trucks like dolls. It's an insult to his audience. What was his point, anyway? That she'll grow up and flunk calculus? That she'll get a job in a daycare center?

If Summers wants to know why women are underrepresented in math and science, he should do his homework, beginning with Nancy Hopkins's pathbreaking 1999 study of bias against female faculty at MIT. And then he should ask them.

●◄ FEBRUARY 21, 2005 ►●

Invisible Women

Women don't shout. Women don't like politics. Women shrink from intellectual debate. Women don't *try*. It's time for another round of "What's Wrong with Women?" Last month's category was science. This month it's punditry, sparked by a testy (well, nasty) letter from syndicated columnist and FOX-TV commentator Susan Estrich to Michael Kinsley, the courtly editorial and opinion editor of the *Los Angeles Times*, pointing out the lack of female talent on his op-ed pages: In nine weeks, only 20 percent of pieces were written by women. Now everybody's jumping in: "Feminists Get Hysterical" (Heather Mac-Donald in *City Journal*) is a typical sentiment.

"There ought to be more women on op-ed pages in general. Over time, I intend to make that happen," said Fred Hiatt, editorial page editor of the *Washington Post,* which counts one woman, Anne Applebaum, among its nineteen pundits; in the first two months of 2005 one in ten op-ed pieces were by women. Take your time, Mr. Hiatt! As Applebaum warns, you don't want to hire untalented women who'll just write about "women's issues." *Her* friends got their bylines by "having clear views, knowing their subjects, writing well and learning to ignore the ad hominem attacks that go with the job." And you know how few women meet those lofty criteria! "The pool of available people doing opinion writing is still tilted toward men," said *New York Times* editorial page editor Gail Collins. "There are probably fewer women, in the great cosmic scheme of things, who feel comfortable writing very straight opinion stuff, and they're less comfortable hearing something on the news and batting something out." Come April, the *Times* will have seven male op-ed columnists, plus Maureen Dowd. Not to worry, though, Dowd writes, there are "plenty of brilliant women. . . . We just need to find and nurture them."

Oh, nurture my eye. It may be true that more men than women like to bloviate and "bat things out"—socialization does count for something. So do social rewards: I have seen men advance professionally on levels of aggression, self-promotion, and hostility that would have a woman carted off to a loony bin—unless, of course, she happens to be Ann Coulter. But feminine psychology doesn't explain why all five of *USA Today's* political columnists are male, or why *Time's* eleven columnists are male— down to the four in Arts and Entertainment—or why at *Newsweek* it's one out of six in print and two out of thirteen on the Web. According to *Editor and Publisher,* the proportion of female syndicated columnists (one in four) hasn't budged since 1999. The tiny universe of political-opinion writers includes plenty of women who hold their own with men, who do not wilt at the prospect of an angry e-mail, who have written cover stories and bestsellers and won prizes—and whose phone numbers are likely already in the Rolodexes of the editors who wonder where the women are. How hard could it be to "find" Barbara Ehrenreich, who filled in for Thomas Friedman for one month last summer and wrote nine of the best columns the *Times* has seen in a decade? Or Dahlia Lithwick, legal correspondent for *Slate,* another Friedman fill-in, who actually possesses a deep grasp of the field she covers—which cannot always be said for John Tierney, who begins his *Times* column in April? What about Susan Faludi? The *Village Voice's* Sharon Lerner? Debra Dickerson? Wendy Kaminer? *The Progressive's* Ruth Conniff? Laura Flanders? Debbie Nathan? Ruth Rosen, veteran of the *L.A. Times* and the *San Francisco Chronicle*? Our own Patricia Williams and Naomi Klein? Natalie Angier, bestselling author and top *New York Times* science writer, would be a fabulous op-ed columnist. And, not to be one of those shrinking violets everyone's suddenly so down on, what about me? Am I a potted plant?

You'll note I've mostly named liberals and feminists—I'm sure there are good women writers on the right out there, too, and their job prospects are probably a lot rosier. A conservative woman who endlessly attacks feminists, like *The New Yorker's* Caitlin Flanagan or the *Los Angeles Times's* departed Norah Vincent or the *Boston Globe's* Cathy Young— what could be hotter than that?

Besides being false and insulting, all this fuss about women not having the *cojones* for no-holds-barred debate overlooks the fact that, as Deborah Tannen pointed out in the *L.A. Times,* there are many ways to write political commentary. Not every male columnist is a fire-breather, an instant expert, a tub-thumper, an obnox. Think of the *Washington Post*'s E. J. Dionne, Jr., or *USA Today*'s Walter Shapiro, both mannerly and sweet-natured to a fault. Some columnists use their perch to do crusading reporting—Bob Herbert's great strength—to tell stories, to analyze ideas and policies, to ask questions, to skewer received opinion with wit and humor. And then there are the ones who just drone boringly on. Surely there are women capable of that!

That opinion writing is a kind of testosterone-powered food fight is a popular idea in the blogosphere. Male bloggers are always wondering where the women are and why women can't/don't/won't throw bananas. After all, anyone can have a blog, right? In the wake of the Estrich-Kinsley contretemps, the *Washington Monthly* blogger Kevin Drum mused upon the absence of women bloggers and got a major earful from women bloggers, who are understandably sick of hearing that they don't exist. "I'm staring you right in the face, Kevin," wrote Avedon Carol (sideshow.me.uk), "and even though you've said you read me every day you don't have me on your blogroll. It's things like this that make me tear out my hair when people wonder why women are underrepresented. . . ." There are actually lots of women political bloggers out there—spend half an hour reading them and you will never again say women aren't as argumentative as men! But what makes a blog visible is links, and male bloggers tend not to link to women (to his credit, Kevin Drum has added nineteen to his blogroll). Perhaps they sense it might interfere with the circle jerk in cyberspace—the endless mutual self-infatuation that is one of the less attractive aspects of the blogging phenom.

Or maybe, like so many op-ed editors, they just don't see women, even when the women are right in front of them.

•◄ APRIL 4, 2005 ►•

Backward Christian Soldiers

Maybe, just maybe, the religious right and its Republican friends have finally gone too far with the Terri Schiavo case. Americans may tell pollsters the earth was created in six days flat and dinosaurs shared the planet with Adam and Eve, but I don't believe they want Tom DeLay to be their personal physician. I don't think they want fanatics moaning and praying outside the hospital while they're making hard decisions. I don't think they want people getting arrested trying to "feed" their comatose relatives, or issuing death threats against judges and spouses in the name of "life." I don't think John Q. Public wants Jeb Bush to adopt his wife or Newt Gingrich to call her by her first name or Senator Frist to diagnose her by video, or Jesse Jackson to pop in at the last minute for a prayer and a photo-op.

The Terri Schiavo freak show is so deeply crazy, so unhinged, such a brew of religiosity and hypocrisy and tabloid sensationalism, just maybe it is clueing people in to where the right's moral triumphalism is leading us. Before Congress jumped into the act, Republicans may have seen a great opportunity to paint the Democrats as the "party of death." No thanks to the Dems, who mostly cowered, the stratagem backfired: The weekend after Schiavo's feeding tube was withdrawn, 75 percent of Americans told CBS pollsters they wanted government to stay out of end-of-life issues, and 82 percent thought Congress and the President should have kept away. Jesse Jackson seems not to have gotten the memo—he's calling for the Florida legislature to overturn thirty years of carefully crafted medical ethics and pass a previously rejected bill requiring patients in a persistent vegetative state to remain on life support forever, unless they've left a written directive to the contrary. If that's the "religious left," forget it.

It's about time Americans woke up. The Schiavo case only looks unprecedented: For decades, women seeking to terminate pregnancies have faced gauntlets of screamers, invasions of privacy, violence in the name of "saving babies," charges of murder and of evil motives, politically motivated legal obstacles, spurious medical "expertise" (abortion causes breast cancer; Terri Schiavo just needs therapy). There is the same free-floating vitriol: Abortion is the "Silent Holocaust," while, according to Peggy Noonan, those who support Ms. Schiavo's right to die are on "a low road that twists past Columbine and leads toward Auschwitz" (that would be the same road that Tom DeLay and his family went down when they withheld life support from his critically injured father—the same road, in fact, that Robert Schindler, Terri's father, took when he turned off his mother's life support). Randall Terry, the Operation Rescue showman who wants to make America a "Christian nation" and to "execute" doctors who perform abortions, is the Schindlers' chief strategist; other Operation Rescuers in the hospice parking lot include the Reverend Pat Mahoney, who freely gives out Michael Schiavo's home address; Cheryl Sullenger, who served two years for conspiring to bomb an abortion clinic in 1987; and Scott Heldreth, a convicted sex offender who told an AP reporter that driving long hours to the hospice and getting arrested was all his ten-year-old son's idea.

In this transposition of the abortion drama, Terri Schiavo is the defenseless fetus; her husband, Michael, is the callous "convenience" aborter; and the Schindlers are the would-be adoptive couple doomed to childlessness by tyrannical judges. But there's a difference. Abortion happens to women—bad girls, sluts. Because of the shame and secrecy around abortion, you can believe, probably wrongly, that you don't know anyone who's had one and, thanks to your virtuous life, that you would never need one yourself. But anyone can fall into a permanent coma, and death comes to us all. Millions of people have had to make end-of-life decisions for loved ones or for themselves; they've had to think about what a life is—a pulse? a reflex? a thought?—and what a person is, and what that person would have wanted. And because of this collective experience, most Americans know that to "err on the side of life," as the enthusiastic death-penalty fan and Medicaid-cutter George W. Bush advises, is just a slogan. Your wife with Alzheimer's who's stopped eating and drinking is alive. Do you intubate or not? Your father in a stroke-induced coma is alive. Do you treat his pneumonia or see it as "the old man's friend"? When do you go for aggressive treatment, when do you let the person go, when do you decide the person has already gone and only their body is there in the bed? Over three decades, Americans won the right to make these painful, intimate decisions for themselves. That right—not disability rights or the possibility of medical miracles—is what is at stake in the Schiavo case. Most people, especially young people like Terri Schiavo, are never going to write living wills. Should no weight at all be given their spoken wishes or the conviction of their loved ones that, like Tom DeLay's father, they "would never have wanted to live like this"?

For many ordinary Americans, the stem-cell debate was the first time the religious right strove to deprive them of something valuable. It's one thing to make women pay for sex with childbirth, or to deprive your children of modern scientific education, or to ostracize homosexuals, but it's going too far to value a frozen embryo more than Cousin Jim with Parkinson's. Now, with the Schiavo case, Americans have another opportunity to ask themselves if they really want to live in Randall Terry's world, where the next Michael and Terri Schiavo could be any one of us.

•◀ APRIL 18, 2005 ▶•

Andrea Dworkin, 1946–2005

I first heard of Andrea Dworkin in 1968. She had been arrested in an antiwar demonstration and jailed at the old Women's House of Detention in Greenwich Village, where male doctors subjected her to brutal internal exams. Her name was in the news because she had gone public with her story. My good, kind, radical, civil libertarian parents thought this was ridiculous. What did she expect, this privileged white woman, this "Bennington girl"? It wasn't that they didn't believe her, exactly. It was that they didn't see why she was making such a big, princessy fuss. It was like getting arrested and complaining about the food.

Andrea Dworkin died on April 9 at fifty-eight—she of the denim overalls and the wild hair and wilder pronouncements. Although she denied ever uttering the most famous sound bite attributed to her, that all intercourse is rape, she came pretty close: "Fucking is the means by which the male colonizes the female"; "in seduction, the rapist often bothers to buy a bottle of wine." She argued that pornography was an instruction manual for rape, that women had the right to "execute" rapists and pedophiles; toward the end of her life she declared that maybe women, like the Jews, should have their own country. The counsel of despair, and crazy, too—but by then Dworkin was ill, not much in demand as a speaker, and several of her major books were out of print. The 1980s were long over: On campus, the militant anti-rape marches and speak-outs of Take Back the Night had morphed into cheery V-Day, which marries antiviolence activism to a celebration of women's sexuality.

The antipornography feminism Dworkin did so much to promote seems impossibly quaint today, when Paris Hilton can parlay an embarrassing sex video into mainstream celebrity and the porn star Jenna Jameson rides the *New York Times* bestseller list. But even in its heyday it was a blind alley. Not just because porn, like pot, is here to stay, not just because the Bible and the Koran—to say nothing of fashion, advertising, and Britney Spears—do far more harm to women, not even because of the difficulty of defining such slippery terms as "degrading to women," a phrase that surely did not mean the same thing to Dworkin as it did to the Christian conservatives who helped make the antiporn ordinance she wrote with Catharine MacKinnon briefly law in Indianapolis. Like the temperance movement, antiporn activism mistook a symptom of male dominance for the cause. Nor did it have much to do with actually existing raped and abused women. "For God's sake, take away his Nina Hartley videos" is not a cry often heard in shelters or emergency rooms. If by magic pornography vanished from the land, women would still be the second sex—underpaid, disrespected, lacking in power over their own bodies. Rape, battery, torture, even murder would still be hugely titillating to both sexes, just as in Shakespeare's day, and women would still be blamed, by both sexes, for the violence men inflict on them. What made Dworkin's obsession with pornography so bizarre is that she herself should have known it for a diversion. After all, she frequently pointed out that male dominance is entwined with our very notion of what sex is, with what is arousing, with what feels "right." Like Foucault (who, as Susan Bordo pointed out, usually gets credit for this insight), Dworkin showed how deeply and pervasively power relationships are encoded into our concepts of sexuality and in how many complex ways everyday life normalizes those relationships. "Standards of beauty," she wrote in *Woman-Hating* (1974), "describe in precise terms the relationship that an individual will have to her own body. They prescribe her motility, spontaneity, posture, gait, the uses to which she can put her body. They define precisely the dimensions of her physical freedom. And of course, the relationship between physical freedom and psychological development, intellectual possibility, and creative potential is an umbilical one." Somewhere along the way, she lost interest in the multiplicity and the complexity of the system she did much to lay bare.

Dworkin was an oversimplifier and a demagogue. She wouldn't debate feminists who opposed her stance on porn, just men like Alan Der-showitz, thus reinforcing in the public mind the false impression that hers was the only feminist position and that this was a male-female de-bate. There is some truth to Laura Miller's quip in *Salon* that "even when she was right, she made the public conversation stupider." But, frankly, the public conversation is usually not very illuminating and on the subject of women has been notably dim for some time. At least Dworkin put some important hidden bits of reality out there on the table. There *is* a lot of coercion embedded in normal, legal, everyday sex-uality. Sometimes the seducer *is* a rapist with a bottle of wine. A whole world of sexist assumptions lay behind my parents' attitude back in 1968: This is what happens to women who take chances, male brutality is a fact of life, talking about sexual violence is shameful, "Bennington girls" should count their blessings. Polite, liberal, reasonable feminists could never have exploded that belief system.

Andrea Dworkin was a living visual stereotype—the feminist as fat, hairy, makeup-scorning, unkempt lesbian. Perhaps that was one reason she was such a media icon—she "proved" that feminism was for women who couldn't get a man. Women have wrestled with that charge for decades, at considerable psychic cost. These days, feminism is all sexy uplift, a cross between a workout and a makeover. Go for it, girls—breast implants, Botox, face-lifts, corsets, knitting, boxing, prostitution. Whatever floats your self-esteem! Meanwhile, the public face of organi-zational feminism is perched atop a power suit and frozen in a deferential smile. Perhaps some childcare? Insurance coverage for contraception? Legal abortion, tragic though it surely is? Or maybe not so much legal abortion—when I ran into Naomi Wolf the other day, she told me she had just finished an article calling for the banning of abortion after the first trimester. Cream and sugar with that abortion ban, sir?

I never thought I would miss unfair, infuriating, over-the-top An-drea Dworkin. But I do. And even more I miss the movement that had room for her.

●◀ MAY 2, 2005 ▶●

Practice What You Preach

Pharmacists think they have the right to deny women birth control and the morning-after pill. Senator Frist thinks God wants more ultraconservative judges on the federal bench and if you disagree, well, you know where you're going. Forget common ground, it's time to divide up the country. The red-state blue-state map is too crude—too many blue pegs in red holes and vice versa. In the great tradition of American individualism and modern in-depth polling procedures, let's make everyone respond, in writing, to a detailed questionnaire on hot-button "values issues" and then be legally compelled to live by the answers they give. It's a glorious blend of academic right and left—rational choice theory (people make decisions in their own best interests) meets postmodernism (there is no one truth).

Consider what happened in Louisiana, Arkansas, and Arizona, where engaged couples can opt for a more restrictive form of marriage. Despite its popularity among conservative pundits and preachers, covenant marriage—which allows only a select few grounds for divorce, like infidelity—has attracted less than 2 percent of marrying couples. That tells us something important about the way people want to live as opposed to the way they think other people should live, and what people choose when they have to live with the results. Let's apply that principle more broadly. For example:

1. *Stem-cell research.* According to an NBC/*Wall Street Journal* poll, 22 percent of the population think extracting stem cells from pre-embryos frozen in fertility clinics is unethical. These tender souls have prevailed upon the Bush administration to restrict federal funds for

stem-cell research. This has resulted in a bidding war among states eager to lure researchers, which nobody sees as the best way to do the science. Why not split the difference? Bring back federal funding, but those who oppose it can take the appropriate tax cut. The catch is, they agree to forgo any cures stem-cell research might yield: They'll have to live with their Parkinson's, diabetes, Alzheimer's, or cancer, which, since they believe stem-cell research is wrong, is surely what they would want to do anyway.

2. *Creationism.* According to NBC, 44 percent of Americans believe that the biblical account of Creation—God, six days, species created individually in the forms that now exist—is literally true. According to Gallup, 45 percent believe the Earth is at most 10,000 years old. A CBS News poll found that 65 percent believe these versions of events should be taught in school alongside evolution, and that given the opportunity 37 percent would ditch Darwinism altogether. Under the new plan, creationists could continue their efforts to wreck science education and dumb down their kids—but first, they would pledge to abstain from any real-life benefits of evolutionary theory. Flu vaccines, for example, rely for their effectiveness on yearly reformulation to account for the evolution of the influenza virus. No evolution? Achoo for you!

3. *Terri Schiavo–like situations.* According to a Fox News/Opinion Dynamics poll, 24 percent of the population worry they'll be allowed to die if their brain turns into boiled squash. Sixty-one percent fear that they'll be kept alive forever in a boiled-squash state. Under the new plan, everyone signs a living will, to be updated yearly. Those who opt for life are enrolled in the private squash-maintenance program of their choice— Comatose for Christ, Operation Get Randall Terry on TV, Concerned Women for Zucchini. Those who prefer a quick exit go off in a delightful NORML-funded haze of controlled substances—they'll be totally unaware of it, unfortunately, but it's a nice thought.

4. *Teen sex.* Every school will offer both abstinence-only and comprehensive sex ed—parents can sign their kids up for the course they prefer. In states with notification/consent laws, parents will remain free to dis-

courage or prevent their daughters from having abortions. The catch is, if they choose this route, they are legally responsible for the total financial support through college of the babies their underage daughters produce. After all, if a girl is too young to learn about birth control, too young to have sex, and too young to decide on her own to have an abortion, she's obviously too young to be a mother. Having made the choice for her, the parents should bear the consequences. If they don't like this system, they can try to extract child support from the baby's father (or his parents), and good luck to them.

5. *Capital punishment.* Against it? Should you be convicted of murder or the like, instead of lethal injection you get a long stay at a Swedish-style prison with college classes, a salad bar, and condom dispensers in every shower room. Pro–death penalty? Uh-oh, there's Sister Helen Prejean. Your appeal must not be going well. You should have more carefully evaluated your propensity for mayhem and/or the fallibility of the justice system.

6. *English only.* Do you blow a gasket when your ATM asks you if you'd like to bank *en español*? Check the English-only box, and get priority on tract housing in Utah or Idaho. But first, just to make sure your own linguistic skills do justice to the language of Shakespeare, Woolf, and Baldwin, you'll be enrolled in a free, intensive, yearlong literature class taught by brilliant, dedicated, culturally conservative professors who firmly believe they failed to get tenure at Ivy League universities because of their resistance to grade inflation and what passes for education these days. Less than a B sends you back to the land from which your ancestors most recently escaped.

7. *The judiciary.* Guardians of liberty or power-hungry perverts? Maybe a little of both? If you think the courts should say what's constitutional, your lawsuits get decided by judges, and, yes, that includes Antonin Scalia. If you think judges have too much power, so be it: Your lawsuits go before a panel made up of marital counselors, rational choice theorists, postmodernists, and the people who decide whether your HMO covers your hospital bills.

Check your mailbox for the values questionnaire, and think very, very carefully about your answers. For the first time in history, you will be stuck with them.

•◀ MAY 16, 2005 ▶•

Virginity or Death!

Imagine a vaccine that would protect women from a serious gyneco-logical cancer. Wouldn't that be great? Well, both Merck and Glaxo-SmithKline recently announced that they have conducted successful trials of vaccines that protect against the human papilloma virus. HPV is not only an incredibly widespread sexually transmitted infection but is responsible for 93 percent of cases of cervical cancer, which is diag-nosed in 10,000 American women a year and kills around 4,000. The new vaccines target two strains that between them cause 70 percent of cervical cancer cases. Wonderful, you are probably thinking, all we need to do is vaccinate girls (and boys too for good measure) before they be-come sexually active, around puberty, and most HPV—and eventually most cervical cancer—goes poof. Not so fast: We're living in God's country now. The Christian right doesn't like the sound of this vaccine at all. "Giving the HPV vaccine to young women could be potentially harmful," Bridget Maher of the Family Research Council told the British magazine *New Scientist,* "because they may see it as a license to engage in premarital sex." Raise your hand if you think that what is keeping girls virgins now is the threat of getting cervical cancer in midlife from a disease they've probably never heard of.

I remember when people rolled their eyeballs if you suggested that opposition to abortion was less about "life" than about sex, especially sex for women. You have to admit that thesis is looking pretty solid these days. No matter what the consequences of sex—pregnancy, disease, death—abstinence for singles is the only answer. Just as it's better for gays to get AIDS than use condoms, it's better for a woman to get cancer than have sex before marriage. It's honor killing on the installment plan.

Christian conservatives have a special reason to be less than thrilled about the HPV vaccine. Although not as famous as chlamydia or herpes, HPV has the distinction of not being preventable by condoms. It's Exhibit A in those gory high school slide shows that try to scare kids away from sex, and it is also useful for undermining the case for rubbers generally—why bother when you could get HPV anyway? In 2000, Congressman (now Senator) Tom Coburn of Oklahoma, who used to give gruesome lectures on HPV for young congressional aides, even used HPV to propose warning labels on condoms. With HPV potentially eliminated, the anti-sex brigade will lose a card it has regarded as a trump unless it can persuade parents that vaccinating their daughters will turn them into tramps, and that sex today is worse than cancer tomorrow. According to *New Scientist,* 80 percent of parents want the vaccine for their daughters—but their priests and pastors haven't worked them over yet.

What is it with these right-wing Christians? Faced with a choice between sex and death, they choose death every time. No sex ed or contraception for teens, no sex for the unwed, no condoms for gays, no abortion for anyone—even for that poor thirteen-year-old pregnant girl in a group home in Florida. I would really like to hear the persuasive argument that this middle-schooler with no home and no family would have been better off giving birth against her will, and that the state of Florida, which totally failed to keep her safe, should have been allowed, against its own laws, to compel this child to bear a child. She was too young to have sex, too young to know her own mind about abortion— but not too young to be forced onto the delivery table for one of the most painful experiences human beings endure, in which the risk of death for her was three times as great as in abortion. Ah, Christian compassion! Christian sadism, more likely. It was the courts that showed humanity when they let the girl terminate her pregnancy.

As they flex their political muscle, right-wing Christians increasingly reveal their condescending view of women as moral children who need to be kept in line sexually by fear. That's why anti-choicers will never answer the call of pro-choicers to join them in reducing abortions by making birth control more widely available: They want it to be *less* available. Their real interest goes way beyond protecting fetuses—it's in keeping sex tied to reproduction to keep women in their place. If pre-venting abortion was what they cared about, they'd be giving birth con-trol and emergency contraception away on street corners instead of supporting pharmacists who refuse to fill prescriptions and hospitals that don't tell rape victims about the existence of EC. Dr. David Hager would never use his position with the FDA to impose his personal views of sexual morality on women in crisis. Instead of blocking nonprescrip-tion status for emergency contraception on the specious grounds that it will encourage teen promiscuity, he would take note of the six studies, three including teens, that show no relation between sexual activity and access to EC. He would be calling the loudest for Plan B to be stocked with the toothpaste in every drugstore in the land. How sexist is denial of Plan B? Anti-choicers may pooh-pooh the effectiveness of condoms, but they aren't calling to restrict their sale in order to keep boys chaste.

While the FDA dithers, the case against selling EC over the counter weakens by the day. Besides the now exploded argument that it will let teens run wild, opponents argue that it prevents implantation of a fer-tilized egg—which would make it an "abortifacient" if you believe that pregnancy begins when sperm and egg unite. However, new research by the Population Council shows that EC doesn't work by blocking im-plantation; it only prevents ovulation. True, it's not possible to say it never blocks implantation, James Trussell, director of the Office of Pop-ulation Research at Princeton, told me, and to anti-choice hard-liners once in a thousand times is enough. But then, many things can block implantation, including breast-feeding. Are the reverends going to come out for formula-feeding now?

"It all comes down to the evils of sex," says Trussell. "That's an ide-ological position impervious to empirical evidence."

•◀ May 30, 2005 ▶•

Stiffed

Penises were all over the news as I sat down to write this column. On May 22 faces blushed scarlet in New York State when it came to light that over the past five years Medicaid has handed out free Viagra to 198 sex criminals. Apparently the state thought federal rules required no less. The next day, researchers released a study showing excellent results for Johnson & Johnson's dapoxetine, a drug that prevents premature ejaculation and intensifies the male orgasm. True, rapists' access to taxpayer-funded stiffies vanished within hours, and they will probably have to buy their own dapoxetine too. But you have to admit, men are moving right along, sexually. They have drugs to help them get up and stay in and get out in a shower of sparks, and an array of private and public health plans to pay for these fleshly maneuvers. Last year Medicaid laid out approximately $38 million for impotence drugs; Medicare will start providing them for seniors next year at an estimated cost of nearly $2 billion over the following decade. Even the Defense Department covers them. Need I add that men don't have to worry that their pharmacist will ask to see a marriage license or plug their name into the sex-offender registry before handing over those little blue pills?

No, the double standard still waves over the nation's bedrooms. The only new birth-control method coming up soon is actually a nostalgia item, the Today Sponge, beloved by *Seinfeld*'s Elaine, which will be returning to drugstores later this year. Two decades into the AIDS epidemic, the only woman-controlled means of protection against HIV—now the leading cause of death among black women age twenty-five through thirty-four—is the aesthetically repulsive, cumbersome, and hard-to-find female condom. Hormone replacement therapy, promoted since the 1950s as the fountain of feminine youth and sexual vitality, looks to be mostly hype, with the possibility of heart attack, stroke, and breast or ovarian cancer.

And what about sex aids for women? Where's that female Viagra they're always promising us? Most newspapers didn't even report that in December an FDA panel turned down Procter & Gamble's application for Intrinsa, a testosterone patch intended to raise libido in women whose ovaries have been removed. The problem wasn't that Intrinsa didn't work (the panel voted 14 to 3 that the manufacturers' trials showed a meaningful improvement in desire and pleasure); the issue was health risks as well as the potential for "off-label use" by women who had simply lost their mojo. A "lifestyle drug" for women! Can't have that. Men, of course, have been known to use Viagra recreationally, and Viagra, moreover, is not without risk: It has been associated with fatal heart attacks and eye damage. Here's what gets me, though: FDA panelist Dr. David Hager voted against Intrinsa. Yes, *that* David Hager— the right-wing Christian ob-gyn accused of persistent marital rape by his former wife and now under scrutiny for his secret role, first revealed in *The Nation,* in killing over-the-counter status for emergency contraception. Maybe there are enough questions about Intrinsa's safety to justify the turn-down—but letting Hager vote on female sex drugs is like letting the Taliban vote on women's hemlines.

It didn't have to be this way. When it first came out, it looked like Viagra was going to be women's best friend. So precipitately did private insurers and government programs rush to cover the magical impotence remedy, the longstanding refusal by many insurers to cover contraception stood out, finally, as indefensibly sexist. (Viagra coverage was justified because impotence makes men depressed—poor Bob Dole! As we all know, fear of pregnancy has no such effect on women.) Pushed by feminist activists, twenty-one state legislatures since 1998 have mandated that private insurers cover birth control the same as other drugs. Even in those states, however, coverage remains spotty, thanks to business-friendly loopholes. And federal coverage is far from perfect: Medicare, which insures not just the elderly but also many young disabled people, does not cover contraception.

The biggest threat to contraception, though, is the right-wing

Christians who have put themselves in charge of the nation's wombs. (Viagra is pro-life, the Pill is pro-death—sperm rules!) It's not enough that they call emergency contraception—high doses of certain birth control pills, taken within seventy-two hours of intercourse—a "mini-abortion" (in fact, as I wrote last time, studies by the Population Council show that EC does not work by blocking implantation of a fertilized egg; it prevents ovulation). Now they've persuaded states to shift funds from family planning to "abortion alternatives." For the past two fiscal years and the upcoming one, Missouri has abolished state funding for family planning and boosted programs intended to encourage child-birth. More than 30,000 women who relied on state-funded birth control are now on their own—though if they get pregnant, the state will be happy to kick in some baby clothes or arrange an adoption. Likewise, the Texas legislature has just voted to divert funds from family planning to anti-choice "crisis pregnancy" centers, and Minnesota is considering a similar move.

It's all enough to make a girl go on sex strike—at least until Intrinsa gets the okay. After all, as President Bush seemed to be suggesting in a photo-op with babies who had been "adopted" as abandoned embryos, why get hot and bothered when you can be implanted with one of the thousands of leftover embryos languishing in fertility-clinic freezers, and save that clump of cells from certain death in the lab? Yes, thanks to the wonders of reproductive science, if you pay attention in abstinence-only sex-ed class, you too can have a virgin birth.

•◀ June 13, 2005 ▶•

If the Frame Fits . . .

In the wake of the 2004 election, Democrats have embarked on an orgy of what the linguist George Lakoff calls "reframing"—repositioning their policies linguistically to give them mass moral appeal. Prime candidate for a values makeover? Abortion, of course. It's as if the party, with its longstanding, if lukewarm, support for reproductive rights, were a family photo with Uncle Lou the molester right in the middle. Maybe if we cropped it to put him way off to the side? Or Photoshopped a big shadow onto his face? Or just decided to pretend he was nice Uncle Max? In "The Foreign Language of Choice," posted on AlterNet, Lakoff writes that he doesn't like "choice"—too consumerist. In fact, he doesn't even like "abortion"—too negative. He wants to "reparse" abortion in four ways. Dems should talk about it as an aspect of personal freedom from government interference, and as the regrettable outcome of right-wing opposition to sex ed and contraception. They should reclaim "life" by talking about the fact that "the United States has the highest rate of infant mortality in the industrialized world," thanks to poverty and lack of healthcare, which are the fault of conservatives, "who have been killing babies—real babies . . . [who] have been born and who people want and love" and damaging their health through antienvironmental policies that put toxins in mother's milk. Finally, they should talk about the thousands of women each year who become pregnant from rape: "Should the federal government force a woman to bear the child of her rapist?"

George Lakoff is really smart and eager to help, so why does this way of talking about "medical operations to end a pregnancy" make me want to reparse myself to a desert island? Is it the sly reference to rape victims coerced by the "federal government," object of much red-state loathing, when surely he knows that the relevant policies—on giving out emergency contraception in ERs, for example, or using Medicaid funds for abortions—are set at the state level, like most abortion laws? Is it the singling out of rape victims as uniquely deserving, which tacitly accepts the conservative "frame" of abortion as a way for sluts to evade the wages of sin? In fact, most American voters who favor abortion restrictions already make an exception for rape. The ones who don't—the 11 percent who would ban abortion completely—have already framed it to their satisfaction: Yes, the government should force rape victims to carry to term because the "child" should not be murdered for its father's crime.

Perhaps I'm naïve, but I keep thinking that reframing misses the point, which is to speak clearly from a moral center—precisely not to mince words and change the subject and turn the tables. I keep thinking that people are so disgusted by politics that the field is open for progressives who use plain language and stick to their guns and convey that they are real people, at home in their skin, and not a collection of blow-dried, focus-grouped holograms. I think this despite ample evidence to the contrary, like the successful Republican reframings of the estate tax as the "death tax" and George W. Bush as a salt-of-the-earth rancher. But, honestly: They say abortion, we say mercury in the breast milk? What if anti-choicers suggest going halfsies? Some abortion opponents—progressive evangelicals, seamless-garment Catholics—do care about babies after they are born.

Still, reframing proceeds apace. Hillary Clinton talks about abortion as sorrow, while calling on Republicans to join her in passing the Prevention First Act promoting contraception and, with Patty Murray, going after acting FDA head Lester Crawford for failing to make emergency contraception available over the counter. Howard Dean says he wants the "pro-life" vote, and before you know it, anti-choice Democrats get the nod to run for the Senate—Bob Casey in Pennsylvania and Jim Langevin in Rhode Island (who has since bowed out). NARAL, or, as it has reframed itself, NARAL Pro-choice America, placed an ad in *The Weekly Standard* calling on conservatives to "Please, Help Us Prevent Abortion" through better access to birth control. Responding to a poll showing that only 22 percent of Americans say abortion should be "generally available," NARAL is emphasizing "freedom and responsibility"—birth control, sex ed, emergency contraception. Responsibility is surely a bedrock American value. The trouble is, as William Saletan pointed out in a perceptive column on *Slate,* it means different things to different people. It can mean moral autonomy and free will, or it can mean suffering the consequences, accepting punishment. To NARAL, "freedom and responsibility" means knowing your body and using contraception, with EC or abortion as unmentioned backup. To an antichoicer, the same words might mean abstinence, with childbirth as the price of getting carried away.

There's a word that doesn't show up much in the new abortion frames: "women." Maybe it doesn't poll well. "Reframing" abortion is actually a kind of deframing, a way of taking it out of its real-life context, which is the experience of women, their bodies, their healthcare, their struggles, the caring work our society expects them to do for free. Lynn Paltrow, the brilliant lawyer who runs National Advocates for Pregnant Women, thinks the way to win grassroots support for abortion rights is to connect it to the whole range of reproductive and maternal rights: the right to have a home birth, to refuse a cesarean section, to know that a miscarriage or stillbirth—or simply taking a drink—will not land you in jail. The same ideology of fetal protection that antichoicers wield against abortion is used against women with wanted pregnancies. More broadly, Paltrow argues that the right to abortion would have more support if it were presented as just one of the things women need to care for their families, along with paid maternity leave, childcare, quality healthcare for all, economic and social support for mothers and children, strong environmental policies that protect fetuses and children.

But when was the last time you heard a Democrat talk about paid maternity leave? It's been reframed right out of the picture.

•◄ JULY 11, 2005 ►•

Should *Roe* Go?

S hould pro-choicers just give up and let *Roe* go? With the resigna-
tion of Sandra Day O'Connor, more people are asking that question. Democratic Party insiders quietly wonder if abandoning abortion
rights would win back white Catholics and evangelicals. A chorus of
pundits—among them David Brooks in the *New York Times* and the
Washington Post's Benjamin Wittes writing in *The Atlantic*—argue that
Roe's unforeseen consequences exact too high a price: on democracy, on
public discourse, even, paradoxically, on abortion rights. By the early
1970s, this argument goes, public opinion was moving toward relaxing
abortion bans legislatively—New York got rid of its ban in 1970, and
one-third of states had begun to liberalize their abortion laws by 1973.
By suddenly handing total victory to one side, *Roe* fueled a mighty backlash (and lulled pro-choicers into relying on the courts instead of cultivating a popular mandate). In 1993 Justice Ruth Bader Ginsburg caused
a flurry when she seemed to endorse this view: *Roe,* she declared in a
speech, had "halted a political process that was moving in a reform direction and . . . prolonged divisiveness and deferred stable settlement of
the issue." It's not an insane idea, even if most of its proponents (a) are
men; (b) think *Roe* went too far; and (c) want abortion off the table because they are tired of thinking about it.

But of course, if the court overturned *Roe,* abortion would not be
off the table at all. It would be front and center in fifty state legislatures.
According to *What If Roe Fell: The State-by-State Consequences of Overturning Roe v. Wade,* a report published this past fall by the Center for
Reproductive Rights, abortion rights would be at immediate high risk in
twenty-one states, moderate risk in nine, and "secure" in only twenty.

Short of a takeover by the Taliban, it's hard to imagine abortion being banned outright in New York or California or Connecticut. But it is equally hard to imagine liberal abortion laws passing in the Deep South, Utah, or South Dakota. And when you consider that Florida, Tennessee, Minnesota, and West Virginia are listed as "secure"—all states that have seen recent anti-choice victories and increasing Republican strength— you can see how volatile the abortion map could quickly become. Over- turning *Roe* would definitely energize pro-choicers and wake up the young featherheads who think their rights are safe because they have al- ways had them. That's why some staunch pro-choicers have "Bring it on!" moments: "Overnight," writes Susan Estrich in a recent syndicated column, "every election, for every state office, would become a referen- dum not on parental consent or partial birth abortion, but on whether regular old middle-class adult women could get first-trimester abor- tions. When you think about it that way, you have to ask: What could be better for Democrats?" Estrich rejects the thought, however, be- cause—something the boy pundits forget—criminalizing abortion, however briefly, means many, many women would suffer atrociously.

The trouble is, getting rid of *Roe* would energize anti-choicers too. Even in pro-choice states, they might be able to win spousal notification requirements, bans on "partial-birth" abortions or even on all second- trimester procedures except to preserve life and health. A national con- sensus on abortion might or might not develop over time, but any such would not likely be as permissive as *Roe*. Meanwhile—and possibly per- manently—fortunate women in anti-choice states would fly to New York or Los Angeles or Chicago, and the less lucky—the poor, the young, the trapped—would have dangerous, illegal procedures or un- wanted children. It would be a repeat of 1970–73, when women who could get to New York—but only they—could have a safe, legal version of the operation that was killing and maiming their poorer sisters back home. The blatant class and racial unfairness of this disparity, in fact, was one of the arguments that pushed the court to declare abortion a constitutional right. If *Roe* goes, that same disparity will reappear, rela- beled as local democracy. And I'm not persuaded that the right to abor- tion will ever be the norm in, say, the South, where the religious right is strong, antiabortion sentiment is high, and the political culture is inbred and hostile to women. Even now, there's only one abortion clinic in Mississippi, and the promised pro-choice masses—the "regular old adult middle-class women"—have yet to arise.

Legislative control might be more "democratic"—if you believe that a state senator balancing women's health against a highway for his district represents democracy. But would it be fair? The whole point about constitutional protection for rights is to guarantee them when they are unpopular—to shield them from majority prejudice, opportunistic politicians, the passions and pressures of the moment. Freedom of speech, assembly, worship, and so on belong to us as individuals; our neighbors, our families, and our legislators don't get to vote on how we use these rights or whether we should have them in the first place. Alabamans may be largely anti-choice, but what about the ones who aren't? Or the ones who are but even so don't want to die in childbirth, bear a hopelessly damaged baby, or drop out of school at fifteen—or twenty-five? If *Roe* goes, whoever has political power will determine the most basic, intimate, life-changing and life-threatening decision women—and only women—confront. We will have a country in which the same legislature that can't prevent some clod from burning a flag will be able to force a woman to bear a child under whatever circumstances it sees fit. It is hard to imagine how that woman would be a free or equal citizen of our constitutional republic.

I NOTE WITH SORROW the death of longtime *Washington Post* columnist Judy Mann, a vigorous voice for women's equality and, as she herself noted in her farewell column, one of a dwindling band of prominent women opinion writers with strong feminist and progressive views. Demoted from the Metro section to a slot next to the comics in 1992, Mann retired in her prime and died, of breast cancer, much too soon. I missed her column, and now, I'll miss hoping I'd come upon her byline, somewhere, again.

•◄ AUGUST 1, 2005 ►•

Feminists for (Fetal) Life

Can you be a feminist and be against abortion? Feminists for Life claims to be both, and if you listen long enough to its voluble and likable president, Serrin Foster, you might almost think it's true. FFL is on a major publicity roll these days, because Jane Roberts, wife of Supreme Court nominee John Roberts, is a pro bono legal adviser, former officer, and significant donor (she gave between $1,000 and $2,499 in 2003). When I caught up with Foster at the end of a long day that included an hour on NPR's *On Point,* she talked a blue and quite amusing streak, and although it can be hard to follow an aria that swoops from Susan B. Anthony to telecommuting to water pollution, while never quite answering the actual question, I'm sure she means every word of it. How can you argue with FFL's contention that America does not give pregnant women and mothers the support they need? Feminists, the pro-choice kind, have been saying this for years. So far as I can tell, FFL is the only "prolife" organization that talks about women's rights to work and education and the need to make both more compatible with motherhood. It has helped bring housing for mothers and children to Georgetown University and supports the Violence Against Women Act; Foster reminded me that she and I had been on the same side in the mid-1990s in opposing family caps, the denial of additional benefits to women who had more children while on welfare. Why, she wondered, couldn't we all just work together to "help pregnant women"?

The problem is that FFL doesn't just oppose abortion. FFL wants abortion to be illegal. All abortions, period, including those for rape, incest, health, major fetal defects, and, although Foster resisted admitting this, even some abortions most doctors would say were necessary to save the woman's life. (Although FFL is not a Catholic organization, its rejection of therapeutic abortion follows Catholic doctrine.) FFL wants doctors who perform abortions to be punished, possibly with prison terms.

It was extremely difficult to get Foster to say what she thought would happen if abortion was banned. At one point she would not concede that women would continue to have abortions if it was recriminalized; at another she argued that criminalization was no big deal: Instructions on self-abortion were posted on the Internet. I had to work to get her to admit that illegal abortion was common before *Roe,* and that it was dangerous—numbers on abortion deaths were concocted by pre-*Roe* legalization advocates, she told me. Yet the FFL website prominently features gory stories of abortion mishaps and discredited claims that abortion causes breast cancer. (Challenged on the cancer connection, Foster says they just want women to have medical information. Asked why they don't then link to the 2004 *Lancet* article debunking their cancer claims, she says they are not medical experts and have considered taking the cancer pages down.) So legal abortion is dangerous but illegal abortion would be safe? When I pointed out that in countries where the operation is banned, such as Brazil and Peru, rates are sky-high and abortion a major cause of injury and death, she professed ignorance.

I got similarly evasive answers when I asked why FFL didn't promote birth control and when I asked if FFL considered the Pill an "abortifacient." She did tell me that "birth control doesn't work" for swing-shift nurses because they lose track of their body clock—interesting, if true—or for teenagers, which I know to be false. "We just want to focus on meeting the everyday needs of women," she told me. But when I asked how the everyday needs of women with unwanted pregnancies would be served by encouraging them to bear children and place them for adoption, Foster didn't answer. Instead, she extolled the benefits of open adoption.

In the FFL view, women have abortions because they are victims—of shamed parents, abusive boyfriends, pro-choice propaganda, and a society hostile to motherhood. Only a "few percent" of women who have abortions have what they need to choose childbirth instead—the rest are like prostitutes, Foster told me, coerced women falsely said to be making a free choice. The FFL vision is that women should embrace motherhood whenever a wayward sperm meets an egg, and that this is what women really want to do, and would do if given support. When I pointed out that Scandinavia provides a raft of benefits for mothers and children, yet many women there still seek abortions for about a million reasons, Foster conceded the point and moved right along.

It is indeed feminist to say no woman should have to abort a wanted child to stay in school or have a career—FFL's line is thus an advance on the more typical anti-choice position, which is that women have abortions to go to Europe or fit into their prom dress. You can see why their upbeat, rebellious slogans—"Refuse to Choose," "Question Abortion," "Women Deserve Better"—appeal to students. (But what do those students think when they find that the postabortion resources links are all to Christian groups and that FFL's sunny pregnancy-assistance advice includes going on food stamps or welfare?) Exposing the constraints on women's choices, however, is only one side of feminism. The other is acknowledging women as moral agents, trusting women to decide what is best for themselves. For FFL there's only one right decision: Have that baby. And since women's moral judgment cannot be trusted, abortion must be outlawed, whatever the consequences for women's lives and health—for rape victims and twelve-year-olds and fifty-year-olds, women carrying Tay-Sachs fetuses and women at risk of heart attack or stroke, women who have all the children they can handle and women who don't want children at all. FFL argues that abortion harms women—that's why it clings to the outdated cancer claims. But it would oppose abortion just as strongly if it prevented breast cancer, filled every woman's heart with joy, lowered the national deficit, and found Jimmy Hoffa. That's because they aren't really feminists—a feminist could not force another woman to bear a child, any more than she could turn a pregnant teenager out into a snowstorm. They are fetalists.

•◀ August 29, 2005 ▶•

Theocracy Lite

So now we know what "noble cause" Cindy Sheehan's son died for in Iraq: Sharia. It's a good thing W stands for women, or I'd be worried. The new Constitution, drafted under heavy pressure from the administration, sets aside the secular personal law under which Iraqis have lived for nearly half a century in favor of theocracy lite. "Islam is the official religion of the state and is a basic source of legislation," Article 2 begins—the spin is that this language is a victory because Islam is not *the* source. "(a) No law can be passed that contradicts the undisputed rules of Islam." On the other hand, "(b) No law can be passed that contradicts the principles of democracy" and "(c) No law can be passed that contradicts the rights and basic freedoms outlined in this constitution"—as in, for example, Article 14: "Iraqis are equal before the law without discrimination because of sex," religion, ethnicity, and so on.

There's enough right here to keep a conclave of political theorists busy for years. Equal before which law? How can women be equal before Islamic law, according to which they are unequal? How can a non-Muslim be equal in a Muslim state? Who decides which Islamic rules are undisputed and which are, well, disputable? As with our own multiple versions of Christianity, doesn't that depend on which imam is holding the Koran? And what happens when (a) Islam conflicts with (b) democracy, or either (a) or (b)—or both—conflicts with (c) human rights? Don't laugh, it could happen. Fortunately, the Constitution has come up with just the thing to settle those knotty questions—a Supreme Federal Court "made up of a number of judges and experts in Sharia (Islamic Law) and law." As prowar pundits are quick to remind us, it's a lot like our own Constitution—except for the official religion part, and that's not for lack of effort by Justice Scalia.

Bush has professed himself delighted with the document. "This Constitution is one that honors women's rights and freedom of religion," he announced in Arizona, where he was taking a vacation from his vacation. The freedom-of-religion bit alludes to a slightly bewildering provision that seems to hold out the possibility of separate courts for each religion. Ayatollah Ahmad Jannati, the head of Iran's ultra-Shiite Guardian Council, isn't too worried by this ecumenical gesture: "Fortunately, after years of effort and expectations in Iraq, an Islamic state has come to power and the Constitution has been established on the basis of Islamic precepts."

We don't yet know what any of this means concretely, but if Iraq turns out to resemble Iran—and boosting Iran's regional influence was another thing Casey Sheehan died for—women have a lot to look forward to: being married off at the age of nine, being a co-wife, having unequal rights to divorce and child custody, inheriting only half as much as their brothers, having their testimony in court counted as half that of men, winning a rape conviction only if the crime was witnessed by four male Muslims, being imprisoned and flogged for premarital sex, being executed for adultery, needing mandatory permission from husband or father to work, study, or travel. Bush supporters who find any of this disturbing—hello? Independent Women's Forum?—can console themselves with the thought that, as former CIA official Reuel Marc Gerecht said on *Meet the Press*, "Women's social rights are not critical to the evolution of democracy." Another plus: Ayatollah al-Sistani is anti-choice. According to his website, www.sistani.org, even a rape victim can have an abortion only if her relatives would murder her for getting pregnant. So Iraqi fetuses are all set.

Is this what all those purple fingers were about? What looked like a nation demanding democracy from reluctant occupiers was really an ethnic and religious power grab? In 2004, Iraqi women's groups, quietly backed by then–U.S. occupation chief Paul Bremer, forced the Governing Council to rescind Resolution 137, which would have replaced secular family law with Sharia. That was reassuring to those who wanted to believe that the U.S. government was on some sort of Wilsonian human-rights mission. This time around we're supposed to take comfort in the promise of secular courts for those who prefer them, in the banning of honor killings, and in the Constitution's transitional 25 percent set-aside for women in Parliament, even as Sunni and Shiite theocratic gangs assault and murder unveiled educated and professional women who venture out alone.

"We have lost all the gains we made over the last thirty years," said Safia Taleb al-Souhail, last seen sitting in the balcony with Laura at the State of the Union address, smiling and waving her purple finger. "It's a big disappointment." Even blunter words come from Dr. Raja Kuzai, an obstetrician and secular Shiite who served in the assembly's Constitution-writing committee and, as the President tells it, greeted him as "My Liberator" when she visited the Oval Office in 2003: "I think it is over now," she writes in the *San Antonio Express-News.* "I want the American people to know that our dreams are gone, our work was in vain. There will be no future for our children and our grandchildren in the new Iraq. The future is for the clerics. They will lead the country. . . . This is not the democracy we dreamed of. This is the dictatorship of the majority!" Dr. Kuzai has announced that she is leaving Iraq.

It always seemed a little strange to me that Bush was carrying the standard of secularism and pluralism and women's rights in the Muslim world when he is so keen against all three here at home. In the liberal hawks' fantasy war, Bush was the love child of Mary Wollstonecraft and Voltaire, striding forth to battle the combined forces of Osama bin Laden and Jacques Derrida. Sometimes I thought that to Bush, as an evangelical Christian, even the Enlightenment was better than Islam, the rival faith. But given the way things are turning out, it's clear that Bush's world is big enough for two kinds of religious mania: America gets creationism, Iraqis get Sharia. Fundamentalists get both countries, and women get the shaft.

•◀ SEPTEMBER 19, 2005 ▶•

Intelligible Design

Sometimes I wonder if the future, in some strange metaphysical way, reaches down into our psyches and readies us to accept what is to come. Maybe we know things before we know them. By the time change is plain to see, we've unconsciously adapted to it and have learned to call it something else—God's will, human nature, life.

Let's say, for example, that the American Empire is just about over. Let's say China and India and other countries as well are set to surge ahead in science and technology, leaving reduced opportunities for upward mobility for the educated, while capital continues to roam the world in search of cheap labor, leaving a shattered working class. Let's say we really are becoming a society of fixed status: the have-nots, an anxious and defensive middle, and what George W. Bush famously calls his base, the have-mores. What sort of shifts in culture and social structure would prepare us for this looming state of affairs? A resurgence of Christian fundamentalism would fill the bill nicely.

Intellectually, scientifically, even artistically, fundamentalism—biblical literalism—is a road to nowhere, because it insists on fidelity to revealed truths that are not true. But religious enthusiasm is not all bad. Like love or political activism, it can help troubled souls transform their lives. And if what we're looking at is an America with an ever-larger and boxed-in working class and tighter competition for high-paying jobs among the elite, fundamentalism is exactly the thing to manage decline: It schools the downwardly mobile in making the best of their lot while teaching them to be grateful for the food pantry and daycare over at the church. At the same time, taking advantage of existing currents of anti-intellectualism and school-tax resistance, it removes from the pool of potential scientists and other creative professionals vast numbers of students, who will have had their minds befuddled with creationism and its smooth-talking cousin, intelligent design. Already, according to a study by University of Minnesota biology professor Randy Moore, 40 percent of high school biology teachers don't teach evolution, either because it's socially unacceptable in their communities or because they themselves don't believe in it.

If you think of current behavior as an advance accommodation to what is on the way, some things make sense that otherwise are mysterious. Why, at the very moment that we are talking obsessively about academic "excellence" and leaving no child behind, are we turning our public schools into factories of rote learning and multiple-choice testing, as if learning how to read and count were some huge accomplishment? Well, if your fate is to be a supermarket checker—and that's a "good job" these days—you won't be needing Roman history or art or calculus. By the same token, cutting state university budgets, burdening students with debt, and turning college into a kind of middle-management trade school make sense, if shrinking opportunities for the professional elite lie ahead. Why create more competition for the graduates of the Ivy League?

Another mystery potentially explained: government's determination to keep working-class women from controlling their fertility. Why does it set a biological trap that dooms them to years of struggle with repercussions for everyone around them, including their children? (It's true that teen pregnancy rates are going down, but they're still astronomical by the standards of any other industrial nation—six times the rate in the Devil's own country, France.) For all our talk about single-parent families—the reason for the terrible poverty of black New Orleans, if we are to believe right-wing columnists Rich Lowry and David Brooks—we act to bring about more of them, and of the most vulnerable, makeshift kind. Somehow single motherhood is supposed to be the fault of the left, but it's the right that has cut public funding for family planning, denied over-the-counter status to emergency contraception, restricted abortion, flooded the schools with useless abstinence-only sex ed, and now even threatens to bar confidentiality to girls seeking birth control. If you wanted a fatalistic, disorganized working class, a working class too worn out by the day-to-day to do much more than get by, saddling girls with babies is a great idea.

Hurricane Katrina was heartbreaking—and it was shocking too. The realities it laid bare—the stark class and race divisions of New Orleans, the callousness and cluelessness and sheer shameless incompetence of the Bush administration, the long years of ecological mismanagement of the Gulf region—show how far the process of adaptation to decline has already gone. Bush's ownership society turns out to be the on-your-ownership society. The rising tide that was supposed to lift all boats is actually a flood that only those who already have a boat can escape.

For decades the right has worked day and night to delegitimize concepts without which no society can thrive, or maybe even survive—the common good, social solidarity, knowledge and expertise, public service. God, abstinence, and the market were supposed to solve all our problems. Bad news—climate change, rising poverty, racial and gender disparities, the mess in Iraq—was just flimflam from liberals who hate freedom. Is there another world power that lives in such a fantasy world? Now, in old people left to drown in their nursing-home beds, in police who reportedly demanded that young women stranded on rooftops bare their breasts in return for rescue, in the contempt for public safety shown by Bush's transformation of FEMA into a pasture for hapless cronies—we can all see what those fantasies obscured. A government that doesn't believe in government was a disaster waiting to happen.

That disaster was Katrina, and it's swept us to a crucial political moment. It's as if we're being given something people rarely get: a chance to take a hard look at the future we are preparing for ourselves, an America that has used up its social and economic and intellectual capital and in which it's every man for himself, and every woman, too.

Is that the future we want? Because if we let this moment slip away, that is where we are heading.

•◄ October 3, 2005 ►•

Desperate Housewives
of the Ivy League?

September 20's prime target for press critics, social scientists, and feminists was the *New York Times* front-page story "Many Women at Elite Colleges Set Career Path to Motherhood," by Louise Story (Yale '03). Through interviews and a questionnaire e-mailed to freshmen and senior women residents of two Yale colleges (dorms), Story claims to have found that 60 percent of these brainy and energetic young women plan to park their expensive diplomas in the bassinet and become stay-home mothers. Over at *Slate*, Jack Shafer slapped the *Times* for using weasel words ("many," "seems") to make a trend out of anecdotes and vague impressions: In fact, Story presents no evidence that more Ivy League undergrads today are planning to retire at thirty to the playground than ten, twenty, or thirty years ago. Simultaneously, an armada of bloggers shredded her questionnaire as biased (hint: If you begin with "When you have children," you've already skewed your results) and denounced her interpretation of the answers as hype. What she actually found, as the writer Robin Herman noted in a crisp letter to the *Times,* was that 70 percent of those who answered planned to keep working full or part time through motherhood. Even by Judith Miller standards, the Story story was pretty flimsy. So great was the outcry that the author had to defend her methods in a follow-up on the *Times* website three days later.

With all that excellent insta-critiquing, I feared I'd lumber into print too late to add a new pebble to the sling. But I did find one place where the article is still Topic No. 1: Yale. "I sense that she had a story to tell, and she only wanted to tell it one way," Mary Miller, master of Saybrook, one of Story's targeted colleges, told me. Miller said Story met with whole suites of students and weeded out the women who didn't fit her thesis. Even among the ones she focused on, "I haven't found that the students' views are as hard and fast as Story portrayed them." (In a phone call Story defended her research methods, which she said her critics misunderstood, and referred me to her explanation on the Web.) One supposed future homemaker of America posted an anonymous dissection of Story's piece at www.mediabistro.com. Another told me in an e-mail that while the article quoted her accurately, it "definitely did not turn out the way I thought it would after numerous conversations with Louise." That young person may be sadder but wiser—she declined to let me interview her or use her name—but history professor Cynthia Russett, quoted as saying that women are "turning realistic," is happy to go public with her outrage. Says Russett, "I may have used the word, but it was in the context of a harsh or forced realism that I deplored. She made it sound like this was a trend of which I approved. In fact, the first I heard of it was from Story, and I'm not convinced it exists." In two days of interviewing professors, grad students, and undergrads, I didn't find one person who felt Story fairly represented women at Yale. Instead, I learned of women who had thrown Story's questionnaire away in disgust, heard a lot of complaints about Yale's lack of affordable childcare, and read numerous scathing unpublished letters to the *Times,* including a particularly erudite one from a group of sociology graduate students. Physics professor Megan Urry had perhaps the best riposte: She polled her class of 120, using "clickers" (electronic polling devices used as a teaching tool). Of forty-five female students, how many said they planned "to be stay-at-home primary parent"? Two. Twenty-six, or 58 percent, said they planned to "work full time, share home responsibilities with partner"—and good luck to them, because 33 percent of the men said they wanted stay-home wives.

The most interesting question about Story's article is why the *Times* published it—and on page one yet. After all, as Shafer pointed out, it had run an identical story, "Many Young Women Now Say They'd Pick Family over Career," on the front page December 28, 1980. (He even turned up one of its star subjects, Princeton alum Mary Anne Citrino, who says she was completely misrepresented by the *Times*: She never wanted to stay home and never did.) I'm particularly grateful to Shafer for digging up that old clip, because somehow I had formed the erroneous impression that the *Times* used to be less sexist than it is now—the week Story made the front page also saw an article uncritically reporting a drug-company study that claimed female executives are addled by menopause, and a Styles piece about the menace to society posed by mothers pushing luxury strollers on Manhattan sidewalks. All that was missing was one of those columns in which John Tierney explains that women, bless their hearts, lack the competitive drive to win at Scrabble.

Story's article is essentially an update on Lisa Belkin's 2003 *Times Magazine* cover story about her Princeton classmates, whose marginalization at work after having children was glowingly portrayed as an "opt-out revolution" and which claimed that women "don't run the world" because "they don't want to." What's painful about the way the *Times* frames work-family issues is partly its obsessive focus on the most privileged as bellwethers of American womanhood—you'd never know that most mothers who work need the money. But what's also depressing is the way the *Times* lumps together women who want to take a bit of time off or work reasonable hours—the hours that everybody worked not so long ago—with women who give up their careers for good. Cutting back to spend time with one's child shouldn't be equated with lack of commitment to one's profession. You would not know, either, that choices about how to combine work and motherhood are fluid and provisional and not made in a vacuum. The lack of good childcare and paid parental leave, horrendous work hours, inflexible career ladders, the still-conventional domestic expectations of far too many men, and the industrial-size helpings of maternal guilt ladled out by the media are all part of it.

Wouldn't you like to read a front-page story about that?

•⊣ OCTOBER 17, 2005 ⊢•

If Not Miers, Who?

Dear Karl Rove,

I understand you're getting a lot of flak over the nomination of Harriet Miers to that pesky slot on the Supreme Court. Just in case it doesn't work out, I would like to propose another candidate: me. I realize my name might not be on your short list, since this is a new ambition of mine, and I haven't had time to organize a big shmoozy campaign like some people I could mention. It was actually the Miers nomination that gave me the idea—some people thought, Why her? but I thought, Why not me? To save time in case you have to move quickly, I've prepared a list of reasons I would be the perfect person to refute the kinds of nasty, rude, unfair arguments being made by Ms. Miers's opponents. I think you will see I have all her strengths, and then some!

1. I am a woman and, moreover, have been one for years. I realize that means I will be subjected to a lot of sexist comments: The media will do silly pieces about my cooking and clothes and whether I am really as bad a mother as all that. Your enemies, of course, will say you chose me because of my sex. Here's the perfect double-whammy defense: While Laura Bush suggests that anyone who criticizes me is a creepy misogynist, which happens to be what I think too (perhaps she could also mention that my daughter has no actual criminal record and surely that counts for something), you point out that there are currently around 113 million adult women in the United States. Obviously if you just wanted a woman, you would never have chosen me. You would have chosen one of those other women—a reactionary judge like Edith Jones

or Priscilla Owen, or maybe Jennifer Aniston because Brad has been so mean.

2. I am not a Christian. This may not strike you as an advantage, given the nature of your base, but think about it. Right now, the Christian right is split: James Dobson says you told him something on the phone about Miers that reassured him greatly, but Gary Bauer doubts she is "a vote for our values." At Miers's own evangelical church, the congregation stood up and applauded; but at other churches the pews are in revolt. Honestly, who can figure these people out? They only stopped burning each other at the stake a few centuries ago. Nominating me will unify them instantly: I'm a half-Jewish half-Episcopalian atheist. When they make a fuss, just tell them God told the President to pick me. Given the other advice God's been giving him—to invade Iraq, for example—it could even be true.

3. I am not a lawyer. George Will and William Kristol and a lot of other pundits complain that Miers isn't qualified for the court because she's not a judge, and her area of legal expertise is serving the President, which is not the same as constitutional law—at least not yet. In my opinion these whiners are just elitist lawyer-haters. But you know what? Everyone seems to hate lawyers, so why not throw George and Bill a bone and nominate me? You'll please the snobs who pooh-pooh Miers's lack of credentials—I have many credentials; they just happen to be in areas other than the law—and you'll please the populists, who don't think credentials matter. That seems to be your guiding philosophy too—Michael Brown went from horses to hurricanes, Karen Hughes is traipsing about the Middle East marketing America to Muslims—and who is to say you're wrong? As Oklahoma senator Tom Coburn observed in defense of Julie Myers, nominated to head the Immigration and Customs Enforcement Agency despite her complete lack of relevant experience, "She doesn't know what can't be done." I can promise you, neither do I!

4. I am not a woman of mystery. Everyone's trying to figure out Miers's views on abortion. We know she's against it—she goes to an anti-choice

church; she gave money to Texans United for Life; when she was president of the Texas Bar Association in the early 1990s she lobbied to get
the ABA to rescind its official support for *Roe v. Wade.* But is she really,
really against it? The President tried to calm his base by saying he knew
her and she would never change, wink-wink. But that was just confusing. After all, she changed once—she used to be a Catholic and a Democrat, and in 1998 she even helped start a feminist lecture series at
Southern Methodist University (first speaker: Gloria Steinem)—so how
can the President be so sure she won't change again? You could turn
around one day and see her sitting up there, next to Antonin Scalia, in
a burqa. My views on abortion, by contrast, are a matter of endless, possibly even tedious, record, and they have been the same since I knew
what abortion was. There will be no need to play the old game of trying
to persuade both sides that the candidate is with them without actually
saying what the candidate thinks. If people ask you what my position on
abortion is, you can just tell them!

What else? Unlike Miers, no one can say I'm a crony—I've never
even met the President, and the only Republicans I know were so disgusted by the Katrina thing they might as well be Democrats. Another
plus: I'm a quick study, so I'm not too worried about the learning curve
if I get on the bench. Besides, the Constitution isn't very long; I could
probably even memorize it if that would help me bond with the other
justices. The President says he expects the court merely to apply the law,
not make the law, and that doesn't sound very difficult, does it? The justices probably go on about what a tough job they have just so we'll think
they're so smart. But if I do have questions, I can always ask Ruth Bader
Ginsburg.

Looking forward to hearing from you, perhaps sooner than you
think!

Sincerely yours,
Katha Pollitt

cc: President George W. Bush

Madam President,
Madam President

I can't help it. I love *Commander in Chief.* Sure, it's cheesy and under-written and not as good as *The West Wing.* More story lines, please! More characters! More witty banter and moral ambiguity and multiple crises all coming to a head at the same time! But in a TV season in which the major network roles for women over thirty are as desperate house-wives in size 0 stretch pants, this feminist fantasy about the first woman President gives me a thrill every Tuesday night at nine. Maybe there's more to life than Wisteria Lane, after all. I love Geena Davis as President Mackenzie "Mac" Allen, so unflappable and warm and confident and kind and clever, to say nothing of gorgeous and six feet tall. But then I've loved Geena Davis ever since she wrote a letter to *Newsweek,* at the height of the "date rape hype" hysteria, pointing out that speaking out against rape wasn't embracing the role of victim but rejecting it. *Commander in Chief* makes you realize how rarely on TV you get to see a woman in charge who isn't a dragon or a bundle of nerves—or a likable one who isn't incompetent, clumsy, silly, or self-hating. Imagine, the show's been on since September 27, and Mac hasn't—yet—dissolved into a puddle of tears from the stress of running the free world while raising three kids and foiling the plots of sexist Republican Speaker of the House Nathan Templeton, played with delicious malice by Donald Sutherland.

Even more amazing, her husband, Rod Calloway (Kyle Secor), isn't sulking and acting out, even though one of Mac's first official acts when she moved up from being Vice President was to fire him as her chief of staff because otherwise people would assume he was running the show. He takes being First Gentleman with a sense of humor, pitches in equally with the kids, and still wants to have sex. More miraculous still, so does Mac. Well, I said it was a fantasy. (Update: Looks like trouble is brewing in paradise. Sigh.)

Pundits wonder out loud if *Commander in Chief* will pave the way for a real-life woman President, like—oh let's just pick a name out of a hat—Hillary Clinton. Far be it from me to suggest that TV dramas don't affect Americans' real-life attitudes—I'd never even heard of cosmopolitans before *Sex and the City* and now I drink them all the time. The show may persuade some voters that it would be cool to have a woman President—"Madam President" has a nice ring to it. But it's unlikely to reach the gender-prejudiced. The substantial minority of voters who, according to polls, wouldn't vote for a woman nominated by their own party probably aren't watching the show, and besides, they're most likely Republicans (20 percent, versus 7 percent of Democrats) who would sooner admit the Earth is more than 10,000 years old than vote for Hillary. Mac Allen, moreover, is so androgynously terrific—even her name is unisex—she's less like a real woman politician than like one of Shakespeare's cross-dressing heroines—Rosalind, or Portia. It's hard to think of a woman within a thousand miles of the White House she doesn't make look frumpy and fussy and old and short.

But then, Mac isn't a politician—she doesn't even belong to a political party. She's an idealistic ex-congresswoman turned academic who rather improbably accepted the vice presidential slot on the Republican ticket, despite being a liberal and understanding that she was there to win women's votes. So little interested is Mac in power that she's all set to heed the President's dying wish and step aside so Templeton can take over—the Speaker of the House is next in line of succession, a fact that must brighten Denny Hastert's life considerably. But then Templeton makes one coarse, woman-hating remark too many and next thing you know, President Allen is sending in the Navy to rescue a Nigerian woman scheduled to be stoned for sex out of wedlock, sending in the Air Force to restore democracy to an unnamed Latin American country by threatening to destroy its coca crop, and using her summit meeting with the arrogant and sexist Russian president to win freedom for imprisoned dissident journalists. Can a woman be tough enough to lead the free world? Take that, misogynists and drug lords and enemies of free speech! In future episodes Mac will capture Osama bin Laden, rewrite the Iraqi Constitution, and raise SAT scores by 75 points—all while dealing with a sullen teenage daughter who wishes Pat Buchanan had her mother's job.

There's a lot of paint-by-numbers feel-good feminism here: See Mac cope when her younger daughter spills juice on the presidential blouse just before she addresses the nation; see Mac and the former First Lady bond over the old joke about how if Moses had been a woman she would have asked for directions and been in Israel in a week; see Mac elegantly trump man after man who makes the mistake of talking down to her. I'm not happy about the show's penchant for calling out the troops, but feel-good feminism? I'll take it. In the real world, after all, it's hard to read the paper without coming across a Larry Summers soundalike. "Women don't make it to the top because they don't deserve to," the important British advertising executive Neil French told a posh Toronto audience in October. "They're crap." French went on to call women "wimps" who inevitably "go suckle something." (Interestingly, the *New York Times* made no mention of the crude language in its report.) French resigned, but that didn't stop Brit celebrity chef Gordon Ramsay from announcing that "the girls" these days "can't cook to save their lives." Harriet Miers is ridiculed for her eyeliner, her thank-you notes, and her lack of hot dates, and attacked as a mediocrity—which she is, but I don't want to hear about it from people who think Clarence Thomas is a brilliant jurist. New data showing that in Minnesota women now get more academic degrees than men at every level is reported as a problem, not just for men but for women. Whom will they marry, poor overeducated dears? Funny how no one worried about marriage when the numbers went the other way.

As the backlash gets daily more open and absurd, our real-life female politicians seem paralyzed. It's up to television now: Run, Geena, run!

•┤ NOVEMBER 14, 2005 ├•

The World According to Dowd

Maureen Dowd doesn't read my column. I know this because in her new book, *Are Men Necessary?*, she uncritically cites virtually every fear-mongering, backlash-promoting study, survey, article, and book I've debunked in this space. She falls for that 1986 Harvard-Yale study comparing women's chances of marrying after forty to the likelihood of being killed by a terrorist, and for the half-baked theories of Sylvia Ann Hewlett (ambitious women stay single or childless), Lisa Belkin (mothers give up their careers), Louise Story (even undergraduates understand this now), and other purveyors of the view that achievement and romance/family are incompatible for women. To be fair, Dowd apparently doesn't read Susan Faludi or Susan Douglas either, or *The American Prospect, Slate, Salon,* or even *The New Republic,* home of her friend Leon Wieseltier, much thanked for editorial help in her Introduction—all of which have published persuasive critiques of these and other contributions to backlash lit. Still, it hurts. I read her, after all. We all do.

Are Men Necessary? is a Feminism Is Dead polemic, put through a Dowdian styleblender. Like her *New York Times* column, it's funny and free-associative and not afraid of self-contradiction, full of one-liners and puns: Women who let men grab the check are "fem-freeloading" a "quid profiterole" (ouch). Like her column, too, it's heavy on media fluff: silly trend stories, women's magazine features and interviews with editors of same, dubious gender-difference studies. It's annoying to read pronouncements about feminism based mostly on chats with her friends in the media about men, clothes, TV shows, and Botox. Why not call up some people who actually do feminist work?

Dowd sees young women dashing back to the 1950s as fast as their Manolos will carry them: making a bestseller of *The Rules,* changing their names when they marry, obsessing about their looks. There were moments when I felt Dowd and I live on different planets—is pay in-equity really now dismissively referred to as "girl money"? Are young women in search of boyfriends really "cultivating the venerable tricks of the trade: an absurdly charming little laugh, a pert toss of the head, an air of saucy triumph"? The young women I know—most of whom, con-trary to stereotype, have no problem calling themselves feminists—are so far ahead of where I was at their age, so much more confident and multicompetent and worldly wise, I only wish I could hire one to re-negotiate my girl-money salary for me.

But glamorous gams, trademark dyed red hair and all, Dowd at least gets it that the problem today isn't that old-school feminists once frowned on Barbie. She doesn't applaud today's retro/raunch gender politics as the return of sanity and fun. And it's hard to deny that there's a reality out there of which she gives a slapdash, cartoon, Style-section version. There is some truth to Dowd's horrified depiction of the hyper-sexualized culture of "hotness" vividly described in Ariel Levy's much-discussed polemic *Female Chauvinist Pigs: Women and the Rise of Raunch Culture.* (Dowd mentions a piece by Levy in her book; Levy's lovestruck profile of Dowd—it mentions that red hair nine times!—made the cover of *New York.*) Eating disorders, breast implants, stripper chic, Queen for a Day weddings, the resurgence of "girl" and "chick"—it's not a happy story.

But these troubling cultural trends aren't the whole story either. How many young women flash their breasts for the camera or flog themselves academically all the way to the Ivy League merely to snag a rich husband? More than minor in women's studies, volunteer for rape-crisis hotlines, have black belts in karate or Ph.D.s in physics or raise Macedonian sheepdogs? Do we know that more women want the man to pay the bill than want to share it or, if that's too mechanical, work out some other arrangement that feels equal? It's a myth that my generation and Dowd's were a unified band of sisters, forging ahead in our sneakers and power suits. By many measures young women today are far more independent than we were—more likely to finish college and have advanced degrees, to work in formerly all-male occupations, to have (or acknowledge having) lesbian sex, to refuse to suffer in silence rape, harassment, abuse. If we're going by anecdotal evidence from our circles of friends, I know young women who've made the finals in the Intel science contest and worked on newspapers in Africa, who've had sperm-bank babies alone or with other women, who play rugby, make movies, write feminist/political/literary blogs, organize unions, raise money for poor women's abortions.

"You're always so glass-half-full in public," my editor says at this point. "But in private you're as down as Dowd." Well, not quite that down. But yes, I thought we'd be further along by now. I feel for young women today—somehow, between the irony and the knowingness and the 24/7 bath in pop celebrity culture and its repulsive values, it can be harder for them than it was for us to call a sexist spade a spade. They've been bombarded from birth with consumerism and Republicanism and hyperindividualism, and told in every possible way that feminism is deeply uncool and unhot. Dowd is such a credulous audience for backlash propaganda it doesn't occur to her that she is promoting, not reporting, the problem she describes. I'm amazed, actually, that feminism is still around, given the press it gets.

Dowd, for example, thinks feminism may be a "cruel hoax" because it keeps women single—men are scared of spunky, successful women. (In interviews Dowd denies she's attributing her own unmated state to her fame and fabulousness, but that's how she's been read.) Well, some men definitely want the young compliant type. But—anecdotal evidence again—most women in my circle are paired, and we are all feminists and really, really great. Men hold a lot of cards in the mating game, but fewer than they used to, and women hold more than before. There has never been a better time in all world history to be a fifty-three-year-old single woman looking for romance. Besides, as ferocious young Jessica Valenti put it over at www.feministing.com, "Feminism isn't a f***ing dating service." Out of the mouths of babes.

•◀ NOVEMBER 28, 2005 ▶•

Girls Against Boys?

I went to Radcliffe, the women's wing of Harvard, at a time when the combined undergraduate student body was fixed at four male students for every female one. I don't remember anyone worrying about the boys' social lives, or whether they would find anyone to marry—even though nationally, too, boys were more likely to go to college and to graduate than girls. When in 1975 President Derek Bok instituted equal-access admissions, nobody said, "Great idea, more marital choice for educated men!"

What a difference a few decades and a gender revolution make. Now, although both sexes are much more likely to go to college than forty years ago—the proportion of the population enrolled in college is 20 percentage points higher today than in 1960—girls have edged ahead of boys. Today, women make up 57 percent of undergraduates, and the gap is projected to reach 60/40 in the next few years. This year, even manly Harvard admitted more girls than boys to its freshman class. So of course the big question is, Who will all those educated women marry? "Advocates for women have been so effective politically that high schools and colleges are still focusing on supposed discrimination against women," writes John Tierney in a recent *New York Times* column. "You could think of this as a victory for women's rights, but many of the victors will end up celebrating alone." If the ladies end up cuddling with their diplomas, they have only themselves—and those misguided "advocates for women"—to blame. Take that, you hyper-educated spinster, you.

The conservative spin on the education gender gap is that feminism has ruined school for boys. "Why would any self-respecting boy want to attend one of America's increasingly feminized universities?" asks

George Gilder in *National Review.* "Most of these institutions have flounced through the last forty years fashioning a fluffy pink playpen of feminist studies and agitprop 'herstory,' taught amid a green goo of eco-motherism and anti-industrial phobia." Sounds like fun, but it doesn't sound much like West Texas A&M, Baylor, Loyola, or the University of Alabama, where female students outnumber males in about the same proportion as they do at trendy Berkeley and Brown. Even Hillsdale College, the conservative academic mecca that became famous for rejecting federal funds rather than comply with government regulations against sex discrimination, has a student body that is 51 percent female. Other pundits—Michael Gurian, Kate O'Beirne, Christina Hoff Sommers—blame the culture of elementary school and high school: too many female teachers, too much sitting quietly, not enough sports and a feminist-friendly curriculum that forces boys to read—oh no!—books by women, or worse—books *about* women.

For the record, in middle school my daughter was assigned exactly one book by a woman: Zora Neale Hurston's *Their Eyes Were Watching God.* In high school she read three, *Mrs. Dalloway, Beloved,* and *Uncle Tom's Cabin.* Required reading included male authors from Sophocles, Shakespeare, and Fitzgerald to (I kid you not) James Michener and Richard Adams, author of *Watership Down.* Four books in seven years: Is that what we're arguing about here? Furthermore, I don't know where those pundits went to school, but education has always involved a lot of sitting, a lot of organizing, a lot of deadlines, and a lot of work you didn't necessarily feel like doing. It's always been heavily verbal—in fact, today's textbooks are unbelievably dumbed down and visually hyped compared with fifty years ago. Conservatives talk as if boys should be taught in some kind of cross between boot camp and Treasure Island— but what kind of preparation for modern life would that be? As for the decline of gym and teams and band—activities that keep academically struggling kids, especially boys, coming to school—whose idea was it to cut those "frills" in the first place if not conservatives?

If the mating game worked fine when women were ignorant and helpless and breaks down when they smarten up, that certainly tells us something about marriage. But does today's dating scene really consist of women who love Woolf and men who love Grand Theft Auto?

College may not create the intellectual divide elite pundits think it does. (Just spend some time looking at student life as revealed at www.facebook.com if you really want to get depressed about American universities.) For most students, it's more like trade school—they go to get credentials for employment and, because of the sexist nature of the labor market, women need those credentials more than men. Believe it or not, there are still stereotypically male jobs that pay well and don't require college degrees—plumbing, cabinetry, electrical work, computer repair, refrigeration, trucking, mining, restaurant cuisine. My daughter had two male school friends, good students from academically oriented families, who chose cooking school over college. Moreover, sex discrimination in employment is alive and well: Maybe boys focus less on school because they think they'll come out ahead anyway. What solid, stable jobs with a future are there for women without at least some higher ed? Heather Boushey, an economist with the Center for Economic Policy and Research, noted that women students take out more loans than their male classmates, even though a BA does less to increase their income. The sacrifice would make sense, though, if the BA made the crucial difference between respectable security and a lifetime as a waitress or a file clerk.

This is not to say that boys make the right choice when they blow off school, or even that it always is a choice. People's ideas about life often lag behind reality—some boys haven't gotten the message about the decline of high-paying blue collar work, or the unlikeliness of rap or sports stardom, the way some girls haven't gotten the message that it is foolish, just really incredibly stupid, to rely on being supported by a man. Most girls, however, have read the memo about having, if not a career exactly, career skills. Their mothers, so many of them divorced and struggling, made sure of that. As for the boys, maybe they will just have to learn to learn in a room full of smart females.

•◄ JANUARY 30, 2006 ►•

Pro-Choice Puritans

D o you think abortion is tragic and terrible and wrong, that *Roe v. Wade* went too far and that the pro-choice movement is elitist, unfeeling, overbearing, overreaching, and quite possibly dead? In the current debate over abortion, that makes you a pro-choicer. As the nation passes the thirty-third anniversary of *Roe*, it is hard to find anyone who will say a good word in public for abortion rights, let alone for abortion itself. Abortion has become a bit like flag burning—something that offends all right-thinking people but needs to be legal for reasons of abstract principle ("choice"). Unwanted pregnancy has become like, I don't know, smoking crack: the mark of a weak, undisciplined person of the lower orders.

On the *New York Times* op-ed page, William Saletan argues that pro-choicers should concede that "abortion is bad, and the ideal number of abortions is zero," and calls for "an explicit pro-choice war on the abortion rate." Sounding a "clear anti-abortion message," pro-choicers should promote a basket of "solutions" to unintended pregnancy: the Prevention First Act, which calls for federal funding for family planning programs; expanded access to health insurance and emergency contraception; comprehensive sex education. "Some pro-choice activists" are even "pushing for more contraceptive diligence in the abortion counseling process, especially on the part of those women who come back for a second abortion." Give those sluts the lecture they deserve.

Saletan is a very shrewd analyst of political framing. Indeed, plenty of Democrats have already picked up the "I hate abortion" mantra. I seem always to be reading calls from pro-choicers to anti-choicers to work together on contraception. Calling their bluff sounds so clever. Why isn't it working?

The problem is, although of course many abortion opponents support birth control, the organized anti-choice movement hates it. To the movement, the most effective birth control methods—the Pill, emergency contraception, the IUD—are "abortifacients" and "mini-abortions," and even barrier methods like the condom promote a "contraceptive mentality": a selfish, licentious attitude that leads straight to abortion hell. Wherever anti-choicers have political power, they've slashed funds for family-planning clinics, passed laws enabling pharmacists to deny women EC and the Pill, and promoted abstinence-only sex ed that tells kids condoms don't work. In 2003 the Republican-controlled Missouri state legislature handed over the entire state family-planning budget for poor women to "abortion alternatives" centers. Among anti-choicers, the political will to mount a significant public-health campaign for contraception, safe sex, and accurate information simply does not exist. Democrats for Life of America is pushing "95-10," a plan they claim would reduce abortions by 95 percent in ten years. It doesn't even mention birth control. And that's the liberals!

And there's another problem too. Inevitably, attacking abortion as a great evil means attacking providers and patients. If abortion is so bad, why not stigmatize the doctors who perform them? Deny the clinic a permit in your town? Make women feel guilty and ashamed for choosing it and make them sweat so they won't screw up again? Ironically, improvements in contraception have made unwanted pregnancy look more like a personal failing. "Why was I so careful? Because I never wanted to have an abortion," wrote thirty-two-year-old Laurie Gigliotti in response to Saletan's op-ed, describing her super-vigilant approach to safe sex. You can just see how unwanted pregnancy will join obesity and smoking as unacceptable behavior in polite society. But how is all this censoriousness supposed to help women control their fertility? If half of all pregnancies are unplanned, it doesn't make sense to treat them as individual sins.

Fact is, there will never be zero abortions. Half the women who abort are using birth control already—there are no perfect methods or perfect people, except maybe Laurie Gigliotti. Even in small, tidy, prosperous Sweden and the Netherlands, there are abortions. So how can there be zero abortions in America, with our ramshackle health-care system, our millions of poor people, our high school graduates who can't even read a prescription information sheet?

The trouble with thinking in terms of zero abortions is that you make abortion so hateful you do the anti-choicers' work for them. You accept that the zygote/embryo/fetus has some kind of claim to be born. You start making madonna-whore distinctions. In the *New York Times Magazine,* Eyal Press, a contributing writer to *The Nation,* writes of his father, a heroically brave and dedicated abortion doctor: "Had the women . . . been free-love advocates for whom the procedure seemed a mere matter of convenience, he would not have been so angry" at the anti-choice protesters who hounded him and his patients. Why not? Because a sexy single woman should suffer for not suffering? Nobody's proposing the walk of shame for men who don't or won't use condoms, or stern lectures for them in the clinic waiting room either.

In 1989 a number of polls asked respondents whether abortion should be legal or not depending on the reason for seeking it. After life/health, rape/incest, and fetal deformity, majorities of Americans disapproved of every reason on the list: can't afford a child (40 percent approval), too many children (40 percent), emotional strain (35 percent), to finish school (28 percent), not married (25 percent). Assuming opinion hasn't drastically changed, most Americans think women should be denied abortions for the reasons the vast majority of procedures are performed. They think women should carry unwanted children to term, even if they can't support them, have no partner, have to drop out of school, shortchange their other children, or can't cope emotionally.

Now, maybe those respondents don't really want abortion to be illegal so much as they want to express their disapproval. Either way, these answers don't suggest to me that injecting more anti-abortion moralism into the debate will help keep abortion legal and accessible. I'd say the debate is too moralistic already.

•◀ FEBRUARY 13, 2006 ▶•

Betty Friedan, 1921–2006

Betty Friedan is dead at eighty-five—a brilliant, pugnacious woman who lived a big life and wrote a big book, a book that helped change our world, in every way for the better. The far-right magazine *Human Events* knew what it was doing when it put *The Feminine Mystique* on its list of the Ten Most Harmful Books of the Nineteenth and Twentieth Centuries. It might not have been as profound as *The Second Sex* or as radical as the stream of articles and pamphlets that a few years later would pour from the mimeograph machines of the women's liberation movement. But for millions of American women it was as profound and as radical as it needed to be.

If you ever doubt how thoroughly dead the 1950s are, try teaching *The Feminine Mystique* to young women, as I did six years ago. You might as well be teaching Jane Austen. The way you'd have to explain about curates and Bath and entailed estates, you'd have to tell them how women dressed up to go to the market, how women's magazines obsessed about the fragile male ego, and how dropping out of college to get married was indulgently viewed because you weren't going to use your education anyway. The vast American obliviousness that shrouds in a kind of Gothic mist everything that happened before last Tuesday has swallowed up the system of laws, social practices, and cultural understandings Friedan described. My students felt a bit exasperated by Friedan's suburban wives, their low-level depression and seething dissatisfactions, their "problem that had no name." If they were so unhappy, why didn't they, you know, do something about it? None of my students planned to spend their days waxing the kitchen floor; even their mothers hadn't done that. But if they did, it would be—the magic word—their choice.

Well, maybe. Or maybe what looked like choice would be a new incarnation of the mystique in a hot new downtown outfit, wheeling a designer stroller. Or maybe the mystique is gone but the structural obstacles it obscured are still there: job discrimination, the old boys' network, workaholic job cultures, lack of childcare. After all, naming a problem is not the same as solving it. The Women's Strike for Equality, which Friedan helped organize in 1970, called for twenty-four-hour childcare centers, abortion on demand, and equal opportunity in education and employment. Not one of those thirty-six-year-old demands has been fulfilled.

In a spirited, much-discussed polemic in the December *American Prospect,* retired law professor Linda Hirshman argues that it's not a media myth that educated young women are going back home in droves; it's really happening, and it's feminists' fault for replacing the language of justice with the language of choice: Whatever you decide is fine, if that's what you really want! For Hirshman work is everything: She counts as slackers even new mothers who take a few years off or go part-time. And work means a high-paying career with a corner office in your sights: None of your poverty-wage, idealistic, do-good jobs for her, so eat your hearts out, *Nation* staffers. Hirshman wants feminists to assert that stay-home mothers waste their talents, buy into domestic subordination, and perpetuate inequality in the public realm. Even if she's right in some abstract, theoretical way, and even if there were some central committee of feminism to issue these fatwas, it would be hard to think of a better recipe for political suicide—as if American women don't already feel attacked by the cartoon feminist in their heads!

In *Salon's* roundup of tributes, Hirshman claims Friedan as her muse. But what strikes me about *The Feminine Mystique* is the absence of one-size-fits-all pronouncements. In her political battles, Friedan may have been rigid and dogmatic—young feminists were "man-haters," lesbians were "the lavender menace." Her 1980 follow-up, *The Second Stage,* is marred by her obsessive hostility to the movement she helped create. But in her first book she spoke in a different voice. Rarely has a writer addressed readers more empathetically and more intimately. She doesn't say, "Well, if you think you need to be home with your children, that just shows what a failure you are." Or, "By washing your husband's shirts you perpetuate the subordination of women, you traitor." She says, "If you feel there's more to life, you're right. You're not the problem, society is."

The Feminine Mystique didn't change my life; I was only thirteen when it came out, and even then I didn't see myself as a Future Homemaker of America. The book I loved was Kate Millett's *Sexual Politics,* which was about literature. Still, whenever I open Friedan's manifesto I'm carried away by its directness and pungency, its moral seriousness, its Emersonian call to women to use their best energies and be true to their best selves. It is so contrary to the caricature of feminism put forward in the media down to this day—child-hating feminazis in power suits— and it is not really Hirshman's feminism either. Friedan doesn't disparage love or motherhood (in fact, for women's liberationists, she was far too devoted to conventional domestic arrangements); she doesn't insist you get up from the delivery table and go straight back to your desk; she doesn't, like Hirshman, belittle majoring in English or art history as a ticket to nowhere. Still less did Friedan—whose major experience of fulltime employment was as editor of the left-wing United Electrical Workers union newspaper—advise women to drop their foolish predilection for socially meaningful work and go for that big corporate paycheck. I doubt she would say, with Hirshman, that domesticity is inherently "not interesting" even if she thought it. She would simply say it is not enough for a whole human life. Cooking and cleaning and shopping are not why we are here.

The Feminine Mystique has a larger and deeper vision: Women, like men, have a duty to their minds and talents and selves that cannot be fulfilled by living vicariously through husbands and children. An equal cannot live a happy subordinate life; an adult cannot thrive in a culture that infantilizes her. If Rousseau had not been a mad misogynist, he would have applauded Friedan.

•◀ FEBRUARY 27, 2006 ▶•

Acknowledgments

Deep thanks to Katrina vanden Heuvel and Victor Navasky, for offering me a page of my own at *The Nation,* and to my editor, Betsy Reed, for her wisdom, skill, and good humor in the face of imminent deadlines. Thanks also to Roane Carey, Judy Long, and Mark Sorkin at the copy desk, and to the many *Nation* interns who patiently researched and fact-checked these columns. For ideas, conversation, stories, arguments, quips, and quotes, I'm grateful to Anna Fels, Katherine Bouton, Michele Barry, Mark Cullen, Richard Kim, Josh Freeman, Dinitia Smith, David Nasaw, JoAnn Wypijewski, Doug Henwood, Patricia Williams, Emily Gordon, Barbara Ehrenreich, Alan Wallach, Randy Cohen, Ann Snitow, Jennifer Baumgardner, and the History in Action list. Most of all, my thanks are to Steven Lukes, who was always ready to listen to yet another draft, and to my daughter, Sophie Pollitt-Cohen, who graciously allowed me to share a few of her thoughts with the reader.

PHOTO: ANDREA SPERLING

KATHA POLLITT is a poet, essayist, and columnist for *The Nation*. She has won many prizes and awards for her work, including the National Book Critics Circle Award for her first collection of poems, *Antarctic Traveller*, and two National Magazine Awards for essays and criticism. She lives in New York City.